THE ROUGH GUIDE TO

BIG ISLAND
OF HAWAII

Forthcoming titles include

The Algarve • The Bahamas • Cambodia
The Caribbean • Costa Brava
New York Restaurants • South America • Zanzibar

Forthcoming reference guides include

Children's Books • Online Travel • Videogaming
Weather

Rough Guides online

www.roughguides.com

Rough Guide Credits

Text editor: Mary Callahan
Series editor: Mark Ellingham
Production: Zoë Nobes, Andy Turner
Cartography: Maxine Repath

Publishing Information

This third edition published November 2001
by Rough Guides Ltd,
62–70 Shorts Gardens, London WC2H 9AH

Distributed by the Penguin Group:

Penguin Books Ltd, 80 Strand, London WC2R 0RL
Penguin Putnam, Inc., 345 Hudson Street, New York 10014, USA
Penguin Books Australia Ltd, 487 Maroondah Highway,
PO Box 257, Ringwood, Victoria 3134, Australia
Penguin Books Canada Ltd, 10 Alcorn Avenue,
Toronto, Ontario, Canada M4V 1E4
Penguin Books (NZ) Ltd,
182–190 Wairau Road, Auckland 10, New Zealand

Typeset in Bembo and Helvetica to an original design by Henry Iles.
Printed in Spain by Graphy Cems.

© Greg Ward, 2001
352pp, includes index
A catalogue record for this book is available from the British Library.

ISBN 1-85828-850-9

THE ROUGH GUIDE TO

BIG ISLAND
OF HAWAII

by Greg Ward

ROUGH
GUIDES

We set out to do something different when the first Rough Guide was published in 1982. Mark Ellingham, just out of university, was traveling in Greece. He brought along the popular guides of the day, but found they were all lacking in some way. They were either strong on ruins and museums but went on for pages without mentioning a beach or taverna. Or they were so conscious of the need to save money that they lost sight of Greece's cultural and historical significance. Also, none of the books told him anything about Greece's contemporary life – its politics, its culture, its people, and how they lived.

So with no job in prospect, Mark decided to write his own guidebook, one which aimed to provide practical information that was second to none, detailing the best beaches and the hottest clubs and restaurants, while also giving hard-hitting accounts of every sight, both famous and obscure, and providing up-to-the-minute information on contemporary culture. It was a guide that encouraged independent travelers to find the best of Greece, and was a great success, getting shortlisted for the Thomas Cook travel guide award, and encouraging Mark, along with three friends, to expand the series.

The Rough Guide list grew rapidly and the letters flooded in, indicating a much broader readership than had been anticipated, but one which uniformly appreciated the Rough Guide mix of practical detail and humor, irreverence and enthusiasm. Things haven't changed. The same four friends who began the series are still the caretakers of the Rough Guide mission today: to provide the most reliable, up-to-date and entertaining information to independent-minded travelers of all ages, on all budgets.

We now publish more than 200 titles and have offices in London and New York. The travel guides are written and researched by a dedicated team of more than 100 authors, based in Britain, Europe, the USA and Australia. We have also created a unique series of phrasebooks to accompany the travel series, along with an acclaimed series of music guides, and a best-selling pocket guide to the Internet and World Wide Web. We also publish comprehensive travel information on our website: www.roughguides.com

Help us update

We've gone to a lot of trouble to ensure that this Rough Guide is as up to date and accurate as possible. However, things do change; all suggestions, comments and corrections are much appreciated; and we'll send a copy of the next edition (or any other Rough Guide if you prefer) for the best letters.

Please mark letters "**Rough Guide Big Island Update**" and send to:

Rough Guides, 62–70 Shorts Gardens, London WC2H 9AH, or Rough Guides, 4th Floor, 345 Hudson St, New York, NY 10014.

Or send email to: mail@roughguides.co.uk

Online updates about this book can be found on Rough Guides' website (see opposite)

The author

Greg Ward has worked for Rough Guides since 1985, in which time he has also written Rough Guides to Hawaii, Honolulu, Maui, Southwest USA, Las Vegas, Essential Blues CDs, and Brittany and Normandy, as well as co-authored the *Rough Guide to the USA* and the *Rough Guide to Online Travel*. He has edited and contributed to numerous other Rough Guides, and worked on travel guides for Fodors and Dorling Kindersley as well.

Acknowledgments

Thanks once again to Samantha Cook for her encouragement, support andpatience, and for all the fun too. At Rough Guides, thanks to Mary Callahan for her thorough and conscientious editing, and to Andrew Rosenberg, Andy Turner, Melissa Baker, Suzanne Welles and Sharon Martins for their hard work. For their generous assistance with my research for this new edition, I'd also like to thank John Alexander, Barbara Andersen, Laura Aquino, Barbara Campbell, Jim Davis, Sharon McKeague, Lori Michimoto, Laurence Mountcastle, Toni Robert, and everyone who sent e-mails via the Rough Guides' website.

Readers' letters

Paul Norfolk, Calvin Lau, Dwight Adams, Liz Capaldi, Eihway Su, Paul Matsuda, Jan Bishop, John and Kristin McDonnell, Francine Marshall, all the many business operators who wrote in, and those whose e-mail addresses or signatures were totally inscrutable or just plain missing.

CONTENTS

MAP LIST

MAP LIST

ix

MAP SYMBOLS

———————	Major road	⁖	Ancient site
··········	Minor road	♥	Museum
- - - - - -	Trail	⚘	Public gardens
———————	Waterway	�☆	Viewpoint
✈	Airport	▲	Peak
▣	Accommodation	⅃	Waterfall
◉	Places to eat and drink	♦	General point of interest
⚐	Campsite	✚	Church (town maps)
☦	Church (regional maps)	▨	Park
✉	Post office	▧	National Park
ⓘ	Information office	▨	Lava flow

Introduction

The Hawaiian islands are the weatherbeaten summits of a chain of submarine volcanoes, poking from the Pacific more than two thousand miles off the west coast of America. Only on the **Big Island of Hawaii** are those volcanoes still active and continuing to shape one of the most remarkable places on earth. Nowhere else in the state, let alone in the rest of the US, can match the sheer rawness of its newborn landscapes. That might sound like an unlikely tourist destination, but the island also offers everything you might want from a tropical vacation – dependable sunshine, superb sandy beaches, warm turquoise fish-filled waters, swaying coconut palms, and pristine rainforest.

Though tourism has become crucial to the local economy, the Big Island lags well behind Oahu and Maui in terms of the number of annual visitors. It holds nothing to match the skyscrapers of Waikīkī, and neither is there the large-scale strip development of the west Maui shoreline. In the 1960s it was confidently expected that the Big Island would emerge as the first serious rival to Oahu. Large sums were spent on building a highway system to cope with the anticipated influx, and luxury resorts were grafted onto what was once bare lava, while a wide range of more reasonably priced hotels began to spring up in the

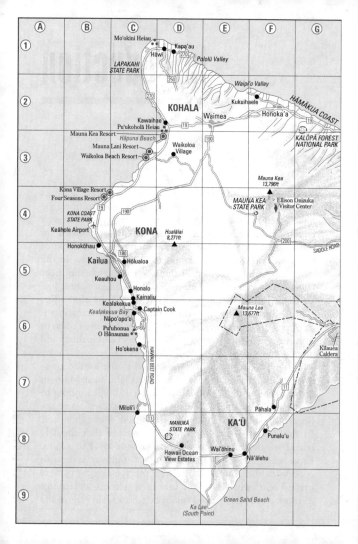

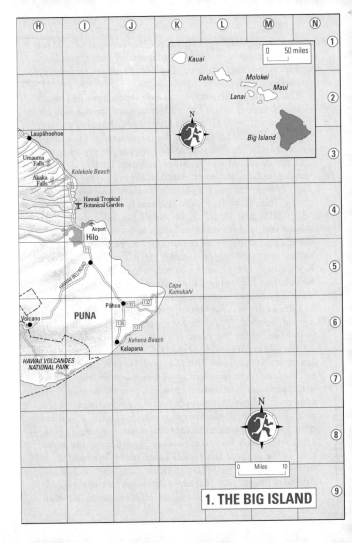

1. THE BIG ISLAND

Kailua area. As things turned out, however, it was Maui that mushroomed, to become plagued by traffic problems and overcrowding, while the Big Island remains remarkably stress-free.

The Big Island is not the cheapest destination in Hawaii – though it does have a few budget inns and hostels – and it can't compete with Honolulu for frenzied shopping or wild nightlife. The entire island has the population of a medium-sized town, with fewer than 150,000 people spread across its four thousand square miles; it holds its fair share of restaurants, bars, and so on, but basically it's a rural community. This is the place to come if you're looking for the elusive "real Hawaii"; it's also unbeatable if you just want to relax. "Hanging loose," as the locals put it, is the island's watchword, and no one ever seems to be too busy to "talk story." There's plenty of opportunity to be active – hiking in the state and national parks, deep-sea fishing off the Kona Coast, golfing in the Kohala resorts, or snorkeling in Kealakekua Bay – but most visitors are content to while away days on end meandering between beach and brunch.

Thanks to massive immigration, modern Hawaii is among the most ethnically diverse places in the world. The population of the Big Island is roughly 27 percent Hawaiian or part-Hawaiian, 25 percent Caucasian, 22 percent Japanese, 10 percent Filipino, and 16 percent "other," although as more than half of all marriages are classified as interracial, such statistics grow ever more meaningless. However, as befits the birthplace of King Kamehameha, the first man to rule all the Hawaiian islands, the Big Island has maintained a strong continuity with its Polynesian past. Little more than two centuries have passed since the isolation of its original inhabitants came to an end, and their *heiaus* (temples), petroglyphs (rock carvings), and abandoned villages are scattered throughout the island. Otherwise, though many of its smaller towns have an

As explained on pp.305–306, the Hawaiian alphabet consists

HAWAIIAN SPELLINGS

As explained on pp.305–306, the Hawaiian alphabet consists
of just twelve letters, together with two punctuation marks, the
macron and the glottal stop. Strictly speaking, the word Hawaii
should be written Hawai'i, with the glottal stop to show that
the two "i"s are pronounced separately. Convention has it,
however, that words in common English usage are written
without their Hawaiian punctuation. Although we've done our
utmost to use correct Hawaiian spellings in this book, therefore, all the island names – Hawaii, Oahu, Kauai, and so on –
appear in their familiar English form.

appealing air of the nineteenth-century West about them,
with their false-front stores and wooden boardwalks, few of
the island's historical attractions are likely to lure you away
from the beaches. Any time you can spare to go sightseeing
is better spent exploring the waterfalls, valleys, and especially
the volcanoes that were themselves so entwined with the
lives of the ancient Hawaiians.

Around the island

All the Hawaiian islands share a similar topography, having
been formed in the same way and exposed to the same
winds and rains. Because the tradewinds blow consistently
from the northeast, each island is much wetter on its north
and east – **windward** – coasts, which are characterized by
steep sea cliffs, inaccessible stream-cut valleys, and dense
tropical vegetation. The islands' west and south – **leeward** –
sides are drier and less fertile.

Only for the last sixty years or so has the title "Big
Island" been widely used, to spare outsiders the confusion
between the name of the state and the name of the island.
It's an appropriate nickname; not only is this the biggest

Hawaiian island – it would comfortably hold all the others put together – but thanks to **Mauna Loa** and **Kīlauea** volcanoes it's getting bigger by the day. Mauna Loa may be the largest object on earth, if you consider its huge bulk underwater, but it's not the highest mountain on the island. That honor goes to extinct **Mauna Kea**, slightly to the north and around 100 feet taller at 13,796 feet.

Mauna Kea is high enough to be capped with snow for a few months each year, which makes an incongruous sight when you're swimming from the Kohala beaches. However, like all Hawaiian volcanoes it's a shield volcano, which means it has a deceptively gradual profile. Most visitors have seen so many photos of precipitous coastal cliffs that they are surprised to discover how very gentle the slope is in most places; on the leeward Kona coast the lava is often all but flat when it reaches the ocean.

The Kona coast, and **Kailua** in particular, is where the great bulk of the island's tourist activity is concentrated. Although the five-mile stretch of Ali'i Drive that connects it to Keauhou has in the last few decades acquired a quick-fire succession of hotels and condos, Kailua itself remains recognizable as the sleepy little town where Kamehameha the Great had his royal palace. To the south lies the prime coffee-growing country of **South Kona**, and Kealakekua Bay, where Captain Cook met his end, while northwards are the island's main airport and a handful of secluded beaches.

The safest and sandiest of the Big Island's beaches are located at the foot of the island's oldest volcano, **Kohala Mountain**, further north. The fact that this region also consists of barren lava flats did not deter the entrepreneurs responsible for the creation of the lavish resorts now tucked into inlets all along the coastline. These include the Disney-like *Hilton Waikoloa Village* and, on the loveliest beach of all, the newer *Hapuna Beach Prince*.

Continuing around the island, beyond the upland cattle ranches of **Waimea** and broad green **Waipiʻo Valley**, you come to the lush **Hāmākua Coast**. After a century of hard work growing sugar, the small towns here are reeling from the recent closure of the plantations, as is the Big Island's capital and only city, **Hilo**. Attempts to attract tourists to Hilo in any quantity have always been swamped by the rainfall, but it's an attractively low-key community, renowned for spectacular orchids and other flowers.

Finally, the south of the island is dominated by **Hawaii Volcanoes National Park**, a compelling wilderness where you can explore steaming craters and cinder cones, venture into the rainforest, and at times approach within feet of the eruption itself. This is one of the world's most exciting hiking destinations, with scores of trails running through the still-active craters. Here and there along the southern shore in either direction the volcanoes have deposited beaches of jet-black sand, while near South Point – the southernmost point of the United States – you can hike to a remote beach composed of green(ish) sand.

Climate and when to go

Despite the power of the tropical sun, the **Hawaiian climate** is not prone to extremes. Of all major US cities, Honolulu has the lowest average annual maximum temperature; it also has the highest average minimum, which goes to show just how small the seasonal variations are.

Throughout the year, sea-level Big Island thermometers rarely drop below the low seventies Fahrenheit (around 22°C) or climb beyond the low eighties (around 28°C) in the daytime; at night the temperature seldom falls below the low sixties. Average daily temperatures in Hilo range from 71°F in February to 76°F in August, while Kailua fluctuates between 72°F and 77°F. Waimea has similar daily maximums, but cooler nights, dropping to the lower fifties (around 11°C). The highest temperature ever recorded in the whole state was 100°F (38°C) at Pāhala on the Big Island, while the temperature at the summit of Mauna Kea ranges from 31°F up to 43°F.

In general, the rainiest months are from December to February, but where you are on the island makes far more difference than what time of year it is. Hilo is the wettest city in the US, with an annual rainfall of 128 inches, while the Kona Coast receives very little rain at any time, and the Kohala resort area is even drier. Kawaihae in Kohala gets a mere ten inches of rain each year.

The only seasonal variation of any great significance for tourists is the state of the **ocean**. You can expect to be able to swim all year round along protected stretches of the shoreline, which consistently offer beautiful seas and water temperatures from 75°F to 82°F (24–28°C). Between October and April, however, high surf can render unsheltered beaches dangerous in the extreme, and some even lose all their sand. Conditions on specific beaches are indicated throughout this book; see also the section on ocean safety on p.44.

For most of the year, the tradewinds blow in from the northeast, though they're occasionally replaced by humid "Kona winds" from the south; the promontories at both the northern and the southern tips of the island are notoriously dangerous for their swirling winds. Despite the much-publicized onslaught of Hurricane Iniki on Kauai in September 1992, hurricanes are very rare. However, *tsunamis* (often erroneously called tidal waves) do hit from time to time, generally as a result of earthquakes or landslides caused by volcanic eruptions.

Mention should also be made of a unique Big Island phenomenon. While the summits of Mauna Loa and Mauna Kea have the clearest air on earth – and astronomical observatories to take advantage of it – down below, when the tradewinds drop, the island is prone to a choking haze of sulphurous volcanic emissions known as "**vog**." The pollution on such days hits worse levels than in Los Angeles or London; the only spot on the island that is consistently downwind of Kīlauea, the Ka'ū Desert, is a lifeless wasteland.

BASICS

Getting there from the US and Canada

The Big Island has two main airports. Keāhole Airport, seven miles north of Kailua and the point of arrival for most tourists, is universally known as Kona Airport, while General Lyman Field is on the outskirts of Hilo.

Only a handful of nonstop flights come straight to the Big Island from the US mainland, all to Kona: United offers two daily services from Los Angeles, and one from San Francisco, while Aloha Airlines flies from San Francisco four times weekly. All other journeys involve touching down elsewhere in Hawaii, usually Honolulu on Oahu, from which Hawaiian Airlines and Aloha operate around sixty flights daily to the Big Island. The last flight each day is around 8pm. For more details, see p.14.

The **journey time** from LA or San Francisco to Honolulu is roughly five and a half hours, while flying from Honolulu to the Big Island takes forty minutes.

FARES AND CUTTING COSTS

There is no high or low season for flights to Hawaii, and

fares remain relatively consistent year-round. However, at **peak periods** – June to August, and around Thanksgiving, Christmas, and New Year's Day – services tend to be booked long in advance, and you might have to pay a slight premium. Flying on a weekday rather than a weekend saves anything from $50 to $200 on a round-trip.

The simplest way to save money is to buy a **package** deal including both flight and accommodation. If you buy a flight only through a **specialist flight agent**, aim to pay around $350 for a round-trip to Honolulu from the West Coast, more like $670 from New York.

AIRLINES AND FLIGHT AGENTS IN NORTH AMERICA

Airlines
Air Canada ⓣ 1-888/247–2262, ⓦ www.aircanada.ca
Aloha ⓣ 1-800/367-5250, ⓦ www.alohaairlines.com
American ⓣ 1-800/433-7300, ⓦ www.aa.com
Canadian ⓣ 1-888/247-2262, ⓦ www.aircanada.ca
Continental ⓣ 1-800/523-3273, ⓦ www.continental.com
Delta ⓣ 1-800/221-1212, ⓦ www.delta.com
Hawaiian ⓣ 1-800/367-5320, ⓦ www.hawaiianair.com
Northwest ⓣ 1-800/225-2525, ⓦ www.nwa.com
TWA ⓣ 1-800/221-2000, ⓦ www.twa.com

United ⓣ 1-800/241-6522, ⓦ www.ual.com

Flight agents
Airhitch ⓣ 1-800/326-2009, ⓦ www.airhitch.org
Cheap Tickets ⓣ 1-888/922-8849, ⓦ www.cheaptickets.com
Council Travel ⓣ 1-800/226-8624, ⓦ www.counciltravel.com
Expedia ⓦ www.expedia.com
High Adventure Travel ⓦ www.airtreks.com
Hotwire ⓦ www.hotwire.com
Orbitz ⓦ www.orbitz.com
Priceline ⓦ www.priceline.com
Qixo ⓦ www.qixo.com

STA Travel Ⓣ 1-800/777-0112,
ⓦ www.sta-travel.com

TicketPlanet
ⓦ www.ticketplanet.com

Travelocity
ⓦ www.travelocity.com

Travelscape
ⓦ www.travelscape.com

NORTH AMERICAN TOUR OPERATORS

American Airlines Vacations
Ⓣ 1-800/321-2121,
ⓦ www.aa.com

Backroads Ⓣ 1-800/462-2848,
ⓦ www.backroads.com

Continental Airlines Vacations
Ⓣ 1-800/634-5555,
ⓦ www.coolvacations.com

Crane Tours Ⓣ 1-800/653-2545

Delta Certified Vacations Ⓣ 1-800/654-6559, ⓦ www
.deltavacations.com

Elderhostel Ⓣ 1-877/426-8056,
ⓦ www.elderhostel.org

Globus and Cosmos
ⓦ www.globusandcosmos.com

New England Hiking Holidays
Ⓣ 1-800/869-0949

Pacific Quest Ⓣ 1-800/776-2518

Pleasant Hawaiian Holidays
Ⓣ 1-800/7HAWAII,
ⓦ www.2hawaii.com

Questers Worldwide Nature Tours Ⓣ 212/251-0444 or
1-800/468-8668,
ⓦ www.questers.com

Sierra Club Ⓣ 415/977-5522,
ⓦ www.sierraclub.org

Tauck Tours Ⓣ 1-800/788-7885, ⓦ www.tauck.com

TWA Getaway Vacations
Ⓣ 1-800/GETAWAY,
ⓦ www.twa.com

United Vacations Ⓣ 1-800
/328-6877, ⓦ www
.unitedvacations.com

World of Vacations Ⓣ 416/620-8050, ⓦ www.macktravel.ca

FLIGHTS FROM THE WEST COAST

United's direct service from **Los Angeles** to Kona leaves at 11.25am and 5.40pm daily, while the flight from **San Francisco** to Kona departs at 9.35am. Aloha flies from **Oakland** airport, in the Bay Area, at 8.40am on Friday, Saturday, Sunday and Monday. A number of airlines offer flights to Honolulu from various US cities: Hawaiian, United, American, Continental, Northwest, and Delta fly from **LA**; Hawaiian, United, American, and Delta fly from **San Francisco**; American flies from **San Jose**; Hawaiian and Northwest fly from **Seattle**; and Hawaiian flies from **Las Vegas**, **Portland** and **San Diego**.

FLIGHTS FROM THE EAST COAST

There are no nonstop flights from the **East Coast** to Hawaii, so most visitors fly via California. American, however, flies direct to Honolulu from **Chicago** and **Dallas**, Northwest from **Minneapolis**, Continental from **Houston**, Delta from **Atlanta**, and TWA from **St Louis**; all take 8–10 hours.

FLIGHTS FROM CANADA

Getting to Hawaii from any **Canadian** city apart from Vancouver will almost certainly require you to change planes on the US mainland. From **Toronto**, United offers routings via San Francisco for around CDN$1250, while its fares **from Vancouver** are more like CDN$700–850. Better from Vancouver is Northwest, with fares starting at CDN$650, via Seattle. If you're flying from either **Toronto** or **Montréal**, you can go via Chicago or Dallas with American (CDN$1300); via Detroit or Minneapolis on Northwest (CDN$1250); or via Atlanta on Delta (CDN$1350).

Canadians flying to Hawaii need passports, but not visas.

Air Canada flies daily to Honolulu from **Toronto** (CDN$1200) via **Vancouver** (CDN$700). Canadian has daily nonstop flights to Honolulu from **Vancouver**, with fares around CDN$700, and flights three times weekly

(Tues, Wed & Fri) from **Toronto** starting around CDN$1000. Through trips from **Montréal**, via Vancouver, start at around CDN$1050.

INSURANCE

Your existing insurance may offer full coverage when you're away from home. Some homeowners' policies are valid on vacation, and credit cards such as American Express often include medical or other insurance. Most Canadians are covered for medical mishaps overseas by their health plans.

If you're not already covered, either contact a specialist travel insurance company, or consider Rough Guides' own travel insurance, customized for our readers and available for anyone, of any nationality, traveling anywhere in the world. There are two main plans: Essential, for basic, no-frills coverage, and Premier, which offers more generous benefits. You can also take out annual multi-trip insurance, which covers you for any number of trips (maximum sixty days each) throughout the year. If you intend to be away for the whole year, the Adventurer policy will cover you for 365 days. Each plan can be supplemented with a "Hazardous Activities Premium" if you plan to indulge in sports considered dangerous, such as scuba diving.

For a policy quote, call the Rough Guide Insurance Line: ℡1-866/220-5588 (US toll-free), ℡0800/015 0906 (UK), or, if you're calling from elsewhere ℡44 1243/621046. Alternatively, get an online quote at ⓦwww.roughguides .com/insurance.

Getting there from Australia and New Zealand

To get to the Big Island from Australia or New Zealand, you have to fly via **Honolulu**. There's no shortage of flights, and very little price difference between airlines. Five airlines operate daily services, with journey times of around nine hours.

Fares vary seasonally by about AUS/NZ$200–300. **Low** season includes mid-January through February, and all of October and November; **high** season runs from mid-May to August and December to mid-January; and **shoulder** season is the rest of the year.

From Australia, most flights to Honolulu are out of **Sydney**, with daily nonstop service on Qantas, American Airlines and Air Canada for around AUS$1500 in low season or AUS$1750 in high season. For around the same price, United flies via Auckland.

From New Zealand, the best deals to Honolulu are

those offered by the United/Air New Zealand partnership out of Auckland; flights cost NZ$1599 in low season and NZ$1899 in high season, whether you fly nonstop or via Fiji, Tonga or Papeete. Air Canada also flies nonstop from Auckland, while Qantas can take you from Auckland to Honolulu via either Sydney or Western Samoa.

AIRLINES AND AGENTS IN AUSTRALIA AND NEW ZEALAND

Airlines
Air New Zealand ☏ 13 2476 (Aus), ☏ 0800/737 000 (NZ), ⓦ www.airnz.com
Air Pacific ☏ 1800/230 150 (Aus), ☏ 09/379 2404 (NZ), ⓦ www.airpacific.com
Cathay Pacific ☏ 13 1747 (Aus), ☏ 09/379 0861 (NZ), ⓦ www.cathaypacific.com
Qantas ☏ 13 1313 (Aus), ☏ 0800/808 767 (NZ), ⓦ www.qantas.com.au
Singapore ☏ 13 1011 (Aus), ☏ 0800/808 909 (NZ), ⓦ www.singaporeair.com

Flight agents
Anywhere Travel, Sydney ☏ 02/9663 0411, ⓔ anywhere@ozemail.com.au
Budget Travel, Auckland ☏ 09/366 0061
Destinations Unlimited, Auckland ☏ 09/373 4033

Flight Centre, Sydney ☏ 02/9235 3522; Auckland ☏ 09/358 4310, ⓦ www.flightcentre.com.au
Northern Gateway, Darwin ☏ 08/8941 1394, ⓔ oztravel@norgate.com.au
STA Travel ☏ 1300/360 960 (Aus); ☏ 09/366 6673 (NZ), ⓦ www.statravel.com.au

Specialist agents
Creative Holidays, Sydney ☏ 02/9386 2111, ⓦ www.creativeholidays .com.au
Hawaiian Island Golf Tours, Sydney ☏ 02/968 1778
Padi Travel Network, Sydney ☏ 02/9417 2800, ⓦ www.padi.com.au
Sydney International Travel Centre, Sydney ☏ 02/9299 8000, ⓦ www.sydneytravel .com.au

ENTRY REQUIREMENTS

Under the visa waiver scheme, Australian and New Zealand
passport holders who stay less than ninety days in the US
do not require visas, so long as they have an onward or
return ticket. For longer stays, a twelve-month US tourist
or business visa costs AUS$85.50/NZ$108. You'll need an
application form – available from the US visa information
service (☏1-902/262 682) – one signed passport photo and
your passport. For details, contact the US Embassy (Aus: 21
Moonah Place, Canberra ☏02/6214 5600; NZ: 29
Fitzherbert Terrace, Thorndon, Wellington). In both countries, you can apply and pay for US visas at all post offices.

INSURANCE

Travel insurance, including medical cover, is essential in
view of the high costs of health care in the US. For details
of Rough Guides' own policies, see p.7.

Getting there from Britain and Ireland

Much the quickest and cheapest route from the UK or Ireland to Hawaii is to fly via the mainland United States or Canada, so your options are more or less the same as they are for North Americans. With a ten-hour flight across the Atlantic to the West Coast, and a five-hour flight over the Pacific, plus potentially a short inter-island hop, that makes for a very long journey. On the other hand, it is just possible to get to Kona on the same day you set off, thanks to the ten- or eleven-hour time difference (see p.61).

Two airlines can get you all the way **from London** to the Big Island in a single day – United and British Airways both have services to Los Angeles that connect with United's 5.40pm onward flight to Kona. If you're willing to fly via **Honolulu**, you can also take Virgin and Continental via Los Angeles, United via San Francisco, Delta via Atlanta, Air Canada via Toronto, or British Airways, in conjunction with Air New Zealand, via Vancouver.

From Ireland, Delta provide same-day connections between Dublin and Kona via Atlanta and Los Angeles, and from Shannon to Kona via New York and Los Angeles. Aer

Lingus and American also offer daily services to Los Angeles, where you can join other carriers for the onward leg to the Big Island.

A typical return ticket from London to the Big Island costs around £475 from January to March, up to as much as £800 in July and August.

FLIGHT AGENTS AND AIRLINES

Flight agents

a2btravel ⓦ www.a2btravel.com

The Airline Network
ⓦ www.netflights.com

Bridge The World
ⓣ 020/7911 0900,
ⓦ www.bridgetheworld.com

Ebookers
ⓦ www.ebookers.com

1stnetflights
ⓦ www.1stnetflights.com

Flynow ⓦ flynow.com

Seaforths Travel
ⓦ www.telme.com

STA Travel ⓣ 0870/160 6070,
ⓦ www.statravel.co.uk

Trailfinders ⓣ 020/7628 7628,
ⓦ www.trailfinders.com

Travel Bag ⓣ 0870/900 1350,
ⓦ www.travelbag.co.uk

usit CAMPUS
ⓣ 0870/240 1010,
ⓦ www.usitcampus.co.uk

usit NOW Dublin ⓣ 01/602
1777, ⓦ www.usitnow.ie

Airlines

Aer Lingus ⓣ 020/8899 4747;
ⓣ 01/705 3333 (Dublin),
ⓦ www.aerlingus.ie

Air Canada ⓣ 0870/524 7226,
ⓦ www.aircanada.ca

Air New Zealand ⓣ 020/8741
2299, ⓦ www.airnz.co.uk

American ⓣ 0845/778 9789,
ⓦ www.aa.com

British Airways
ⓣ 0845/773 3377,
ⓦ www.britishairways.com

Continental ⓣ 0800/776464,
ⓦ www.flycontinental.com

Delta ⓣ 0800/414767;
ⓣ 1800/414 767 (Dublin),
ⓦ www.delta.com

Hawaiian ⓣ 01753/664406,
ⓦ www.hawaiianair.com

KLM/Northwest ⓣ 0870/507
4074, ⓦ www.klmuk.com

United ⓣ 0845/844 4777,
ⓦ www.ual.com

Virgin Atlantic ⓣ 01293/747747,
ⓦ www.virgin-atlantic.com

TOUR OPERATORS IN BRITAIN AND IRELAND

Bon Voyage ☏0800/316 3012,
Ⓦ www.bon-voyage.co.uk

Contiki Tours
☏1-888/CONTIKI,
Ⓦ www.contiki.com

Destination Pacific
☏020/7400 7003

The Hawaiian Dream
☏020/8552 1201

Hawaiian Travel Centre
☏020/7706 4142

North America Travel Service
☏0845/766 0209

Page & Moy ☏0870/010 6250,
Ⓦ www.page-moy.co.uk

ENTRY REQUIREMENTS

Passport holders from **Britain**, **Ireland** and most European countries do not require visas for trips to the United States of less than ninety days. Instead you simply fill in the **visa waiver form** handed out on incoming planes. Immigration control takes place at your point of arrival on US soil, which, if you're flying from Britain, will not be in Hawaii. For further details, contact the **US embassy** in Britain (24 Grosvenor Square, London W1A 1AE; ☏020/7499 9000; premium-rate visa hotline ☏0906/820 0290) or Ireland (42 Elgin Rd, Ballsbridge, Dublin; ☏01/668 8777).

There is no British or Irish **consulate** in Hawaii.

INSURANCE

Travel insurance, including medical cover, is essential in view of the high costs of health care in the US. For details of Rough Guides' own policies, see p.7.

Inter-island travel

The only way to reach the Big Island from any other Hawaiian island is to fly. Except for a few nonstop services from Maui, almost all flights are from or via Honolulu. The last flight each day is always around 8pm.

Hawaiian Airlines flies to **Kona** from **Honolulu** (16 flights daily), from Kahului on **Maui** (2 daily), from **Kauai** (13 daily, via Honolulu), and from **Molokai** and **Lanai** (both 1 daily).

Hawaiian also has regular flights to **Hilo** from **Honolulu** (13 daily), from **Maui** (2 daily), from **Kauai** (5 daily, again via Honolulu), and from **Molokai** and **Lanai** (both 1 daily).

Aloha Airlines flies to **Kona** from **Honolulu** (up to 19 daily), from Kahului on **Maui** (2 daily) and from **Kauai** (17 daily, via Honolulu). Aloha also has 16 daily flights to **Hilo** from **Honolulu**, 2 daily from **Maui** and 9 daily from **Kauai**.

In addition, Pacific Wings (☎887-2104 or 1-888/575-4546, ⓦwww.pacificwings.com) offers daily flights to **Waimea**'s tiny commuter airport from **Honolulu** and from Kahului on **Maui**.

FARES AND DISCOUNTS

Both Hawaiian and Aloha have standard one-way **fares** on all inter-island routes of around $85, although Hawaiian sells cut-price seats on early-morning and late-evening flights

INTER-ISLAND CARRIERS

	Aloha	Island	Hawaiian
Web site	ⓦ www.alohaair .com	ⓦ www.hawaiianair .com	
US & Can	☎ 1-800/367-5250	☎ 1-800/323-3345	☎ 1-800/367-5320
Oahu	☎ 484-1111	☎ 484-2222	☎ 1-800/882-8811
Big Island	☎ 935-5771	☎ 1-800/652-6541	☎ 1-800/882-8811
Kauai	☎ 245-3691	☎ 1-800/652-6541	☎ 1-800/882-8811
Lanai		☎ 1-800/652-6541	☎ 1-800/882-8811
Maui	☎ 244-9071	☎ 1-800/652-6541	☎ 1-800/882-8811
Molokai		☎ 1-800/652-6541	☎ 1-800/882-8811

daily for more like $50. Both airlines offer all sorts of **discount packages**. The most common deal is a "book" of six coupons valid for any inter-island flight; these cost around $380 on Hawaiian or Aloha, and $420 on Island Air, an Aloha affiliate. Hawaiian's Hawaiian Inter-Island Pass allows unlimited travel for five days ($321), one week ($345), ten days ($409), or two weeks ($469), while Aloha's similar Visitor Seven-Day Island Pass costs $321.

Many **discount travel agents** in Hawaii sell airline coupons over the counter, offering individual tickets rather than entire "books" for around $65. Remember also that virtually all the resorts, hotels, B&B agencies and even hostels in Hawaii can arrange discounts on inter-island flights.

Discount travel agents in Hawaii

Cheap Tickets Inc, US
☎ 1-888/922-8849, Oahu
☎ 947-3717, Maui ☎ 242-8094 or 244-7782,
ⓦ www.cheaptickets.com

Cut-rate Tickets, US
☎ 1-800/297-5093, Kailua
☎ 326-2300, Hilo ☎ 969-1944, Kahului ☎ 871-7300, Lahaina ☎ 661-5800,
ⓦ www.cutratetickets.com

FARES AND DISCOUNTS

PACKAGES FROM HONOLULU

Waikīkī travel agents such as Magnum Tickets & Tours, 2134 Kalākaua Ave (℡923-7825), or Aloha Express, 2464 Kalākaua Ave (℡924-4030), offer inexpensive **package tours** to the Big Island. Available at extremely short notice, these are designed to suit short-stay visitors keen to see more of Hawaii than just Oahu. All-inclusive flight, accommodation and rental-car deals cost around $100 per person for one night, $130 for two nights, and $30 for each additional night. Fly-drive deals typically start at around $40 per person one-way.

Information and maps

ast quantities of written information are available about Hawaii. Tourism is big business, and plenty of people and organizations are eager to tell you what's on offer.

Foremost among these is the **Hawaii Visitors Bureau**, which has offices ("chapters") on every island – two on the Big Island, in fact, in Hilo and Waikoloa. Contact the nearest office – listed below – or simply call in when you arrive, and you'll be deluged with handouts and brochures. The most useful is the free annual *Connections Hawaii*, which has detailed listings for accommodation, restaurants, car rental, activities and tour operators. You can also get free copies of the glossy *Islands of Aloha* travel guide (in North America, call ⊤ 1-800/GO-HAWAII).

In hotels, malls and airports, you'll find racks of leaflets including free listings magazines such as *This Week on the Big Island* and *Big Island Gold*. Kailua in particular is full of **activities desks**, kiosks that act as information booths but are primarily concerned with selling tickets for cruises, horse rides, island tours, or whatever. Details on operators can be found on pp.26, 46 and 95.

An ever-increasing amount of information is also available on the **internet**, on sites such as Aloha from Hawaii, at ⓦ www.aloha-hawaii, the official Hawaii Visitors Bureau site at ⓦ www.gohawaii.com, and servers and directories such as ⓦ www.e-hawaii.com.

HAWAII VISITORS BUREAU OFFICES

In Hawaii

Main Office, Waikīkī Business Plaza, Suite 801, 2270 Kalākaua Ave, Honolulu, HI 96815 ⊤ 923-1811, Ⓕ 924-0290, ⓦ www.gohawaii.com
Big Island Visitors Bureau, 250 Keawe St, Hilo, HI 96720

⊤ 961-5797, Ⓕ 961-2126; 250 Waikoloa Beach Drive, Suite B-15, Waikoloa, HI 96748 ⊤ 886-1655, Ⓕ 886-1652, ⓦ www.bigisland.org
Kauai Visitors Bureau, 4334 Rice St, Suite 101, Līhu'e, HI

96766 ⓣ 1-800/262-1400 or
245-3971, ⓕ 246-9235,
ⓦ www.kauaivisitorsbureau.org
Destination Lanai, PO Box
700, Lānai City, HI 96763
ⓣ 565-7600, ⓕ 565-9316,
ⓦ www.visitmaui.com
Maui Visitors Bureau,1727 Wili
Pā Loop, Wailuku, HI 96793
ⓣ 244-3530 or 1-800/525-
MAUI, ⓕ 244-1337,
ⓦ www.visitmaui.com

Molokai Visitors Association,
PO Box 960, Kaunakakai, HI
96748 ⓣ 553-3876, 1-800
/800-6367 (US & Can) or
1-800/553-0404 (HI), ⓕ 553-
5288, ⓦ www.molokai-hawaii
.com
Oahu Visitors Bureau, 733
Bishop St, #1872, Honolulu,
HI 96813 ⓣ 1-877/525-OAHU
or 524-0722, ⓕ 521-1620,
ⓦ www.visit-oahu.com

Elsewhere

Australia ⓣ 02/9955 2619,
ⓕ 9955 2171
Canada ⓣ 604/669-6691,
ⓕ 683-9114

New Zealand ⓣ 09/379 3708,
ⓕ 309 0725
United Kingdom ⓣ 020/8941-
4009, ⓕ 8941-4011

MAPS

The best map of the Big Island is published by the
University of Hawaii at $3.95. Plenty of free maps are avail-
able on the island itself – you'll get a map booklet with
your rental car, for example. These can be useful for pin-
pointing specific hotels and restaurants, but only the
University of Hawaii map is at all reliable for minor roads.

Costs, money, and banks

Although it's possible to have an inexpensive vacation in Hawaii, prices on the islands are consistently higher than in the rest of the USA. With 85 percent of the state's food and 92 percent of its fuel having to be shipped in, the cost of living is around forty percent above the US average.

How much you spend per day is, of course, up to you, but it's hard to get any sort of breakfast for under $6, a cheap lunch easily comes to $12, and an evening meal in a restaurant, with drinks, is likely to be $25–30. Even the cheapest hotel or B&B is likely to charge over $60 for a double room, and a rental car with gas won't cost less than $25 per day. It's easy to spend $75 per person per day before you do anything; pay for a snorkel cruise, let alone a helicopter ride, and you've cleared $100.

The state **sales tax** of four percent on all transactions is almost never included in the prices displayed. Hotels impose an additional 7.25 percent tax, adding a total premium of more than eleven percent to accommodation bills.

MONEY AND BANKS

US dollar **travelers' checks** are the best way to carry significant quantities of money, for both American and foreign visitors, as they offer the security of knowing that lost or stolen checks will be replaced. Foreign currency, whether cash or travelers' checks, can be hard to exchange, so foreign travelers should change some of their money into dollars at home. However, the resort areas of the Big Island are absolutely bursting with **ATM machines** (Kailua's **Lanihau Center** mall holds the widest range), which accept most cards issued by domestic and foreign banks. Call your bank before you leave home to make sure that your ATM card will work in Hawaii.

For many services, it's taken for granted that you'll be paying with a credit card. Hotels and car-rental companies routinely require an imprint of your card whether or not you intend to use it to pay.

Transport and tours

There's no avoiding the fact that if you want to travel around the Big Island you're going to have to **drive**. It's possible to get from either of the airports to your hotel by cab, and there's a limited bus network, but without a car your movements will be extremely restricted.

RENTING A CAR

The demand for rental cars in Hawaii is great, but there's such a plentiful supply that competition among the rental companies is fierce, and prices are among the lowest in the States. All the major rental chains are represented at both the Big Island's main airports. Call the toll-free numbers for reservations; individual offices cannot advise on rates or availability. With so much competition, it's hard to quote specific prices, but a target rate for the cheapest economy car with unlimited mileage should be around $35 per day or $175 per week. No companies rent cars to anyone under 21.

Before you commit yourself to a rate, check whether the airline that flies you to the Big Island or your hotel, B&B, or hostel can offer a discount on car rental.

All the national chains except Avis refuse to provide insurance coverage or emergency help if you drive the cross-island **Saddle Road** (see p.200) or **South Point Road** down to the southern tip of the island (see p.259). Both roads are in fact passable; the ban has more to do with the difficulty of providing assistance should you happen to break down. To explore those areas, rent a **four-wheel-drive vehicle** from Harper Car & Truck Rentals (☎1-800/852-9993; Kona ☎329-6688; Hilo ☎969-1478; ⓦwww.harpershawaii.com) at $60–90 per day.

Car rental chains

Alamo ☎1-800/327-9633 (US, Can & HI); 0870/606 0100 (UK); ⓦwww.alamo.com

Avis ☎1-800/331-1212 (US & Can); 1-800/831-8000 (HI); 020/8848 8733 (UK); 1800/225 533 (Aus); 0800/655 111 (NZ); ⓦwww.avis.com

Budget ☎1-800/527-0700 (US, Can & HI); 0800/181181 (UK); 1300/362 848 (Aus); 0800/652 227 (NZ); ⓦwww.budgetrentacar.com

Dollar ☎1-800/800-4000 (US & Can); 1-800/367-7006 (HI); 01895/233300 (UK); 1800/358 008 (Aus); ⓦwww.dollar.com

Hertz ☎1-800/654-3001 (US & HI); 1-800/263-0600 (Can); 0870/844 8844 (UK); 1800/550 067 (Aus); 0800/655 955 (NZ); ⓦwww.hertz.com.

National ☎1-800/227-7368 (US, Can & HI); 0870/536 5365 (UK); 09/537 2582 (NZ); ⓦwww.nationalcar.com.

DRIVING

The Big Island does not have a lot of roads; in a sense it has just one, the **Hawaii Belt Road**, which circles the entire island. However, thanks to a program of highway improvements carried out in the 1960s and 1970s – at a time when it was assumed that the Big Island and not Maui would be Hawaii's next major tourist destination – traffic problems are all but nonexistent everywhere except Kailua.

If you have to, you can get from anywhere on the island to anywhere else pretty quickly. However, unlike all the other Hawaiian islands, the Big Island is just too big for visitors to comfortably manage a complete island circuit in a single day. Also keep in mind that visiting the volcanoes as a day-trip from Kona won't give you enough time at the park.

Keep a closer eye on your fuel gauge than usual; **gas stations** are common around Kailua and Hilo, but in some areas you can drive fifty miles without seeing one. Typical gas prices are around $2.20 per gallon.

CYCLING

The Big Island makes an ideal choice for a **cycling** vacation. Regions such as North Kohala, South Kona, and the Hāmākua Coast offer superb scenic rides. Unless you know what you're doing, however, don't attempt to cycle to the summit of Mauna Kea; in fact, it's best to avoid the Saddle Road altogether. The nonprofit Big Island Mountain Bike Association (PO Box 6819, Hilo, HI 96720-8934; ⓣ961-4452, ⓦwww.interpac.net/~mtbike) can provide trail maps and suggest routes.

Neither motorbikes nor bicycles are allowed on hiking trails in national or state parks.

Bike and motorbike rental and tours

Chris' Adventures, PO Box 869, Kula, HI 9679; ⓣ326-4600. Mountain-bike tours, some of which also involve hiking, at $60 for a half-day up to $90 for a full day.

DJ's Rentals, 75-5663A Palani Rd, Kailua-Kona ⓣ329-1700 or 1-800/993-4647, ⓦwww.harleys.com. Harley-Davidson motorcycles from $119 per day, plus scooters at $45 and mopeds at $25.

Hawaiian Pedals, Kona Inn Shopping Village, Kailua ⓣ329-2294. Mountain bikes for $20 per day or $70 per week; performance bikes $25/day and $105/week. Tandems are available, too.

Hilo Bike Hub, 318 E Kawili St, Hilo; ☎961-4452. Mountain bikes for rent from around $25 per day.

Kohala Eco Adventures, ☎327-1519. Guided off-road dirt-biking expeditions in North Kohala, for $89.

Kona Coast Cycling Tours, ☎327-1133, ⓦwww.cyclekona.com. Daily guided on-road cycling tours, in North Kohala and South Kona, for $95–145.

Mauna Kea Mountain Bikes, based in C&S Cycle & Surf, Waimea ☎883-0130 or 1-888/682-8687, ⓦwww.bikehawaii.com. Rentals from $25 for five hours to $130 per week, plus customized tours, including Kohala Mountain Road for $80, and downhill rides from the summit of Mauna Kea to the 6700ft level for $120.

BY AIR

If you're really in a hurry, it's possible to take a 25-minute **flight** between Hilo and Kona on Aloha (1 daily Hilo–Kona). Standard inter-island rates apply (see p.14).

LOCAL BUSES

Hilo's Hele On Bus Company (☎961-8744) runs the **Hilo-Kona** bus service detailed opposite, and a weekday-only connection between Hilo and **Hawaii Volcanoes National Park** (see p.222). There are also minimal local services in Kailua and Hilo, and resort shuttle buses between Kailua, Waikoloa and the Kohala resorts, as detailed on p.67 and p.118.

HILO–KONA BUS TIMETABLE

Kona to Hilo Bus

Keālia	5.45am
Hōnaunau	5.55am
Captain Cook	6.00am
Kainaliu	6.15am
Keauhou Kona Surf	6.25am
KAILUA Lanihau Center	6.45am
Waikoloa	7.25am
Waimea Parker Ranch	8.05am
Honoka'a Dairy Queen	8.30am
Laupāhoehoe	8.55am
Honomū	9.25am
Pepe'ekeo	9.30am
HILO Mooheau Bus Terminal	9.45am
HILO Prince Kūhiō Plaza	10.05am

Hilo to Kona Bus

HILO Prince Kūhiō Plaza	1.10pm
HILO Mooheau Bus Terminal	1.30pm
Pepe'ekeo	1.45pm
Honomū	1.50pm
Laupāhoehoe	2.10pm
Honoka'a Dairy Queen	2.40pm
Waimea Parker Ranch	3.20pm
Waikoloa	3.45pm
KAILUA Lanihau Center	4.25pm
Keauhou Kona Surf	4.50pm
Kainaliu	5.05pm
Captain Cook	5.15pm
Hōnaunau	5.20pm
Keālia	5.30pm

Mon–Sat only; fares 75¢–$6. Call ☏ 961-8744 for more details.

HILO–KONA BUS TIMETABLE

BUS TOURS

Circle-island **minibus tours** with Roberts Hawaii (⊤329-1688, ⓦwww.roberts-hawaii.com) cost between $55 and $65 (under-12s $48–57), depending on whether you start from Kona or the Kohala resorts. In addition, as detailed on p.204, three operators run guided tours to the summit of Mauna Kea – a road only four-wheel-drive vehicles should attempt.

FLIGHT-SEEING TOURS

Over the last couple of decades, helicopter **flight-seeing tours** have been one of the few booming sectors of the Hawaiian economy. However, the industry ran into difficulty during the 1990s, after fifteen accidental deaths in three years. Most of those involved plunges over the Nā Pali cliffs of Kauai, but on the Big Island there was a much-publicized incident in which a camera crew crash-landed in Kīlauea and were trapped for two days. New restrictions require all single-engine aircraft, including helicopters, to maintain a minimum altitude of at least 500 feet. Fixed-wing, twin-engine aircraft can still fly low; as they're cheaper than choppers, they make a good-value alternative.

The Big Island is too large to see on one trip, but it has the incomparable attraction of the Kīlauea eruption. Typical **prices** start at around $100–120 for a 45-minute flight, and range up to over $300 for a full loop around Mauna Kea and Mauna Loa plus a good long stare at the eruption. It is, however, well worth shopping around for **discounts** and two-for-one deals; the Activity Connection (⊤329-1038, ⓦwww.beachactivityguide.com) can usually offer up to fifteen percent off the standard rates. If it's the volcano you want to see, opt for a flight from Hilo or Volcano; many of the cheaper ones on the Kona side go up the Kohala coast and skip Kīlauea.

FLIGHT-SEEING OPERATORS

Helicopters

Blue Hawaiian, ⓣ 961-5600, ⓦ www.bluehawaiian.com. Departs from Hilo and Waikoloa.

Safari, ⓣ 969-1259, ⓦ www.safariair.com. Departs from Hilo and Kona.

Sunshine, ⓣ 882-1223, ⓦ www.sunshinehelicopters.com. Departs from Hilo and Hapuna.

Tropical, ⓣ 961-6810, ⓦ www.tropicalhelicopters.com. Departs from Hilo and Kona.

Volcano, ⓣ 967-75. Departs from Volcano.

Fixed-wing

Big Island Air, ⓣ 329-4868, ⓔ bigisle@ilhawaii.net. Departs from Kona.

Island Hoppers, ⓣ 969-2000, ⓔ above@aloha.net. Departs from Hilo and Kona.

Mokulele, ⓣ 326-7070, ⓦ www.mokulele.com. Departs from Kona.

Accommodation

Where you stay on the Big Island, and in what kind of **accommodation**, depends on the sort of vacation you're planning. If you plan to spend a lot of time on the beach, the prime areas are the Kona and Kohala coasts, which are filled with upscale hotels, condos and exclusive resorts. Much the cheapest options on this side of the island are in Kailua, though that town too has its share of luxury properties. Elsewhere, Hilo offers large hotels as well as smaller, more characterful inns, while both the National Park area and Waimea have some medium-scale lodges and an abundance of B&Bs in private homes.

Prospective visitors who think of Hawaii as an expensive destination won't be reassured by the official statistics that show the average cost of a single night's accommodation on the Big Island to be $174. That alarming figure, however, is boosted by the prices at the megaresorts of Kohala, where rates average an amazing $250 per night; the average rate in the Kailua area is around $100 per night, while Hilo's average is well below that.

All these prices are based on the hotels' own **rack rates** – the rate you're offered if you walk through the door and ask for a room. While there's little scope for bargaining in the smaller inns or B&Bs, in the larger hotels it's very possible to cut costs by buying a **package deal**. Those tend to

ACCOMMODATION PRICE CODES

Throughout this book, accommodation prices have been graded with the symbols below, covering the full spectrum of rooms in each establishment and ranging upwards from the quoted nightly rate for the least expensive double room for most of the year, not including state taxes of 11.25 percent.

Hostels, in which dorm beds (rather than double rooms) are usually available for $15–20, have been coded with symbol ❶. Both hostels and budget hotels tend to keep the same rates throughout the year, but in more expensive properties, rooms that are normally priced above $70 often rise by $15–30 in peak seasons – from Christmas to Easter and June to August.

❶ up to $40	❹ $100–150	❼ $250–300
❷ $40–70	❺ $150–200	❽ $300–400
❸ $70–100	❻ $200–250	❾ over $400

require reservations well in advance, but if you're happy to pay full rate it's usually possible to book a room at short notice. See p.51 for details on **camping**.

It's barely possible to see all the Big Island from a single base. While most of your time is likely to be spent on the Kona or Kohala coasts, at the very least you should reckon on spending a night or two in the National Park area or possibly in Hilo. It may even be worth simply not using your prepaid Kona-side room for one night, to give yourself time at the volcanoes.

RESORTS

If you haven't visited a tropical destination before, you may not be familiar with the concept of a **resort**. These gigantic, sprawling enclaves, each holding hundreds or even thousands of rooms, are more than just hotels; located far from any town, they have their own restaurants, stores, swimming pools, beaches, golf courses, tennis courts, walking trails and so on, all designed to ensure that guests can spend their entire vacations without ever feeling the need to leave the property.

The Big Island was a pioneer of this kind of development, and offers some of its most extreme examples. On face value, the Kohala coast is a bleak and inhospitable desert, but in the 1960s entrepreneurs saw it was dependably dry and hot enough to make it worth constructing brand-new oases from scratch. Where beaches didn't exist they were sculpted into the coastline, coconut palms were flown in and replanted and sand poured on top of the lava. The four main resort areas of Waikoloa, Mauna Lani, Mauna Kea and Ka'ūpūlehu now have at least two hotels each. Unless you book as part of a package, there's little prospect of finding a room at any of them for under $200 per night.

HOTELS AND CONDOS

When it comes to guestrooms, standards in the resorts are high, but you can also find high-quality rooms in the conventional hotels of Kailua and Hilo. En-suite bathrooms can be taken for granted, and most rooms have balconies (known as *lānais*). The distinction between a hotel room and a **condominium** apartment is not always clear; the same building may hold some private condos and others rented by the night to short-term guests. An individual condo unit is likely to be more comfortable and better equipped than a typical hotel room, often with a kitchenette, but on the other hand, a condominium building may not have a lobby, daily housekeeping service, restaurants or other hotel amenities. The vast majority of the Big Island's condos are found along Ali'i Drive, stretching south

ROUGH GUIDE FAVORITES: ACCOMMODATION

Pineapple Park, Kealakekua ❶–❷; see p.103
Arnott's Lodge, Hilo ❶–❷; see p.182
Manago Hotel, Captain Cook ❶–❷; see p.103
Kona Tiki Hotel, Kailua ❷; see p.71
Dolphin Bay Hotel, Hilo ❷–❸; see p.183
Waimea Gardens Cottage, Waimea ❹; see p.135
Shipman House B&B Inn, Hilo ❺; see p.185
Hilton Waikoloa Village ❺–❼; see p.115
Hapuna Beach Prince ❽–❾; see p.123
Kona Village Resort ❾; see p.110

from Kailua on the Kona Coast; like the nearby hotels, they tend to charge a little over $100 per night for a double room.

BED AND BREAKFASTS

The definition of a **bed and breakfast** stretches from a simple room or two in a private home, through self-contained, self-catering cottages to luxurious fifteen-room inns. In principle, however, the standards are very high. The cheapest rooms, perhaps sharing a bathroom, start at around $60 per night, while for more like $100 per night you can expect your own well-furnished apartment with all facilities. For information on a variety of hand-picked, top-quality B&Bs on all the islands, with an especially wide range on the Big Island, contact **Hawaii's Best Bed & Breakfasts** (PO Box 563, Kamuela, HI 96743; ☎885-4550 or 1-800/262-9912, ℱ885-0559, ⓦwww.bestbnb.com).

Most small-scale B&Bs tend to be located in areas that otherwise offer little choice of accommodation. The greatest concentrations are in Volcano village, just outside the National Park, and in upcountry Waimea. The owners are often friendly and full of advice on making the most of your vacation.

HOSTELS

At budget **hostels** in **Kailua** (*Patey's Place*; see p.72), **Hilo** (*Arnott's Lodge* and *Pineapple Park*; p.182), **Kealakekua** (*Pineapple Park*; p.103), and **Volcano** (*Holo Holo Inn*; p.251), you can get a bed in a dormitory for under $20 per night. All tend to be geared towards young surfers, and few offer any reduction for members of youth hostel organizations.

Food and drink

f you imagine that eating in Hawaii will consist of an endless feast of fresh fruits and fishes, you'll be disappointed to find that the islands are not bountiful Gardens of Eden: the state produces less than twenty percent of the food it consumes. Polynesian cuisine can mean little more than putting a pineapple ring on top of a burger, and, amazingly, more than half of all the Spam eaten in the United States is consumed in Hawaii.

However, two strong factors work in your favor. First of all, there's the state's **ethnic diversity**. Immigrants from all over the world have brought their national dishes and recipes here, and traditions have mingled to create intriguing new cuisines. Second, the presence of thousands of **tourists**, many prepared to pay top rates for good food, means that the island has some truly superb restaurants.

Food in general is often referred to as **kaukau**, and it's also worth knowing that **pūpūs** (pronounced *poo-poos*) is a general term for little snacks, the kind of finger food that is given away in early-evening Happy Hours.

THE HAWAIIAN TRADITION

Cooking in ancient Hawaii was the responsibility of the menfolk, who prepared food for themselves and their wives in separate calabash gourds and ovens. Women were forbidden to eat pork, bananas or coconuts, as well as several kinds of fish, or to dine with the men.

The staple food was **poi**, a purple-gray paste produced by pounding the root of the taro plant (cultivated in wetlands such as Waipi'o Valley – see p.161). Poi is eaten with the bare hands and comes in three grades – one-finger, two-finger or three-finger – according to how many fingers it takes to scoop a satisfactory portion out of the pot; one-finger is the thickest and best.

These days, there's no such thing as an authentic "Hawaiian" restaurant; the closest you can come to eating traditional foods is at a *lū'au* or "banquet." Primarily tourist money-spinners, and always accompanied by pseudo-Polynesian entertainment, these offer the chance to sample such dishes as **kālua pork**, an entire pig wrapped in *ti* leaves and baked all day in an underground oven known as an *imu*; **poke**, which is raw fish, shellfish or octopus, marinated with soy and Oriental seasonings; and **lomi-lomi**, made with raw salmon. As *lū'aus* always involve mass catering and canteen-style self-service, the food itself rarely provides sufficient incentive to go.

BIG ISLAND LŪ'AUS

There are currently seven regular *lū'aus* on the Big Island, all based at major Kona-side hotels. The *Kona Village Resort's lū'au* wins hands down for atmosphere, due in part to its remote location.

Drums of Polynesia, *Royal Kona Resort* ☎ 329-3111; Mon, Fri & Sat 5.30pm; $55.

Island Breeze, *King Kamehameha Hotel* ☎ 326-4969; Tues–Fri & Sun 5.30pm; $55.

Kona Village Lū'au, *Kona Village Resort* ☎ 325-5555; Fri 5pm; $72.

Legends of the Pacific, *Hilton Waikoloa Village* ☎ 885-1234; Fri 5.30pm; $55.

Mauna Kea Lū'au, *Mauna Kea Beach Hotel* ☎ 882-7222; Tues 6pm; $70.

Royal Lū'au, *Outrigger Waikoloa Beach* ☎ 886-6789; Wed & Sun 6pm; $64.

Traditions at Kahalu'u, *Aston Keauhou Beach Resort* ☎ 322-3441; Thurs & Sun 5.30pm; $68.

LOCAL RESTAURANTS

While the Big Island has its fair share of outlets of the national fast-food chains, typical budget restaurants, diners and takeout stands serve a hybrid cuisine that draws on the traditions of the US mainland along with Japan, China, Korea and the Philippines; the resultant mixture has a slight but definite Hawaiian twist.

ROUGH GUIDE FAVORITES: EATING

These ten top places to eat are drawn from all price categories, and arranged in ascending order of price.

The Coffee Shack, Captain Cook; see p.92

Bamboo Restaurant and Bar, Hāwi; see p.150

Maha's, Waimea; see p.141

The Seaside Restaurant, Hilo; see p.198

Cassandra's Greek Taverna, Kailua; see p.84

Kilauea Lodge, Volcano; see p.252

Merriman's, Waimea; see p.142

Roy's, Waikoloa; see p.118

Hale Moana, *Kona Village Resort*; see p.111

Coast Grille, *Hapuna Beach Prince*; see p.124

Breakfast tends to be the standard fare of eggs, meat, pancakes, muffins or toast. At midday, the usual dish is the plate lunch, a tray of meat, rice, potato or macaroni salad ($5–8). Bento is the Japanese equivalent; in Filipino diners, you'll be offered **adobo**, which is pork or chicken stewed with garlic and vinegar. Korean barbecue, **kal bi** – prepared with sesame – is especially tasty, while **saimin** (pronounced *sy-min* not *say-min*), a bowl of clear soup filled with noodles and other ingredients, is something of a state dish. Finally, the carbohydrate-packed **loco moco** is a fried egg served on a hamburger with gravy and rice.

FINE DINING

Many of the Big Island's best **restaurants** are in its most expensive hotels. The resorts of the Kona and Kohala coasts in particular are blessed with a captive clientele who aren't going to drive forty miles in the dark for a cheap meal in Kailua. These are the places where a distinctive Hawaiian

FINE DINING

cuisine is being created, known variously as **Pacific Rim**, **Euro-Asian**, or **Hawaii Regional**. In its ideal form it combines foods and techniques from all the countries and ethnic groups that have figured in Hawaiian history, using the freshest ingredients possible. The top chefs preserve natural flavors by flash-frying meat and fish like the Chinese, baking it whole like the Hawaiians, or even serving it raw like the Japanese. The effect is enhanced by Thai herbs and spices, and by the sheer inventiveness of modern Californian cooking.

The Big Island also has plenty of conventional **American** shrimp and steak specialists, as well as high-class **Italian**, **Thai**, and **Chinese** places. Many restaurants offer all-you-can-eat **buffets** one or more nights of the week; they all sacrifice quality to quantity, so you might as well go for the cheaper ones. Lastly, to cater for that much-prized customer, the Japanese big-spender, several large hotels have very good **Japanese** restaurants, specializing in discreet sushi and sashimi dining.

LOCAL INGREDIENTS

As well as the **fish** listed opposite, widely used **local ingredients** include **ginger** (the Big Island is the major producer of ginger in the US) and **macadamia nuts** (large, creamy, white nuts said to contain a hundred calories each). Bright-red **'ōhelo berries**, which taste like cranberries, were once sacred to the volcano goddess Pele, and to eat one was punishable by death; now they're served up in gourmet restaurants. **Avocados** are widely grown, and are even richer than you may be used to, as are fruits such as **guava**, **papaya** and **mango**. Watch out also for small yellow **apple bananas**, with their savory tang, and, of course, the ever-present **coconut**.

HAWAIIAN FISH

Although the ancient Hawaiians were expert offshore fishermen, as well as being sophisticated fish farmers, the great majority of the **fish** eaten in Hawaii nowadays is imported. Local fishing is on too small a scale to meet the demand, and in any case many of the species that tourists expect to find on menus thrive in much cooler waters. Thus salmon and crab come from Alaska, and mussels from New Zealand, although Maine lobsters are now being farmed in the cold waters of the deep ocean off Hōnokohau, and aquafarms at Hilo and elsewhere are raising freshwater species.

However, if you feel like being adventurous, you should get plenty of opportunity to try some of the Pacific species caught nearby. If the list below still leaves you in the dark, personal recommendations include **opah,** which is chewy and salty like swordfish; the chunky **'ōpakapaka,**

TYPES OF HAWAIIAN FISH

'ahi	yellow-fin tuna	mano	shark
aku	skipjack tuna	moi	thread fish
a'u	swordfish or marlin	onaga	red snapper
		ono	mackerel or tuna-like fish
'ehu	red snapper		
hapu'upu'u	sea bass	'ōpae	shrimp
hebi	spear fish	opah	moonfish
kākū	barracuda	'ōpakapaka	pink snapper
kalekale	pink snapper	pāpio	pompano
kāmano	salmon	uhu	parrot fish
kūmū	red goat fish	uku	gray snapper
lehi	yellow snapper	ulua	jack fish
mahimahi	dorado or dolphin fish	weke	goat fish

LOCAL INGREDIENTS

37

which, because of its red color (associated with happiness), is often served on special occasions; the succulent white **ono** (which means "delicious" in Hawaiian); and the dark **'ahi**, the most popular choice for sashimi.

To get an idea of the range of fish that lurk in Hawaiian waters, call in at Hilo's early morning Suisan Fish Auction (see p.191).

DRINK

The usual range of **wines** (mostly Californian, though the Big Island does have its own tiny Volcano Winery) and **beers** are sold at Big Island restaurants and bars, but at some point every visitor seems to insist on getting wiped out by a tropical **cocktail** or two. Among the most popular are the **Mai Tai**, which should contain at least two kinds of rum, together with orange curacao and lemon juice, the **Blue Hawaii**, in which vodka is colored with blue curacao, and the **Planter's Punch**, made with light rum, grenadine, bitters and lemon juice.

Tap **water** is safe to drink. If you're hiking, however, never drink untreated stream water.

Mention should also be made of the Big Island's most famous home-grown product, Kona coffee which is widely available in small cafés and espresso bars throughout the island and especially in the South Kona district where the farms are located. For more details, see p.90.

Communications and media

Telephone connections on and between the Hawaiian Islands and to the rest of the US are generally efficient and reliable, but mail service can be slow.

PHONES AND THE MAIL

The **telephone area code** for the entire state of Hawaii is ☏808. Calls from anywhere on the Big Island to anywhere else on the island count as local; you don't need to dial the area code and it costs a flat-rate 25¢ on pay phones. Calling any of the other islands, you have to use the prefix ☏1-808.

Hotels impose huge surcharges, so it's best to use a **phone card** for long-distance calls. In preference to the ones issued by the major phone companies, you'll find it simpler and cheaper to choose from the various **prepaid** cards sold in almost all groceries and general stores.

Post offices usually open between 8.30am and 4pm on weekdays, and for an hour or two on Saturday mornings. **Mail service** is slow, as all the post has to go via Honolulu.

Allow a week for your letter to reach anywhere in the US, two weeks or more for the rest of the world.

To make an international call to Hawaii, dial your country's international access code, then 1 for the US, then 808 for Hawaii. To place an international call from Hawaii, dial 011 then the relevant country code (Britain is 44, Ireland is 353, Canada is 1, Australia is 61 and New Zealand is 64).

NEWSPAPERS AND RADIO

The *Hawaii Tribune-Herald*, a broadsheet based in Hilo, and the tabloid *West Hawaii Today* are the Big Island's two homegrown **newspapers**, both published daily except Saturday, though the *Honolulu Advertiser* and *Honolulu Star-Bulletin* are also widely distributed and cover island issues.

The Big Island has about half a dozen radio stations, both AM and FM, and the average rental-car radio will pick up perhaps another half-dozen the closer you get to Maui and Oahu. Thus there's far more choice, especially of nationally syndicated shows, on the Kona side; in the remoter southern stretches the station selection can be reduced to none at all. The music-minded KIPA on 620 AM is the most ubiquitous; for local news steer your dial towards Hilo's K-BIG FM 98 or KPUA 670 AM.

Entertainment and festivals

I f you're hoping for wild nightlife during your stay in Hawaii, the Big Island is probably the wrong island to choose; it has nothing to compare with the bright lights of Waikīkī. However, there is a wide variety of festivals throughout the year – some traditional Hawaiian celebrations, and some laid on specifically for tourists.

NIGHTLIFE AND ENTERTAINMENT

Almost all the major **hotels** put on some form of entertainment, and many feature live musicians every night. The music tends to consist of anodyne medleys of 1950s Hawaiian hits, but the setting is usually romantic enough for that not to matter. In a typical week, the biggest events are the **lū'aus** listed on p.34, but visiting artists from the other islands or the mainland also make concert appearances. Nearly all such activity happens in the prime tourist areas of Kona and Kohala, but the biggest venue for Hawaiian performers who command strong local followings is the *Crown Room* at Hilo's *Hawaii Naniloa Hotel*. For more about Hawaiian music, see p.296.

BIG ISLAND HOLIDAYS AND FESTIVALS

By far the most important of the Big Island's annual festivals is Hilo's **Merrie Monarch Festival**, a *hula* showcase for which tickets sell out almost immediately. For more details, see p.195.

Jan 1	New Year's Day (public holiday)
3rd Mon in Jan	Dr Martin Luther King Jr's Birthday (public holiday)
3rd Mon in Feb	Presidents' Day (public holiday)
Feb	Mardi Gras, Hilo
Feb	Waimea Cherry Blossom Festival, Waimea
Feb	Tahiti Fête of Hilo
March	Kona Brewers Festival, Kailua
March 26	Prince Kūhiō Day (public holiday)
April	Merrie Monarch Festival, Hilo
Easter Monday	Public holiday
May 1	Lei Day (public holiday)
Last Mon in May	Memorial Day (public holiday)
June 11	Kamehameha Day (public holiday); Floral Parade in Kailua, also ceremonies at Kapa'au
mid-June	Waiki'i Music Festival, Waiki'i Ranch, Saddle Road
Late June	Pu'uhonua O Hōnaunau Cultural Festival
Late June	Kona Marathon, Kailua
July 4	Independence Day (public holiday); Parker Ranch Rodeo, Waimea

An ideal way to taste the local flavor is to visit one of the old-style **community theaters** that still survive in the smaller towns. Most were built to provide entertainment for the plantation laborers; some still have their original Art Deco adornments. Fine examples include the People's Theater in **Honoka'a**, **Kainaliu**'s Aloha Theater, and the Akebono Theater in **Pāhoa**.

mid-July	Kīlauea Cultural Festival, Volcano
mid-July	Slack Key Festival, Hilo
late July	Kīlauea Volcano Wilderness Runs, Volcano
Aug–Oct	International Festival of the Pacific, Hilo
mid-Aug	Hawaiian International Billfish Tournament, Kailua
3rd Fri in Aug	Admissions Day (public holiday)
1st Mon in Sept	Labor Day (public holiday)
early Sept	Queen Lili'uokalani Long-Distance Canoe Races, Kailua
early Sept	Parker Ranch Round-Up Rodeo, Waimea
Sept	Aloha Week Festival, islandwide
2nd Mon in Oct	Columbus Day (public holiday)
early Oct	Ironman Triathlon World Championship, Kailua
Oct	Hāmākua Music Festival, Honoka'a
Nov	Taro Festival, Honoka'a
Nov	Kona Coffee Cultural Festival, South Kona
Nov	Hawaii International Film Festival, island-wide
Nov 11	Veterans' Day (public holiday)
mid-Nov	King Kalākaua Hula Festival, Kona
4th Thurs in Nov	Thanksgiving (public holiday)
Dec	Christmas Parade, Waimea
Dec 25	Christmas Day (public holiday)

HOLIDAYS AND FESTIVALS

Sea sports
and safety

Because the Big Island is the youngest member of the Hawaiian archipelago, it's the least suitable for a beach vacation. That's only relative, of course – it has some magnificent palm-fringed beaches and the facilities to go with them. However, it takes millions of years for a tropical island to acquire a protective reef of coral, and millions more for that coral to break down and produce white sandy beaches. By contrast, much of the Big Island's shoreline has been shaped by new lava flows within the last century, and some of it within the last week. Only along the North Kona and South Kohala coasts – the oldest, most sheltered parts of the island – are conditions really perfect. That's where the beaches are concentrated, and that's where the hotels are too.

According to the state's own figures, the Big Island has 19.4 miles of sandy beach, of which just 1.2 miles are considered **safe beaches**, being clean, accessible and generally suitable for swimming. So long as you observe the necessary precautions, however, there's plenty of scope for enjoyment, with some of the best snorkeling, surfing, scuba diving, and just plain swimming in the world.

SEA SPORTS AND SAFETY

What constitutes the "**best beach**" is a matter of taste, but be sure to visit **Hāpuna Beach** (p.122), **Kona Coast State Park** (p.108), **Old Kona Airport State Recreation Area** (p.78), the black-sand beach at **Kehena** (p.213), and **Green Sand Beach** near South Point (p.261).

OCEAN FUN

With average water temperatures of between 75°F and 82°F (24–28°C), the sea in Hawaii is all but irresistible, and most visitors are tempted to try at least one or two of the state's wide range of **ocean sports**.

SNORKELING

Probably the easiest activity for beginners is **snorkeling**. Equipment is available for rent all over the island, from outlets such as Snorkel Bob's, based near the *Royal Kona Resort* in Kailua (☎329-0770), as well as from most hotels, including all the Kohala resorts.

Among the best snorkeling sites are **Kahaluʻu Beach** in Keauhou, at the southern end of Aliʻi Drive; **Kaunaʻoa Beach** at the Mauna Kea resort; and the beach at the **Puʻuhonua O Hōnaunau** ("City of Refuge") in South Kona. You might also want to join a snorkel cruise; see pp.46 or 95.

DIVING

Scuba diving is both expensive and demanding, but with endless networks of submarine lava tubes to explore, and the chance to get close to some amazing marine life forms, the Big Island is a great dive destination. The prime spots are congregated along the Kohala and Kona coasts, especially

OCEAN FUN

BOAT TRIPS ON THE KONA AND KOHALA COASTS

Most Kona and Kohala coast boat trips depart from Honokōhau Harbor. Precise arrangements vary from day to day; contact the companies below for details. Activities desks in Kailua can usually offer discounted rates. The Activity Desk, in Bougainvillea Plaza (℡ 329-1038, 🌐 www.beachactivityguide.com), is particularly recommended.

Dive boats

One-dive cruises tend to cost $60–80, two-dive trips more like $85–100, with a $20–30 surcharge for unqualified divers, and equipment rental available at $5 per item. Most operators offer two-day certification courses for around $300.

Big Island Divers	℡ 329-6068, 🌐 www.bigislanddivers.com
Eco Adventures	℡ 1-800/949-3483, 🌐 www.ecodive.com
Jack's Diving Locker	℡ 329-7585, 🌐 www.divejdl.com
Kona Coast Divers	℡ 329-8802, 🌐 www.konacoastdivers.com
Rainbow Diver	℡ 325-1687, 🌐 www.rainbowdiver.com
Red Sail Sports	℡ 885-2876, 🌐 www.redsail.com
Torpedo Tours	℡ 938-0405, 🌐 www.torpedotours.com

Snorkel cruises

Typical morning or afternoon snorkel cruises cost $45–70, and double as whale-watching cruises in winter. The prime destination is Kealakekua Bay; for more details, see p.95.

Body Glove	℡ 326-7122, 🌐 www.snorkelkona.com
Captain Zodiac	℡ 329-3199, 🌐 www.captainzodiac.com
Dolphin Discoveries	℡ 322-8000, 🌐 www.dolphindiscoveries.com

Fair Wind	☎ 322-2788, 🌐 www.fairwind.com
Kamanu	☎ 329-2021, 🌐 www.kamanu.com
Rainbow Diver	☎ 325-1687, 🌐 www.rainbowdiver.com
Red Sail Sports	☎ 885-2876, 🌐 www.redsail.com
Sea Quest	☎ 329-7238, 🌐 www.seaquesthawaii.com

Deep-sea fishing

Fishing trips cost from $75 per person for a half-day to $400-plus for a whole boat for a day. For a broad selection of charter vessels, contact the Charter Desk (☎ 329-5735, 🌐 www.charterdesk.com) or Charter Services Hawaii (☎ 334-1881).

Camelot	☎ 325-6421
Cherry Pit II	☎ 326-7781
Hapa Laka	☎ 322-2229
Happy Times	☎ 325-7060
Ihu Nui Sportfishing	☎ 325-1513
Pacific Blue	☎ 325-1775
Reel Action	☎ 325-6811
Sea Dancer	☎ 322-6630

Sightseeing cruises

Atlantis Submarines (☎ 329-6626, 🌐 www.go-atlantis.com; $79 for 1hr trip). Cramped but fascinating ocean-floor cruises, with foolhardy divers trying to entice sharks alongside. Hourly from Kailua Pier.

Dan McSweeney's Whale Watch (☎ 322-0028; $55 for a morning's excursion). Departs 9am daily from Honokōhau. From December to March there's an excellent chance of sneaking up on some humpback whales.

Lilikoi (☎ 936-1470, 🌐 www.dolphinshawaii.com; $45 for half-day trip). Seasonal whale-watching trips from Honokōhau Harbor.

OCEAN FUN: BOAT TRIPS

in the waters in and around Kealakekua Bay. Sadly, however, in many places the seabed has become damaged in recent years by runoff from agricultural and construction sites along the shoreline. On the other hand, the Big Island does offer a couple of unusual treats for divers: many operators run **night dives**, especially around Keauhou, to see manta rays attracted by artificial spotlights, and also **bluewater dives** in the open ocean a few miles offshore, in the hopes of seeing sharks, dolphins, and other pelagic species.

Dive-boat operators are listed on p.46; experienced divers can also enter the water direct from the shoreline, at the same beaches that are recommended for snorkelers. Be sure not to dive within 24 hours of flying or ascending to any significant altitude. The summit of Mauna Kea is certainly out of bounds, and you should ask your dive operator for advice before even driving the main highway through South Kona.

For a taste of what it's all about, you might like to try **snuba** – snorkeling from a boat, with a longer breathing tube. The *Fair Wind* (see box p.95) offers snuba for an extra charge on its snorkel cruises.

SURFING

The place that invented **surfing** – long before the foreigners came – remains its greatest arena. A recurring theme in ancient legends has young men frittering away endless days in the waves rather than facing up to their duties (see p.284); now young people from all over the world flock to Hawaii to do just that. Nowhere on the Big Island quite matches up to Oahu's fabled North Shore, but again the Kona and Kohala coasts offer the best prospects, at beaches such as **'Anaeho'omalu Bay** at the Waikoloa resort. Unless you're a real expert, don't join the locals who surf at spots along the Hāmākua Coast.

OCEAN FUN

At some popular beaches, such as Hāpuna Beach and Spencer Beach Park, surfing is forbidden in order to prevent collisions with ordinary bathers. Use of the smaller **boogie boards**, which you lie on, *is* allowed. **Windsurfing**, too, is rapidly growing in popularity; aficionados can be found off many of the favorite surfing beaches and also in Hilo Bay.

OCEAN SAFETY

It's essential whenever you're in or near the ocean to be aware of **safety issues**. Hawaii is one of the remotest islands on earth, so waves have two thousand miles of the misnamed Pacific Ocean to build up their strength before they come crashing in. People born in Hawaii are brought up with a respect for the sea and learn to watch out for all sorts of signs before they swim. You'll be told to throw sticks into the waves to see how they move, or to look for disturbances in the surf that indicate powerful currents; unless you have local expertise, however, you're better off sticking to the official beach parks and most popular spots, especially those that are shielded by offshore reefs. Not all beaches have lifeguards and warning flags, and unattended beaches are not necessarily safe. Look for other bathers, but whatever your experience elsewhere don't assume you'll be able to cope with the same conditions as the local kids. Always ask for advice and above all **never turn your back on the water**.

The beaches that experience the most accidents and **drownings** are those where waves of four feet or more break directly onto the shore. This varies according to the season, so beaches such as Hāpuna or White Sands, which are idyllic in summer, can be storm-tossed death traps between October and April. If you get caught in a rip current or undertow and are dragged out to sea, stay calm and remember that the vast majority of such currents disappear within a hundred yards of the shore. Never exhaust yourself by trying to swim against them, but allow yourself to be carried out until the force weakens, and swim first to one side and then back to the shore.

Sea creatures to avoid include *wana* (black spiky **sea urchins**), Portuguese men-of-war **jellyfish**, and **coral** in general, which can give painful, infected cuts. **Shark attacks** are much rarer than popular imagination suggests; in 2000, 79 occurred worldwide, of which ten were fatal. Two of the nonlethal attacks were in Hawaii, both off Maui. Those that do happen are usually due to "misunderstandings", such as surfers idling on their boards who look a bit too much like turtles from below.

SUN SAFETY

Only expose yourself to the harsh tropical **sun** in moderation; a mere fifteen to thirty minutes is the safe recommendation for the first day. The sun is strongest between 10am and 3pm, and keep in mind that even on overcast days human skin still absorbs harmful UV rays. Use plenty of **sunscreen** – doctors recommend Sun Protection Factor (SPF) 30 for Hawaii – and reapply after swimming. Note, however, that some marine life sanctuaries, such as Lapakahi State Park, forbid the use of sunscreen by bathers.

OCEAN SAFETY

Camping and hiking

The Big Island is one of the most exciting hiking destinations imaginable. Well-maintained trails guide walkers through scenery that ranges from dense tropical rainforest to remote desert and, above all, offer hikers the chance to experience firsthand the splendor of the world's most active volcanoes. If you're planning to do any hiking, however, it's essential to remember that Hawaii is more than a vacation playground, and you may find yourself in some pretty uncompromising wilderness.

But **camping** on the island need not be a battle with the elements. At several lovely oceanfront campgrounds, all you have to do is drive in and pitch your tent; some offer cabins for rent so you needn't even do that.

CAMPING

If you're **camping**, then you'll almost certainly spend most of your time at the dozen or so **County Beach Parks** along the shoreline. A long stretch of coast to either side of Kailua has no campgrounds, but otherwise there's plenty of choice. **Spencer Beach Park** in Kohala, with its white, sandy beach, and the black-sand beach at **Punalu'u**, are the most popular. Several others, especially on the east coast, aren't really beaches in the usual sense, being set in clifftop woodlands or simply near the edge of a jagged lava shore-line.

All county parks offer showers, toilets, and drinking water and are administered by the Department of Parks and Recreation, 25 Aupuni St, Hilo, HI 96720 (Mon–Fri 7.45am–4.30pm; ☎961-8311, ⓦwww.hawaii-county.com), which has subsidiary offices at Hale Halawai on Aliʻi Drive in Kailua (same hours), Yano Hall in Captain Cook (Mon–Fri noon–2pm), and Waimea Community Center in Waimea (Mon–Fri 8.30–10.30am). Permits are required for all stays, with fees of $3 per day ($1.50 ages 13–17). Maximum lengths of stay, and even whether a particular park is open at all, tend to change at a moment's notice.

In addition, the **state** provides eight-bed cabins with linen and cooking facilities at several of its own parks, including Mauna Kea (not the summit, but the state park on the Saddle Road; see p.207) and Kalōpā (p.169). Precise rates vary; contact the Division of State Parks, 75 Aupuni St, Hilo, HI 96720 (☎974-6200) for details. For information about camping at **Hāpuna Beach**, see p.123.

Hawaii Volcanoes National Park has a number of campgrounds, as detailed in Chapter Eleven. The most accessible of these are the free, first-come, first-served sites at Nāmakani Paio and Kulanaokuaiki; it's also possible to book cabins at Nāmakani Paio through *Volcano House* (☎967-7321; see p.226). Register with the authorities before **backpacking** in the park.

Finally, you can also camp in a couple of out-of-the-way places on the Hāmākua coast. Camping in **Waipiʻo Valley** – see p.168 – is controlled by the Bishop Estate (78-6831 Aliʻi Drive, Kailua-Kona, HI 96740; ☎322-5300), while **Waimanu Valley** beyond – see p.169 – is under the juris-diction of the Department of Forestry in Hilo (1643 Kilauea Ave, Hilo, HI 96720; ☎933-4221).

HIKING

All the best **hiking trails** on the Big Island are described in
detail in the relevant chapters of this book. Other than the
route down to **Kealakekua Bay** (p.93), the Kona coast is
short of interesting trails, but the rest of the island has plenty
to keep you occupied. Favorites include the descents into
Waipiʻo (p.165) and **Pololū** (p.154) valleys, and the coastal
walks to **Green Sand Beach** (p.261) and **Kamehameha's
Birthplace** (p.149).

However, the most unique and fascinating feature of the
island has to be **Kīlauea volcano**, in Volcanoes National
Park. It would be easy to spend a week day-hiking the trails
to current and recent eruption sites without the thrill of
being inside an active volcano wearing off, and there's
potential for countless longer backpacking expeditions. See
Chapter Eleven for full accounts.

EQUIPMENT AND SAFETY

Like all the Hawaiian islands, the Big Island is basically a
large pile of rough lava, and any **footwear** except sturdy
boots is likely to be torn to shreds. Other equipment should
include rain gear, a flashlight, insect repellent, sunscreen
and sunglasses, some attention-seeking device such as a
whistle or a piece of brightly colored clothing, and a basic
first-aid kit. If you're backpacking, you'll need a waterproof
tent and sleeping bag, and if you're heading up Mauna Kea
or Mauna Loa take warm clothing as well.

Never drink untreated water. **Leptospirosis**, a bacterial
disease carried by rats and mice in particular, can be con-
tracted through drinking stream water (filtering alone will
not purify it), or even from wading through fresh water,
especially if you have any kind of open wound or blister.
Symptoms range from diarrhea, fever, and chills through to

kidney or heart failure and appear in anything from two to twenty days. For more information, contact the Big Island's District Health Office on ☎933-4276.

Sports

Competitive sports are not very much in evidence on the Big Island, although the University of Hawaii in Hilo boasts some enthusiastically supported basketball and baseball teams. A number of showpiece events take place each year, however, with the highlight being the **Ironman Triathlon World Championship**, held each October and centered on Kailua (☎329-0063, ⓦwww.ironmanlive.com). Its superhuman participants race to complete a 2.4-mile ocean swim across Kailua Bay, a 112-mile cycle ride and a full 26-mile marathon – all on the same day.

In August, Kailua plays host to the **Hawaiian International Billfish Tournament** (☎329-6155), when sportfishermen from around the world hunt the high seas for blue marlin weighing up to 1000 pounds. Early September sees the Queen Liliʻuokalani World Championship Long-Distance **Canoe Races**, once again held in Kailua (☎ 323-2565).

As for **participant sports**, many of the most popular activities are ocean-related (see p.44). Most of the larger hotels have **tennis courts** for their guests, and there are public courts in Hilo, Kailua and elsewhere (call the Dept of Parks & Recreation for details: ☎ 961-8311).

There are also plenty of **golf courses**. Those at the Kohala resorts, designed to tournament specifications, have the highest reputations, but also the highest **green fees** –

BIG ISLAND GOLF COURSES

Big Island Country Club, Waikoloa; $125; ☎ 325-5044
Hāmākua Country Club, Honokaʻa; $15; ☎ 775-7244
Hāpuna Golf Course, Kohala; $185; ☎ 880-3000
Hilo Municipal Golf Course, Hilo; $25; ☎ 959-9601
Kona Country Club,
 Aliʻi Course, Kailua; $175; ☎ 322-2595
 Ocean Course, Kailua; $175; ☎ 322-2595
Makalei Hawaii Country Club, Kona; $110; ☎ 325-6625
Mauna Kea Beach Golf Club, Kohala; $195; ☎ 882-5400
Mauna Lani Resort,
 Francis H Iʻi Brown, North Kohala; $185; ☎ 885-6655
 Francis H Iʻi Brown, South Kohala; $185; ☎ 885-6655
Naniloa Country Club, Hilo; $40; ☎ 935-3000
Sea Mountain Golf Course, Punaluʻu; $45; ☎ 928-6222
Volcano Golf & Country Club, Volcano; $62.50; ☎ 967-7331
Waikoloa Golf Club,
 Beach Course, Waikoloa; $195; ☎ 886-6060
 Kings' Course, Waikoloa; $195; ☎ 886-7888
Waikoloa Village Golf Club, Waikoloa; $95; ☎ 883-9621
Waimea Country Club, Waimea; $85; ☎ 885-8777

SPORTS

most cost little short of $200, and the reductions for hotel guests are not all that significant. Rates at Hilo's municipal course, by contrast, start around $25.

The annual **Hawaii Golf Guide**, published by the Aloha Section PGA (770 Kapi'olani Blvd, Suite 715, Honolulu, HI 96813; ☎593-2230) carries complete listings. Stand-By Golf (☎1-888/645-2665) specializes in finding discounted and short-notice golfing opportunities.

Crafts and shopping

Many Big Island residents think nothing of flying to Honolulu for the day to shop in Ala Moana mall, and unless you're going to Oahu as well, you may find you fly home with fewer gifts and souvenirs than you expected. To put it simply, shopping is not one of the Big

Island's strong points. The prints, posters, and T-shirts on sale in Kailua and the major tourist areas are OK if you think that whales are interplanetary voyagers from another dimension, or that a gecko on a surfboard is real neat, but stores and galleries selling high-quality indigenous arts and crafts are few and far between.

SHOPS AND GALLERIES

Devoting your days to the search for the perfect gift is probably not a good idea, but it's worth knowing about some of the more interesting places to call in on as you explore the island. **Hōlualoa**, immediately above Kailua, has the main concentration of **galleries** – you never know what locally produced paintings or ceramics might catch your eye in the co-operative Coffee Mill Workshop (see p.90). The Harbor Gallery in **Kawaihae** (p.131) is expensive but offers a wide range of fine arts, as does the better known Volcano Art Center in the National Park (p.225). As well as serving good food, **Hāwī's** *Bamboo Restaurant and Gallery* (p.150) usually has some nice *koa*-wood furniture, and the bizarre Hawaiian Shop in **Honoka'a** (p.158) stocks an amazing tangle of genuine Pacific artifacts and absolute rubbish. **Bookstores** are listed on p.301.

HAWAIIAN CRAFTS AND PRODUCE

Some of the most attractive products of Hawaii are just too ephemeral to take home. That goes for the orchids and tropical flowers on sale everywhere, and unfortunately it's also true of **leis**.

Leis (pronounced *lays*) are flamboyant decorative garlands, usually composed of flowers such as the fragrant *melia* (the plumeria or frangipani) or the Big Island's own bright-red *lehua* blossom (from the *'ō'hia* tree), but sometimes also made from feathers, shells, seeds, or nuts. They're worn by both men and women, above all on celebrations or gala occasions. The days are gone when every arriving tourist was festooned with a *lei*, but you'll probably be way-*leied* at a *lūʻau* or some such occasion, while on Lei Day (May 1) everyone's at it.

Colorful Hawaiian clothing, such as **aloha shirts** and the cover-all "Mother-Hubbard"-style **muʻumuʻu** dress, is on sale everywhere, though classic designs are surprisingly rare, and you tend to see the same stylized prints over and over again. Otherwise, the main **local crafts** are **lau hala weaving**, in which mats, hats, baskets, and the like are created by plaiting the large leaves (*lau*) of the spindly-legged pandanus (*hala*) tree, and **wood turning**, with fine bowls made from native dark woods such as *koa*.

Directory

AREA CODE The telephone area code for the whole state of Hawaii is ⊤808.

CLIMATE For details of the climate in Hawaii, see the "Introduction" on p.xvii.

ELECTRICITY Hawaii's electricity supply, like that on the US mainland, uses 100 volts AC. Plugs are standard American two-pins.

FISHING For full details of Hawaii's fishing regulations, write to Division of Aquatic Resources, Department of Land and Natural Resources, Kalanimoku Building, 1151 Punchbowl St, Room 330, Honolulu, HI 96813.

GAY AND LESBIAN LIFE The greatest concentration of gay activism in Hawaii is in Honolulu, though the state as a whole is liberal on social issues. It's one of 25 states to allow consensual "sodomy," with no criminal laws against private sex acts and a guarantee of privacy in the constitution. Pacific Ocean Holidays (PO Box 88245, Honolulu, HI 96830-8245; ⊤923-2400 or 1-800/735-6600, ⓕ923-2499, ⓦwww.gayhawaii.com/vacation/index.html) organizes all-inclusive **package vacations** in Hawaii for gay and lesbian travelers. It also publishes the thrice-yearly *Pocket Guide to Hawaii*, a useful booklet of gay listings throughout the state (available free in Hawaii, or by mail for $5 per issue, one year's subscription $12). Other useful sources of **information** include Matthew Link's *Rainbow Handbook*

(ⓦ www.rainbowhandbook
.com), a self-published
guidebook to all the Hawaiian
islands available from local
bookstores for $15, and the
various web pages gathered
on ⓦ www.gayhawaii.com.

HOSPITALS Big Island
hospitals can be contacted at
the following numbers: Hilo
ⓣ 974-4700; Waimea ⓣ 885-
4444; Ka'ū ⓣ 928-8331;
Kohala ⓣ 889-6211; Kona
ⓣ 322-9311. In emergencies
call ⓣ 911.

INOCULATIONS No
inoculations or vaccinations
are required by law in order to
enter Hawaii, though some
authorities suggest a polio
vaccination.

PUBLIC TOILETS Some public
toilets are labeled in Hawaiian:
kanes means men, *wahines*
means women.

QUARANTINE Very stringent
restrictions apply to the
importation of all plants and
animals into Hawaii. Cats and
dogs have to stay in
quarantine for 120 days; if you
were hoping to bring an
alligator or a hamster into the
state, forget it. For full
regulations on importing

animals call ⓣ 483-7151; for
the rules regarding plants call
ⓣ 586-0844; or access
ⓦ www.hawaiiag.org.

SENIOR TRAVELERS The
University of Hawaii at Hilo
runs Elderhostel programs
each summer, in which senior
citizens take courses in
Hawaiian culture and history,
with fees covering board,
lodging and tuition; for details
contact the Program Director,
University of Hawaii CCECS,
523 W Lanikaula St, Hilo, HI
96720 (ⓣ 933-3555).
Elderhostel's national
headquarters is at 11 Ave de
Fayette, Boston, MA 02111
(ⓣ 978/323-4141 or
1-877/426-8056,
ⓦ www.elderhostel.org). US
residents aged fifty or over
can join the American
Association of Retired
Persons, 601 E St NW,
Washington, DC 20049
(ⓣ 1-800/424-3410,
ⓦ www.aarp.org), for
discounts on accommodation
and vehicle rental.

TIME Unlike most of the United
States, Hawaii does not
observe Daylight Saving Time.
Therefore, from 2am on the

last Sunday in April until 2am on the last Sunday in October, the time difference between Hawaii and the US West Coast is three hours, not the usual two; the difference between Hawaii and the mountain region is four hours, not three; and the islands are six hours later than the East Coast, not five. Hawaiian time is from ten to eleven hours behind the UK. In fact it's behind just about everywhere else; although New Zealand and Australia might seem to be two and four hours respectively behind Honolulu time, they're on the other side of the International Date Line, so are actually almost a full day ahead.

TIPPING Wait staff in restaurants expect tips of at least fifteen percent, in bars a little less. Hotel porters and bellhops should receive around $1 per piece of luggage, and housekeeping staff $1 per night.

TRAVELERS WITH DISABILITIES

Copies of the *Aloha Guide to Accessibility in the State of Hawaii*, and additional information on facilities for travelers with disabilities on Oahu, can be obtained from the State Commission on Persons with Disabilities, 919 Ala Moana Blvd, Suite 101, Honolulu, HI Ⓣ 96814 (Ⓣ 586-8121). Accessible Vans of Hawaii, 186 Mehani Circle, Kīhei, HI 96753 (Ⓣ 879-5521, Ⓦ www.accessiblevans.com) rent out wheelchair-accessible vans and also run island tours and shuttle services. In Hilo, inexpensive city-run taxi service is provided by Handi-Van (Ⓣ 961-6722). Wheelchairs and other equipment can be rented from Medi-Home Care (Ⓣ 969-1123) and Pacific United Rent-All (Ⓣ 934-2974) in Hilo, or Kona Coast Drugs (Ⓣ 329-8886) and Kona Rent-All (Ⓣ 329-1644) on the Kona side.

WEDDINGS To get married in Hawaii, you need to have a valid state license, which costs $50 from the Department of Health, Marriage License Office, 1250 Punchbowl St, Honolulu, HI 96813 (Mon–Fri 8am–4pm; Ⓣ 586-4545; Ⓦ www.hawaii .gov), and is valid for thirty

DIRECTORY

days. You also need proof of rubella immunizations or screening, which can be arranged through the Department of Health. The Big Island Visitors Bureau website (Ⓦ www.bigisland.org) lists companies who arrange weddings, and most resorts offer their own marriage planners. Among the local wedding specialists are Paradise Weddings Hawaii (Ⓣ 883/9067, Ⓦ planet-hawaii .com/weddings/), and Aloha Weddings in Paradise (Ⓣ 776-1420; Ⓦ www.alohaweddings inparadise.com).

THE GUIDE

Kailua

onsidering that **KAILUA** is the oldest Western-style community on the Big Island – Hawaii's first Christian missionaries arrived here from New England in 1820 – and was before that a favorite home of Kamehameha I, it took a surprisingly long time to grow to its present size. Before the 1980s spurt that made Kailua the Big Island's busiest tourist area, things had stood still for over a century, a fact that has left the town with an oddly dual personality. While the harbor area continues to center around the simple palace and church, built in the 1830s, it's increasingly surrounded by modern malls. The high-rise hotels conspicuous to either side of the center form just a small part of the ribbon of beachfront properties that accommodate several thousand visitors per day. That said, Kailua's heyday as a resort seems already to be over, as the great majority of new investment in hotels is now taking place further up the coast. While the town continues to expand, it is doing so primarily as a residential, rather than a tourist, area.

Kailua is still a very long way from the overkill of Waikīkī, however. When Mark Twain called it "the sleepiest, quietest, Sundayest looking place you can imagine," he meant to be pejorative, but if you've come to relax you'll probably find its low-key pleasures appealing. At least one of the local beaches is bound to suit you, and there are plenty of alternative activities. In particular, sitting on the *lānai* of one of the many waterfront cafés and bars, for a blast of Kona coffee in the morning or for a cocktail at sunset, is enough to make anyone feel that all's right with the world.

Many new arrivals assume that Kailua, not Hilo, is the island's capital. Infuriated residents of Hilo console themselves with the thought that hardly anyone seems to get the name of their rival right. Officially, it's called Kailua, hyphenated by the post office to "Kailua-Kona" to distinguish it from the Kailuas on Oahu and Maui. Most tourists, however, have only heard of Kona and not of Kailua. Compound that with the fact that most of the businesses and other facilities that people generally refer to as being "in Kona" are in fact in Kailua, and you have a recipe for confusion.

The telephone area code for all Hawaii is ℡ 808.

ARRIVAL AND INFORMATION

Keāhole Airport, the Big Island's laid-back main airport, sprawls across the lava seven miles north of Kailua. Most arriving passengers rent a car immediately from the usual outlets (detailed on p.21) or arrange to be picked up by their hotels. **Taxis** from the airport rank cost around $20 to Kailua, $40 to Waikoloa; multipassenger shuttle vans, run by companies such as Speedi Shuttle (℡ 329-5433), which has a courtesy phone in the baggage area, charge slightly less.

Public transport in Kailua town itself is restricted to two shuttle services that run hourly loops along the five-mile length of Ali'i Drive. The Ali'i Shuttle (daily

8.30am–7.30pm; $2 one-way, $5 per day; ☏775-7121) is based at the Lanihau Center, while the Kona Town Trolley (daily 8.45am–8.45pm; $5 per day; ☏331-1582) starts from the *King Kamehameha* hotel. The latter company also runs the Kona Town Express, which operates ten daily loops between the *King Kamehameha* and the King's Shops up in Waikoloa (daily 8am–9.30pm; $5 one-way). Their $15 one-day systemwide pass includes connecting buses that run north from Waikoloa up the Kohala coast (see p.118).

Finally, on Monday through Saturday, a daily bus run by the Hilo-based Hele On Bus Company (☏961-8744) follows the Belt Road all the way to Hilo; for a full timetable see p.25.

Kona-coast boat excursions are listed on pp.46 and 95

Information and services

The **Hawaii Visitors Bureau** (☏329-7787, ⓦwww.bigisland.org) no longer maintains a full-service office in Kailua, but they do have an information booth on the pier, open unpredictable hours. In any case, most of the brochures available at the booth can also be picked up at any of the abundant "**activities desks**" in the seafront malls and hotels, whose primary function is to book tourists onto snorkel cruises, helicopter rides, and the like. One recommended example is the Activity Connection, based in Bougainvillea Plaza just up from the *Kona Seaside* hotel (☏329-1038, ⓦwww.beachactivityguide.com). Free glossies such as *This Week* and *Big Island Gold* are available all over town.

There are **post offices** in the Lanihau Center in downtown Kailua and in the Keauhou Shopping Village, five miles south at the far end of Ali'i Drive. If you need **money**, the branches of the Bank of Hawaii, First Hawaiian Bank, and American Savings Bank in the Lanihau Center hold virtually every ATM under the sun.

Snorkel Bob has an outlet of his inimitable **snorkeling equipment** rental service (daily 8am–5pm; ☎329-0770, ⓦ www.snorkelbob.com) opposite *Huggo's*, near the *Royal Kona Resort*.

ACCOMMODATION

Well over half of all the Big Island's **hotel** and **condo** rooms are concentrated in or near Kailua, the vast majority of them along the roughly five-mile oceanfront stretch of Ali'i Drive. However, in terms of quality the area is falling way behind the resorts to the north. A steady decline in investment has seen standards drop alarmingly, and certain well-known properties, such as the *Kona Surf Resort*, have closed down altogether. That said, there are still some attractive and good-value places to be found, and if you prefer to spend your vacation in a real town rather than a self-contained resort, Kailua is still the best option on the island.

Ali'i Drive also holds a handful of **B&Bs**, though visitors in search of a traditional B&B experience tend to prefer to drive the three miles up from the ocean to the idyllic seclusion of the "coffee town" of Hōlualoa, described on p.89.

If you plan to spend your entire vacation in Kailua, remember that you can get far better rates by booking an all-inclusive package before you leave home. In addition, a wide selection of **condos** along the Kona coast, at all prices, can also be booked through *Sunquest Vacations*, 77-6435 Kuakini Hwy, Kailua-Kona, HI 96740 (☎329-6488, 1-800/367-5168 in the US, 1-800/800-KONA in Canada, ⓕ329-5480, ⓦ www.sunquest-hawaii.com).

ACCOMMODATION PRICE CODES

All accommodation options in this book have been graded
with the following symbols; for a full explanation, see p.29.

❶ up to $40   ❹ $100–150   ❼ $250–300
❷ $40–70   ❺ $150–200   ❽ $300–400
❸ $70–100   ❻ $200–250   ❾ over $400

- -

Hotels and restaurants listed in this
chapter are keyed on maps 2 and 3.

- -

Aston Keauhou Beach Resort

78-6740 Aliʻi Drive ☏ 322-3441
or 1-877/532-8468, or through
Aston 1-800/922-7866 (US &
Can), 1-800/321-2558 (HI),
🖷 322-6586,
🌐 www.aston-hotels.com.
Seven-story hotel jutting into
the sea on a black-lava
promontory at the southern
end of Kahaluʻu Beach Park,
five miles south of central
Kailua. All rooms have been
renovated to a high standard
of comfort, and offer ocean-
view balconies. Facilities
include tennis courts and a
pool immediately below the
Dining Room; trails around
the grounds lead past ruined

temples and petroglyphs, as
well as the site of the twice-
weekly *lūʻau* (Sun & Thurs
5.30pm; $68). The open-air
Verandah Bar is a good spot
for an evening drink, and
often features live Hawaiian
music. Garden view ❺, ocean
view ❻.

Aston Royal Sea Cliff Resort

75-6040 Aliʻi Drive ☏ 329-8021,
or through Aston 1-800/922-
7866 (US & Can), 1-800/321-
2558 (HI), 🖷 326-1887,
🌐 www.aston-hotels.com.
White multilevel complex of
luxurious one- and two-
bedroom condos, dropping
down to the coast a mile

KAILUA: ACCOMMODATION

south of central Kailua, and
laid out around a lush
courtyard garden to
maximize ocean views. You
can't swim in the sea here,
but there are fresh- and
saltwater pools, plus a sauna
and Jacuzzi. Garden view ❺,
ocean view ❻.

Kailua Plantation House
75-5948 Ali'i Drive
Ⓣ 329-3727, Ⓕ 326-7323,
Ⓦ www.tales.com/KPH.
Dramatic oceanfront
mansion, a mile south of
central Kailua, now run as an
upmarket B&B. All five
luxury suites have their own
spacious *lānais*, and they share
use of a pool, Jacuzzi and
living area. ❺–❻

King Kamehameha's Kona Beach Hotel
75-5660 Palani Rd Ⓣ 329-2911
or 1-800/367-6060, Ⓕ 329-4602,
Ⓦ www.konabeachhotel.com.
Long-established family-
oriented hotel, centered
around picturesque, sandy

Kamakahonu Beach (see p.79),
with a small shopping mall,
and an unexceptional
restaurant. You can swim in
the pool or from the beach,
and kayaks, pedaloes and
other watersports equipment
are available for rent. The
lobby hosts Hawaiian music
performances and crafts
displays, while the gardens
make an attractive *lū'au*
setting (Tues–Fri & Sun
5.30–8.45pm; $55). Standard
❹, oceanfront ❺.

Kona Billfisher
75-5841 Ali'i Drive
Ⓣ 329-3333 or 1-800/622-5348
(US & Can), Ⓕ 326-4137,
Ⓦ www.konahawaii.com.
Well-maintained, good-value
condos in a complex of
small, coffee-colored three-
story units that sprawls up the
hillside across from the *Royal
Kona Resort*, just a short walk
south of central Kailua. Each
unit has a kitchen and
balcony. ❸

**Unless otherwise specified, all properties listed
here share the zip code Kailua-Kona HI 96740.**

Kona Islander Inn Resort

75-5776 Kuakini Hwy
Ⓣ 329-3333 or 1-800/622-5348,
Ⓕ 326-4137,
Ⓦ www.konahawaii.com.
These centrally located
1960s condos, just behind
the Coconut Grove
Marketplace, may not seem
the height of style from the
outside, but they're perfectly
adequate inside, and offer
some of the Kona coast's best
rates, right in the heart of
Kailua. Prices rise
significantly from mid-
December through March.
The front desk is also a
reservations office for several
other local condo resorts. ❷

Kona Reef

75-5888 Ali'i Drive Ⓣ 329-2959
or through Castle Resorts
1-800/367-5004 (US & Can) or
1-880/272-5275 (HI), Ⓕ 329-
2762, Ⓦ www.castle-group.com.
Attractive modern condo
development, on the southern
edge of Kailua just beyond
the *Royal Kona Resort*, with

several successive levels of
very comfortable, blue-
roofed, one-, two- and three-
bed units dropping down to
the ocean. No on-site beach,
but a good pool. ❺

Kona Seaside Hotel

75-5646 Palani Rd
Ⓣ 329-2455 or 1-800/560-5558,
reservations also at Ⓣ 922-
1228, Ⓕ 922-0052,
Ⓦ www.sand-seaside.com.
The 223-room property
sprawls across central Kailua
just up from Ali'i Drive; the
main entrance is opposite the
King Kamehameha. Several
three-story wings of small,
good-value air-con rooms are
clustered around a central
pool, while a newer six-floor
building overlooks another,
smaller pool. Reservations for
this Hawaiian-owned chain
are handled in Honolulu. ❹

Kona Tiki Hotel

75-5968 Ali'i Drive
Ⓣ 329-1425, Ⓕ 327-9402.
This three-story, motel-style

For a wide range of inexpensive, small-scale alternatives to
Kailua's hotels, see "South Kona Accommodation" on p.101.

KAILUA: ACCOMMODATION

property, poised inches from the ocean a mile out from central Kailua, is an absolute gem for budget travelers. The winter season is often completely booked up three years in advance. All rooms have private oceanfront balconies, some also have kitchenettes, and rates even include breakfast beside the tiny pool. No TVs, phones or credit cards; three-night minimum stay. ❷

Patey's Place

75-195 Ala-Ona Ona St
Ⓣ326-7018, Ⓕ326-7640,
Ⓔ ipatey@gte.net,
Ⓦ www.hawaiian-hostels.com.
Chaotic, ramshackle and unappealing hostel that's nonetheless popular with backpackers and surfers. It's a few hundred yards *mauka* of the town center, reached by taking Kalani St up from Kuakini Hwy at *McDonald's*, and then the second turning on the left. Minimally furnished, thin-walled doubles for $41.50, or four-bed dorms for $17.50 a bed, plus a communal kitchen and TV room, but no restaurant. As well as the odd $5 barbecue, it offers a $10 airport shuttle service, bikes at $15 per day, and its own cheap island tours. It can also arrange discounts on car rental and airfares. ❶–❷

The only other hostel in the Kailua area is *Pineapple Park*, a dozen miles south near Captain Cook; see p.103.

Royal Kona Resort

75-5852 Ali'i Drive
Ⓣ329-3111 or 1-800/919-8333
(US & Can), Ⓕ329-7230,
Ⓦ www.royalkona.com
The gleaming white pyramids of the *Royal Kona Resort* (originally the *Kona Hilton*), where almost all of the 452 rooms have their own *lānais*, dominate the headland at the southern end of central Kailua. The standard rooms are nothing special, but ones in the more expensive categories are very nice. Its main restaurant, the *Tropics Café*, has beautiful views and serves good-value

buffets of above-average Asian and Pacific food, while the "Drums of Polynesia" *lū'au* (Mon, Fri & Sat 5.30pm; $55), open to nonresidents, is one of the best in town. Garden view ❹, ocean view ❺.

Uncle Billy's Kona Bay Hotel

75-5739 Ali'i Drive ☏329-6488, 1-800/367-5102 (US & Can) or 1-800/442-5841 (HI), ℉935-7903, Ⓦwww.unclebilly.com. Friendly central hotel, run by the same family as the *Hilo Bay* (see p.185). Far from fancy, occasionally noisy, but reasonably comfortable rooms, all air-conditioned and with private bathrooms, are arranged in a crescent around a small pool and *Kimo's* restaurant (see p.82). The parking lot, at the back, is entered off Hualālai Rd. ❸

THE TOWN

Central Kailua still retains something of the feel of a seaside village. Every visitor should set aside an hour or two to take a leisurely oceanfront stroll along the old seawall, whose scenic route runs for a few hundred yards around the bay from the **Ahu'ena Heiau**, jutting into the ocean in front of the *King Kamehameha* hotel, to the **Hulihe'e Palace** and **Moku'aikaua Church**.

At its heart is the jetty of **Kailua Pier**, a small expanse of asphalt popular with anglers, courting couples and surf-bums alike. Until as recently as the 1960s there were still cattle pens here, but these days most commercial boats leave from the marina at Honokōhau Harbor, three miles north (see p.107), and the mood tends to be slightly aimless. At least the time-honored tradition of fishermen displaying their catches in the early evening persists, with the biggest fish of all weighing in during August's International Billfish Tournament. More gleaming flesh is on show in mid-October each year, when the pier is the starting point of the 2.4-mile swimming leg of the **Ironman Triathlon**, which also requires its participants to cycle 112 miles and run a marathon on the same day.

The resort area stretches away to the south, while up from the seafront ever-increasing numbers of **shopping malls** seem to appear each year, catering more to the needs of local residents, and less to those of tourists, the higher you climb from the shoreline. For everyday shopping and services, locals tend to head for Costco or Kmart, on the northeastern edge of town, or the **Lanihau Center** near the main stoplights on the highway.

Ahuʻena Heiau

Map 2, B4.

The **Ahuʻena Heiau**, guarding the mouth of Kailua Bay in a too-good-to-be-true setting beside a sandy little beach, looks as though it was built yesterday to provide an ersatz Polynesian backdrop for the *King Kamehameha* hotel. Few visitors spare it more than a passing glance, but this genuine Hawaiian temple, dedicated to the god Lono, deserves at least a few minutes of your time. Kamehameha the Great held sway from this ancient temple between his return from Honolulu in 1812 and his death here on May 8, 1819. Soon afterwards, his son Liholiho, spurred on by Kamehameha's principal queen, Kaʻahumanu, broke the ancient *kapu* system by hosting a banquet here, and thereby inadvertently cleared the way for the missionaries (see p.273).

Thanks to detailed drawings made in 1816, archeologists have been able to restore the *heiau* to its original appearance, but it still possesses great spiritual significance, and all access to the platform is forbidden. You can get a close-up view by walking to the end of the *King Kamehameha* beach – officially Kamakahonu Beach (see p.79) – or by swimming out a short way. The *heiau* itself is small, but follows the conventional Hawaiian template, consisting as it does of three distinct structures set on a *paepae* (platform) of black volcanic rock. The largest hut is the *hale mana* ("house of spiritual power"), a place of prayer and council. The smaller *hale pahu* ("house of the drum") alongside is thatched with *hala* leaves, while the ramshackle, tapering structure nearby is the *anuʻu* ("oracle tower"), used by the priests to intercede with the gods. In addition, half a dozen *kiʻi akua*, carved wooden images symbolizing different gods, stand on the platform; the tallest, a god of healing known as Kōleamoku, has a golden plover on his head.

After his death, Kamehameha's bones were prepared for burial on a similar rock platform adjacent to the *heiau*, then interred in a location that remains a secret to this day. The platform still exists, though the *hale pōhaku* that stood upon it, in which the ceremonies took place, has long since disappeared.

Huliheʻe Palace

Map 2, C4. Mon–Fri 9am–4pm, Sat & Sun 10am–4pm; $5; ⓉⓉ 329-1877.

Though the four-square, two-story **Huliheʻe Palace**, facing out to sea from the center of Kailua, was built in 1838 for Governor John Adams Kuakini, it soon passed into the hands of the Hawaiian royal family. It was constructed using lava rock, coral, and native hardwoods, but you wouldn't know that from a glance at its coffee-colored modern exterior. Visiting this mildly quaint Victorian private residence is not very enthralling, nor is its limited charm enhanced by the ponderous reverence of the staff. The interior is notable mainly for its massive *koa*-wood furnishings, made to fit the considerable girth of such dignitaries as the four-hundred-pound Princess Ruth, and its countless fading photographs of the bewhiskered King David Kalākaua and his stately relatives.

The room immediately to the left of the entrance holds a small but interesting collection of Hawaiiana, including bone fishhooks and stone adzes and hammers. Alongside a small feather cape, King Kalākaua's desk and guitar, and several bowls made from *koa* wood, there's a narrow replica *hōlua* sled, of the kind once raced by the *ali'i* down artificial slides of grass-covered rock. On display in the master bedroom upstairs are a mighty four-poster bed, a beautiful inlaid table and a colossal and highly ornate wardrobe, all fashioned from dark hardwood.

Pleasant *lānais* run the full length of the ocean side of both the first and second floors. Visitors are free to wander into the well-maintained gardens, which host free *hula* performances on the fourth Sunday of each month (except June & Dec).

Moku'aikaua Church

Map 2, C4. Daily dawn–dusk, Congregational services Sun 8am & 10.30am; free.

The original **Moku'aikaua Church**, directly opposite the palace, was the first church to be built on the Hawaiian islands. It was constructed in 1820 for the use of Reverend Asa Thurston, one of the first two Christian missionaries dispatched to Hawaii from New England, who had arrived in Kailua Bay on April 4 that year. At that time it closely resembled a *heiau*, being just a thatched hut perched on a stone platform. The current building was erected immediately before Hulihe'e Palace by the same craftsmen, using the same methods, and incorporates large chunks of lava into a design clearly related to the clapboard churches of New England.

The church itself is not of great interest, but part of it has been set aside as a museum chronicling the early days of Hawaiian Christianity. Displays include a large model of the ship *Thaddeus*, Hawaii's equivalent of the *Mayflower*,

THE COMING OF THE MISSIONARIES

The Sandwich Islands Mission, which sent the first Christian missionaries to Hawaii, was formed largely as a result of the death of **Henry 'Opukaha'ia**. A *kahuna* priest at the Hikiau *heiau* in Kealakekua Bay (see p.97), he converted to Christianity and went to study at the Foreign Mission School in Connecticut. In 1818, however, still in his early twenties, he died of typhus, lamenting his failure to return home to convert his benighted brethren.

The heartfelt prayer, and hard cash, of New England worthies moved by the young man's untimely end enabled two ministers, **Revd Hiram Bingham** and **Revd Asa Thurston**, to set sail from Boston in the brig *Thaddeus* on October 23, 1819. Their 18,000-mile journey, via Cape Horn, took more than five months, ending eventually in Kailua Bay on April 4, 1820.

Asa Thurston did not immediately take to Hawaii – he described Kailua as "a filthy village of thatched huts . . . on which the fervent sun poured its furnace heat every day of the year." But then, neither did the Hawaiians take to him, and there was great debate as to whether the missionaries should be permitted to land. They arrived just as **Queen Ka'ahumanu** had broken the hold of Hawaii's traditional priesthood by defying the *kapu* system. She was in no mood to replace them with a new set of interfering moralizers.

In the end, the counsel of the aging John Young (see p.129) was decisive, but only Thurston was allowed to remain in Kailua. Bingham was sent to Honolulu, where, scurrilously known as "King Bingham," he was soon denouncing his flock as the "stupid and polluted worshippers of demons." Nonetheless, the missionaries' tactic of focusing their attentions on the ruling class, in the belief that the common people would convert in their wake, soon paid dividends. Even Ka'ahumanu, after she was nursed through a grave illness by Bingham's wife Sybil, became an enthusiastic Christian.

and an exhibition on traditional Polynesian navigational techniques featuring, among other things, a fascinating Micronesian "stick chart," in which an intricate latticework of pandanus (*hala*) twigs and cowrie shells depicts ocean currents, swells, and islands. Such charts were committed to memory rather than carried on board, and served to guide canoes across thousands of miles of the open Pacific.

A bizarre "sausage tree" grows in the grounds of the church. A native of Mozambique, it is named after the pendulous, elongated and foul-smelling fruit that dangles on long cords from its branches. One of only two on Hawaii, it was planted here on a whim in the 1920s.

South along Ali'i Drive

Heading south from both the church and palace, **Ali'i Drive** is at first fringed with modern malls housing T-shirt stores, boutiques and restaurants. Beyond Kailua proper, it stretches five miles along a rugged coastline scattered with tiny lava beaches and lined all the way with hotels and condos. The only thing you could call a "sight" along here is the tiny, blue, and highly photogenic **St Peter's Church**, built in 1880. It takes perhaps a minute to admire its waterfront setting, on a tiny patch of lawn at the north end of Kahalu'u Bay, and to glance in through the open door at the etched glass window above the altar.

BEACHES

Considering its reputation as a resort, central Kailua is surprisingly short of **beaches**. There are enough patches of sand along Ali'i Drive to satisfy those who like the convenience of being able to walk to and from their hotels, but most visitors tend to drive north when they fancy a swim. The Big Island's best beaches – such as the Kona Coast

State Park (p.108), Hāpuna Beach (p.122), and Spencer Beach Park (p.125) – start ten miles or more up the coast, but a good nearby alternative is the Old Kona Airport park, just a few minutes from town.

Note that camping is not permitted on any of the beaches covered in this section.

Old Kona Airport State Recreation Area

Map 3, A2. Daily dawn–8pm.

When Keāhole Airport opened in 1970, the lands of its predecessor on the northern outskirts of Kailua, which had become too small to meet the requirements of the tourist trade, were set aside for public use as the **Old Kona Airport State Recreation Area**. Though it's not all that attractive, it's now Kailua's most extensive and popular beach. Driving in along the long former runways, which run parallel to the sea, is either hair-raising or fun depending on your state of mind, as no one ever seems sure which, if any, of the plentiful road markings to follow.

A strip of coarse, whitish sand lies beyond the fringe of low palm trees, while the shoreline itself consists almost entirely of flat, smooth *pāhoehoe* lava, indented with calm shallow pools that are ideal for children to splash in. Sheltered pavilions and barbecue facilities are scattered all the way along, and despite the lack of food and drink outlets, there always seems to be plenty of people around. The park gates are closed daily at 8pm to prevent nighttime gatherings.

Kamakahonu Beach

Map 2, B4.

Many first-time visitors to Kailua glance at pretty little

Kamakahonu Beach and assume that it belongs to the *King Kamehameha* hotel. However, nonguests are entirely at liberty to sunbathe here or to swim out for a closer look at the Ahu'ena Heiau (see p.74). It can be a delightful spot, but you're not permitted to swim beyond the mouth of the tiny inlet, and in terms of size, calmness and crowds it often feels more like a swimming pool, so only small children are likely to want to linger for any length of time.

Ali'i Drive beaches

The coast along Ali'i Drive south of central Kailua is predominantly made up of black lava flats interspersed with the odd sandy cove. Few of the hotels or condos have adjacent beaches, so the designated beach parks tend to be the only places where it's possible to swim.

If you visit in winter or early spring, you probably won't even be able to find the small **White Sands Beach**, immediately north of St Peter's Church (see p.78), four miles south of central Kailua. Long renowned as an exhilarating surfing beach – the pile of black boulders near the church are the ruins of the **Kue'manu Heiau**, the only temple in the Hawaiian islands known to have been devoted exclusively to surfing – this remains Kona's most popular venue for boogie-boarders and body-surfers. However, the dramatic waves are capable of washing the beach away altogether – hence the name by which it's more commonly known, **Magic Sands**. For most of the year, bathing is safe for children in the inshore area, though experienced divers will enjoy investigating a network of submarine lava tubes. So long as the beach is not devoid of sand, the snorkeling too is superb – especially if you head off to the right.

The largest of the beaches along Ali'i Drive, and even better for snorkeling, is **Kahalu'u Beach**, just south of St Peter's Church. It's more of a slight indentation in the coastline than a bay, but that's enough for it to hang onto a fair-sized spread of white sand. Children play in the lava hollows to either side, snorkelers explore deeper but still sheltered pools, and strong swimmers and scuba divers use the shelving sand to access the open waters of the bay. Large segments remain of a long breakwater, which originally protected the whole area and was supposedly constructed by early Hawaiians – the *menehune* who, according to legend, were here long before the main Polynesian migration of the twelfth and thirteenth centuries – to aid fish-farming.

Generally this is a safe spot, but high surf conditions can create a devastating rip current. Don't venture into the water if you're in any doubt; if you get caught by the current, your best strategy, as ever, is to allow yourself to be swept out beyond its reach rather than exhaust yourself trying to fight it.

EATING

Though Kailua is filled with **places to eat**, it's surprisingly short of anything that could be considered fine dining. Each of its many malls has at least a couple of restaurants, while those that stand more than a block or so up from the ocean, such as the Lanihau Center, also house outlets of every imaginable fast-food chain. Asian cuisines, especially Thai, are strongly represented, and there are plenty of raucous, heavy-drinking, pseudo-Mexican options.

Most of the restaurants along Ali'i Drive are pricier, but offer views of the bay and serve slightly better-quality food. Even along the waterfront, however, there are still some determinedly old-fashioned, inexpensive diners.

Hotels and restaurants listed in this chapter are keyed on maps 2 and 3.

INEXPENSIVE

Kimo's Buffet Restaurant

Kona Bay Hotel, 75-5739 Ali'i Drive ☎ 329-1393.
The palm-fringed and vaguely Polynesian open-air terrace beside the pool of this central Kailua hotel is the venue for plain but good value all-you-can-eat buffets, costing $7 Mon–Fri, $8 Sat & Sun for breakfast, and $11 or $12 for dinner. Daily 7–10am & 5.30–9pm.

King Yee Lau

Ali'i Sunset Plaza, 75-5799 Ali'i Drive ☎ 329-7100.
Large Chinese restaurant at the rear of a modern plaza. Most entrees (such as lemon chicken, beef in oyster sauce, and mussels in black bean sauce) cost around $8. You can also get fresh lobster and crab, as well as budget lunch buffets. Mon–Sat 11am–2pm & 5–9pm, Sun 5–9pm.

Kona Brewing Co

North Kona Shopping Center, 75-5744 Ali'i Drive ☎ 329-2739.
Large brewpub, in an unexciting mall behind the *King Kamehameha*, with lots of indoor and outdoor seating but no views to speak of. As well as home-brewed beers like Longboard Lager and even a Kona Coffee Stout, they sell reasonably inventive salads and sandwiches available in both half and full sizes for $5–10, and inexpensive pizzas made to your precise specifications. Food service stops an hour before closing time. Mon–Thurs 11am–10pm, Fri & Sat 11am–11pm, Sun 4–10pm.

Ocean Seafood

King Kamehameha Mall, 75-5626 Kuakini Hwy ☎ 329-3055.
Indoor Chinese dining in a small mall, one block back from the sea, behind the *King Kamehameha* hotel. There are no views, and the food is served at plain glass-topped tables, but it's tasty and inexpensive: weekday plate lunches such as ribs or barbecue pork cost $6.50, while set meals in the evening start around $12, with sizzling platters for a

little less. Lots of shrimp and scallop entrees are on offer, and there's a small vegetarian selection. Mon–Fri 10.30am–9pm, Sat & Sun 11am–9pm.

Ocean View Inn

75-5683 Ali'i Drive ⊤ 329-9998. Old-style Hawaiian diner, facing the jetty near Hulihe'e Palace, with the drabbest of fittings but magnificent views of the bay. Crowds flock for $8–11 dinner plates such as roast pork or roast beef, plus breakfasts and lunches, good-value sandwiches and all-day cocktails; there's also a large and even cheaper Chinese menu. Tues–Sun 6.30am–2.45pm & 5.15–9pm.

Sibu Café

Banyan Court Mall, 75-5695 W Ali'i Drive ⊤ 329-1112. Popular, informal Indonesian restaurant, with no views but some atmospheric outdoor seating. Tasty $11–14 entrees include a great shrimp *sate*, cooked in coconut milk. Daily 11.30am–3pm & 5–9pm.

Stan's Restaurant

75-5685 Ali'i Drive ⊤ 329-4500. Open-sided dining area, facing the sea in the center of Kailua's most attractive stretch, next to the *Ocean View*. Full breakfasts, including $6 Royal Hawaiian Hotcakes with banana, pineapple, papaya, and coconut syrup, as well as an extensive dinner menu featuring "Granny's 50-Year Fish Recipe" for $8.50, and stuffed *mahimahi* at $11. Daily 7–9.30am & 6–8pm.

MODERATE

Bangkok Houses

King Kamehameha Mall, 75-5626 Kuakini Hwy ⊤ 329-7764. Light, airy Thai restaurant where lunch features $5.50 specials, plus slightly pricier fish and meat salads. The dinner menu includes an $8 appetizer of New Zealand mussels, and plenty of Thai curries, among them a delicious mixed seafood curry for $15. Mon–Sat 11am–9pm, Sun 5–9pm.

Hawaiian food terms are explained on p.33.

Basil's Pizzeria

75-5707 Ali'i Drive ☎ 326-7836.
Unadventurous Italian eatery,
sited immediately north of
Moku'aikaua Church. Seated
near the doorway you can
enjoy sea views; further back
there's little to do but dig into
one of the tasty Italian daily
specials, your choice of a
variety of pasta entrees, or an
individual pizza for $6–11.
Daily 11am–10pm.

Cassandra's Greek Taverna

Kona Plaza, 75-5719 Ali'i Drive
☎ 334-1066.
This friendly European
taverna is a very welcome
addition to Kailua's dining
scene. There are plenty of
outdoor tables, but no views.
At lunchtime a Greek salad
costs $8, while in the evening
traditional appetizers such as
taramasalata or *dolmades* run to
$5–8, a substantial moussaka
is $15, and sensational *uvetsi*
dishes, of shrimps or scallops
baked with feta cheese, are
$19. Mon–Fri

11.30am–10pm, Sat & Sun
4.30–10pm.

Kona Amigos

75-5669 Ali'i Drive ☎ 326-2840.
Mexican restaurant-cum-bar
that sprawls along a large
open-air deck across from the
King Kamehameha. A vast list
of cocktails, plus the usual
array of enchiladas, burritos,
and fajitas priced at around
$11–15 for a full meal. Daily
11am–10pm.

Kona Inn Restaurant

Kona Inn Shopping Village, 75-
5744 Ali'i Drive ☎ 329-4455.
Conventional waterfront fish
place. The *Café Grill*, on an
open-air *lānai* by the sea, sells
bar snacks, salads and
sandwiches; there's a plusher
and more formal dining room
inside. Clam chowder and
sashimi feature among the
dinner appetizers, while
entrees – mostly seafood, but
including steaks – cost around
$20. *Café Grill* daily
11.30am–10pm, dinner daily
5.30–9.30pm.

Kona Petroleum Grill

75-5725 Ali'i Drive ☏ 326-1311.
Diner with a very central
location, spread across a
second-floor terrace opposite
the *Kona Inn*, and filled with
1950s antiques – gas pumps,
vintage signs, and the like –
to create a fun road-food
theme. Lunchtime burgers
and sandwiches for up to $10,
with $1 draft beer and free
pool tables, and rib and steak
dinners for just under $20.
Sun–Thurs 11.30am–10pm,
Fri & Sat 11.30am–11pm.

Thai Rin

Ali'i Sunset Plaza, 75-5799 Ali'i
Drive ☏ 329-2929.
Smart, somewhat minimalist
Thai restaurant, facing the sea
in front of a modern mall,
south of central Kailua
towards *Huggo's*. Weekday
lunch specials go for $7–8;
for dinner, try *satay* or *poocha*
(crab and pork patties) to
start, for $7–8, followed by
either a *tom yum* soup or one
of the many Thai curries
($9–12). Mon–Fri & Sun
11am–2.30pm & 5–9pm, Sat
5–9pm.

EXPENSIVE

Edward's at Kanaloa

Kanaloa at Kona, 78-261
Manukai St ☏ 322-1003.
Hard to find but attractive
and romantic restaurant,
squeezed between the ocean
and the pool in a luxury
condo complex at the (very)
quiet southern end of the
Kailua/Keauhou coastline.
The menu is hard to
categorize but generally
Mediterranean, with a
tendency toward rich sauces.
Appetizers such as escargots,
stuffed mussels, and shrimp
with couscous are either side
of $10, while entrees,
including fresh fish cooked to
your specifications, and rack
of lamb, hover around $25.
By Kailua standards it's very
good, if not quite up to the
level of the Kohala resorts.
Daily 8am–2pm & 5–9pm.

Huggo's

75-5828 Kahakai St
☏ 329-1493.
Large wooden *lānai* right on
the ocean opposite Snorkel
Bob's, where lunch includes

salads, burgers, and sandwiches, for $8–14. The dinner menu features a range of Pacific Rim dishes, including fish stuffed with prawns, grilled lamb chops, and island-raised lobster, typically priced at $25–35. Prices owe as much to the location as to the food, so come while there's light to enjoy the views. There's often live entertainment in the evenings, usually a local easy-listening band. Mon–Fri 11.30am–2.30pm & 5.30–10pm, bar open until 12.30am; Sat & Sun 5.30–10pm.

Kona Beach Restaurant

King Kamehameha's Kona Beach Hotel, 75-5660 Palani Rd ⊤329-2911.
Completely enclosed, not very atmospheric dining room, with a $10 breakfast buffet every morning. Most full dinners, such as steaks or prime rib, cost around $15, though there's a $25 seafood and rib buffet on Friday and Saturday nights, and a $14 Hawaiian one on Monday nights. Sunday's $26

champagne brunch buffet, served 9am–1pm, is the best meal of the week. Mon–Sat 6–10.30am & 5.30–9pm, Sun 6am–1pm & 5.30–9pm.

Oodles of Noodles

Crossroads Shopping Center, 75-1027 Henry St ⊤329-2222.
Extremely successful, rapidly expanding gourmet noodle joint, making the most of its dull mall setting adjoining Safeway, just off Hwy-19 a mile or so up from the ocean. The food is excellent, combining both Asian and Italian flavors; fettuccine dishes range $10–15, while the specialty wok-seared *ahi* (tuna) casserole costs $16. The lunch menu is shorter, with prices $2–4 cheaper. Mon–Fri 11.30am–9pm, Sat & Sun noon–9pm.

Sam Choy's

Kaloko Light Industrial Park, 73-5576 Kauhola St ⊤326-1545.
Living proof that if your restaurant is good enough, decor and even location don't matter. Celebrity Hawaiian chef Sam Choy's original outlet is tucked away amid a

maze of warehouses *mauka* of Hwy-19, three miles north of Kailua, and has basic canteen furnishings, but the crowds still flock for his extra-large portions of local favorites. Lunch is a ludicrously good value, with steak, *poke*, or noodles for well under $10, while dinner entrees that rival the finest Pacific Rim cuisine cost up to $30. Mon 6am–2pm, Tues–Sat 6am–2pm & 5–9pm, Sun 7am–2pm.

SHOPPING

Generally speaking there's little difference between Kailua's various malls, though as a rule those closer to the sea tend to be more firmly geared towards tourists, with the predictable array of T-shirts, sun hats, postcards, and sundry souvenirs on sale, and the odd ABC convenience store thrown in. For everyday shopping and services, locals tend to head for Costco or Kmart, on the northeastern edge of town, or the **Lanihau Center** near the main stoplights on the highway. The **Crossroads Center**, above town on the main Kuakini Highway, boasts a large Borders bookstore and an even bigger Safeway.

The two-part **Kona Marketplace**, near Moku'aikaua Church, immediately south, has a two-screen movie theater, plus assorted galleries, trinket shops, and jewelry stores, while **Kona Plaza**, hidden behind the northern section of the Marketplace, is home to the Middle Earth Bookshoppe, with its copious selection of Hawaiiana. The largest and most tourist-oriented seafront mall, the **Kona Inn Shopping Village** across Ali'i Drive, holds several clothing stores such as the excellent Hula Heaven.

Perched above the sea at the far southern end of Ali'i Drive, the modern **Keauhou Shopping Village** centers on KTA and Longs Drug superstores. It also houses a post office, a *Bad Ass* coffee bar, and a few unexciting fast-food places.

South Kona

outh of Kailua and Keauhou, the Belt Road, as **Hwy-11**, sets off on its loop around the island by rising away from the sea to run through the attractive verdant uplands of **South Kona**. This lush region is best known as the home of one of the world's finest, and most expensive, gourmet coffees – **Kona coffee**. Trees laden with avocados, mangos, oranges, and guavas stand out from the general greenery, and the route is characterized by the blossom of coffee bushes and the occasional aroma of nearby mills.

Kealakekua Bay, along the south Kona coast, is where Captain Cook chose to anchor in January 1779, as it was then both the best harbor and the main population center on the island. It was also, of course, where he was to die the following month. Within a century of that event, the seafront slopes were largely abandoned, and these days even the area higher up is inhabited only by a sparse scattering of old-time farmers and New Age newcomers. Most tourists scurry through, put off perhaps by the lack of beaches and the ramshackle look of the small towns that sprawl along the highway. However, many of these hold one or two welcoming local cafés or intriguing stores, and it's certainly worth dropping down to visit the restored **Puʻuhonua o Hōnaunau**, or "Place of Refuge," which bears atmospheric witness to a vanished Hawaiian way of life and death.

HŌLUALOA

Map 3, F3.

HŌLUALOA, the first and nicest of the coffee-growing towns, stands well above the Belt Road, scarcely three miles out of Kailua, and feels a long way removed from the hurly-burly below. This sleepy village consists of a single quiet road (Hwy-180) that meanders across the flanks of Hualālai, 1400 feet up from the ocean, and is lined on either side with small galleries and workshops, as well as orchards brimming with tropical blooms.

The production of **art** in Hōlualoa remains essentially a cottage industry, though more galleries open each year and several now also display pieces by mainland artists. Prices are seldom low, and the whole place is geared towards selling to tourists rather than locals. However, half a day can enjoyably be spent admiring the paintings and ceramics of the Hōlualoa Gallery, the fine art and sculpture in Studio Seven, and the general creative free-for-all that is the Coffee Mill Workshop, also known as the Kona Arts Center.

Most of Hōlualoa's galleries and workshops are closed on Saturday afternoons and Sundays; some take Mondays off as well.

The friendly German-owned *Hōluakoa Café* (Mon–Sat 6.30am–3pm; ☏322-2233), at the top end of the village, serves **coffees and snacks** in a pleasant garden. On Thursday evenings it also opens from 7pm until 10pm for live music. **Accommodation** in Hōlualoa is reviewed on p.101 onwards.

HŌLUALOA

ALONG HWY-11: THE COFFEE TOWNS

In theory there are four separate towns within the first four miles south of the junction of Hwy-180 and Hwy-11, though where one ends and the next begins is far from obvious. Any points of interest can be easily spotted as you drive through, be they wayside coffee stalls, antiquated general stores, local diners, or simply junkyards.

If you want to sample the atmosphere, the best stop comes just south of tiny Honalo, in the shape of **KAINALIU**'s friendly *Aloha Café* (Sun–Wed 8am–3pm, Thurs–Sat 8am–3pm & 5–9pm; ☎322-3383). Housed in the lobby of the 1930s Aloha Theater – still an active community theater, with performances by local groups and

KONA COFFEE

Succulent, strong-smelling **Kona coffee** has been grown on the Kona coast since the first seedlings arrived from Brazil in 1828. Strictly speaking, the Kona name only applies to beans grown between 800ft and 2000ft up the western slopes of Hualālai and Mauna Loa. This narrow strip, extending from Hōlualoa to Hōnaunau, offers perfect greenhouse conditions: bright sunny mornings, humid rainy afternoons, and consistently mild nights.

Though Kona boasts an enviable reputation, and demand always outstrips supply, large corporations tend to leave the labor-intensive processes of planting and tending the coffee bushes and harvesting the ripe red "cherry" from the tangled branches to small-scale family concerns. Only 1300 acres are now under cultivation in Kona, although the predominantly Japanese farmers have been joined by an influx of back-to-the-land *haoles*.

Independent farmers have long campaigned to restrict the label "Kona" to coffee consisting of one hundred percent pure Kona beans. Hawaiian state law, which allows any coffee visiting musicians, and occasional movie shows – this all-day town forum serves coffees, snacks, pastries, and a limited dinner menu.

To the south of Kainaliu, set back from the highway in a former general store in **KEALAKEKUA**, is the **Kona Historical Society Museum** (Mon–Fri 9am–3pm; $2; ⊤323-3222). This low-key assortment of photographs and heirlooms documents Kona's history from the perspective of its immigrant farmers and also offers tours of a restored old coffee farm nearby (see below). A little further on, across from the *Pineapple Park* **hostel** (see p.103), *Billy Bob's Restaurant* (Mon–Fri 11am–2.30pm & 5–9pm, Sat & Sun 5–9pm; ⊤323-3371) is a cheap and cheerful barbecue joint, which has sadly changed its name from the more colorful

containing at least ten percent Kona-grown beans to be sold as Kona coffee, has had the unfortunate effect of encouraging Californian bulk buyers to use a smattering of Kona beans to improve lesser coffees and then to sell them at inflated prices. In a locally notorious case, the Berkeley-based owner of the Kona Kai brand was recently convicted of a multimillion dollar fraud that involved passing off Costa Rican coffee as true Kona.

Coffee **prices** in the area range from around $15 per pound for the lowest ("prime") grade up to as much as $30 for a pound of the gourmets' favorite, Peaberry, while roadside outlets serve fresh Kona coffee in whatever form may take your fancy. Visitors are welcome at working coffee farms such as the **Bay View Farm**, half a mile north of the Painted Church (daily 9am–5pm; free; ⊤328-9658), and **Greenwell Farms**, just off the highway in Kealakekua (Mon–Sat 8am–4pm; free; ⊤323-2862). In addition, the **Kona Historical Society** offers regular tours of the old Uchida coffee farm, restored to illustrate agricultural life during the 1920s and 1930s (Tues & Thurs 8.30am & 11am, Fri 10am; $30; ⊤323-2006, ⊛www.konahistorical.org).

Billy Bob's Park'n'Pork. Also in Kealakekua, you can stop for an espresso and sandwich at the *Kona Mountain Cafe* (Mon–Sat 6.30am–6pm, Sun 8am–1pm; ☎323-2700), which may look unimpressive from the front but has a terrace with a panoramic view around the back.

Immediately beyond Kealakekua, a minor road branches off the highway to lead down to Nāpo'opo'o Beach (see p.96), at the southern end of Kealakekua Bay. Stay on the main road, however, and you soon find yourself in the small community of **CAPTAIN COOK**, which is most noteworthy as the site of the venerable *Manago* hotel and restaurant, reviewed on p.103.

South of Captain Cook's minimal "downtown," *makai* of the highway near mile marker 108, the *Coffee Shack* (daily 7am–3.30pm; ☎328-9555) is the quintessential South Kona café, serving wonderfully fresh coffee on a terrace perched above gorgeous gardens and enjoying staggering views all the way down to Kealakekua Bay. Their smoothies are sensational too, as are the colossal $7–9 sandwiches made with fresh-baked breads.

KEALAKEKUA BAY

Map 4, D6.

KEALAKEKUA BAY may be familiar because of Captain Cook's fatal encounter with the rulers of old Hawaii – as well as the "Little Grass Shack" of the song – but it's a surprisingly inaccessible spot. Very few visitors make it as far as the actual site of Cook's death, on the north shore of the bay, and most of those who see the obelisk to the navigator's memory do so from the south side, across a mile of shark-infested sea. **Nāpo'opo'o Beach** is the only point that can be reached by car; to see the bay otherwise, you either have to undertake a strenuous hike or come by boat.

The name Kealakekua, which means "pathway of the god,"

KEALAKEKUA ON HORSEBACK

Four-wheel-drive vehicles are out of the question on the narrow track down to Kealakekua Bay, and the only alternative to walking is to go on **horseback**. Individual or group trips can be arranged, with advance notice, through King's Trail Rides O Kona, based at mile marker 111 in Kealakekua (PO Box 1366, Kealakekua, HI 96750 Ⓣ323-2388, Ⓦwww.konacowboy.com). The cost for the enjoyable half-day round-trip is around $95 per person.

refers to the five-hundred-foot cliff that backs the sheltered crescent bay. It was said that this *pali*, which slopes down from north to south, was used as a slide by the god Lono when he needed to leave his mountain home in a hurry. When Cook was here, around 80,000 Hawaiians are thought to have lived on the coastal lava plain that extends to the north and south. Though the mummified bodies of their chiefs, and possibly that of Cook as well, remain entombed in lava-tunnel "caves" high on the cliff face, all that remains below are overgrown walls and ruined *heiaus*.

Plans have been put forward to restore the area around Cook's monument as a state park, with a visitor center atop the cliffs, but at present only the waters of the bay itself are formally protected. As a Marine Life Conservation District, it offers some of the best snorkeling on the island.

Walking to the bay

Walking down to the site where Cook was killed – or, more accurately, walking back up again – is a serious undertaking, though well worth it for keen hikers. With no facilities at the bottom, not even water, you have to carry everything you need; allow a total walking time of at least four hours for the round-trip.

The unmarked trail starts a hundred yards down Nāpoʻopoʻo Road, which leaves Hwy-11 a quarter-mile before Captain Cook. Take a dirt road that drops to the right, and keep going straight when that road veers off to the right within a couple of hundred yards. A rutted track, fringed with bright purple and red flowers, continues down for about a mile through open pastureland and avocado orchards. Eventually the vegetation thins out, and you find yourself on very exposed black lava fields, picking your way over jagged rocks. Avoid climbing this stretch in the midday sun.

From this high vantage point you can discern the worn path of the old **King's Trail** that once encircled the entire island, paved with river-rounded boulders. The trail then drops abruptly down to the foot of the hill, before pushing its way into a tangle of scrubby undergrowth at the bottom. Soon you can make out the ruined black walls of the long-vanished Hawaiian village of **KAʻAWALOA**, half submerged by twisted pandanus trees. Somewhere here stood the house of the high chief Kalaniopuʻu, whose attempted kidnapping by Captain Cook precipitated the final drama of Cook's life.

The trail reaches the sea at the precise spot where Cook died; a bronze **plaque** reposes in a rocky pool under a couple of inches of water. Fifty yards away to the left, on what is legally a small patch of England, stands a white-marble **obelisk**, 27 feet high, that was raised to Cook's memory in 1884. In an ongoing tradition, visiting ships set their own small plaques in the cement at its base. An equally well-established tradition is for such plaques to be prised away by souvenir hunters, so the most interesting ones, together with all earlier memorials, have long since disappeared, though some recent ones remain. The crude copper plaque that Mark Twain saw here in 1866, and described in his book *Roughing It*, is now in Honolulu's Hawaii Maritime Center.

KEALAKEKUA BAY

KEALAKEKUA SNORKEL CRUISES

Much of the bay is very deep, as the sheer *pali* simply drops beneath the surface of the ocean. The shallowest and most sheltered spot is in the immediate area of Captain Cook's monument, where the reef provides perfect conditions for snorkelers. Swarms of yellow butterfly fish and tangs, plus parrotfish, triggerfish and hundreds of other species, can always be found circling near the edge.

For centuries, this area has been a favorite haunt of **"spinner" porpoises**. Marine biologists have yet to explain why, but the porpoises gather here in schools of up to a hundred individuals to while away the afternoons by arching in and out of the water. Mark Twain described them as "like so many well-submerged wheels," but they do vary their routines by rotating on their own axes and even flipping the occasional somersault. At the end of the day, they head out once more to the open sea, to feed on the deep-water fish that come to the surface at night.

Snorkel cruises are extremely popular, so the number of vessels allowed into the bay each day is strictly limited. If possible, choose a boat that starts from Keauhou, as this gives you more time at Kealakekua. Bear in mind that passengers are forbidden to set foot ashore, so snorkeling has to be your priority. The following operators are recommended:

Fair Wind (☎ 322-2788 or 1-800/677-9461, ⓦ www.fairwind .com). A large catamaran sails from Keauhou Pier at 9am ($85; 4hr 30min) and 1.30pm ($50; 3hr 30min) and also offers snuba and scuba. The raft *Orca* leaves Kailua Pier at 8.15am ($69; 4hr) and 12.45pm ($50; 3hr).

Sea Quest (☎ 329-7238, ⓦ www.seaquesthawaii.com). Shadeless, bouncy six-person Zodiac rafts leave from Keauhou at 8am ($69; 4hr) and 1pm ($52; 3hr).

Snorkelers from the cruise boats will ensure that you don't have the place to yourself, although they're not allowed to leave the water. Kayakers, however, tend to use the surround of the monument as a convenient place to haul in their vessels. As there's no proper beach, it's also the easiest launching-point if you want to snorkel yourself.

Fifty yards farther along the coast towards the cliff, look out for the inconspicuous **Queen's Pool**. This spring-fed pool of slightly brackish fresh water, originally lined with gentle river rocks and sealed off from the ocean, makes an ideal spot to rinse off after a swim.

For a full account of the death of Captain Cook, and the many legends and theories that surround it, see p.269.

Nāpo'opo'o Beach County Park

Map 4, D6.

To drive to the south shore of Kealakekua Bay, follow the road down from just before Captain Cook as it twists for four miles around the great *pali*. It reaches sea level at the small, usually crowded, parking lot of **NĀPO'OPO'O BEACH COUNTY PARK**, and then continues a few yards north to dead-end at the "beach" itself. Not that there's much of one; Nāpo'opo'o used to be a reasonably pleasant beach, but all its sand has progressively been whipped away – a process completed by Hurricane Iniki in 1992 – and it now consists of a jumble of black lava boulders.

The snorkeling at Nāpo'opo'o remains as good as ever, however – once you've eased across the rocks at the water's edge. Fish congregate in greater numbers on the far side, near the conspicuous obelisk, but you may be swimming with the sharks for a mile to get there. Most visitors make

the crossing by kayak instead. There aren't any re[...]
down here, but there are plenty in Kailua and on [...]
highway around Kealakekua town. It's only legal [...]
kayaks into the water from the ramp beside the j[...]
parking lot.

Stone steps beside the end of the road climb the stout black-lava tiers of **Hikiau Heiau**, the temple where Captain Cook was formally received in January 1779. During a baffling ceremony that lasted several hours, he was fed putrefied pig, had his face smeared with chewed coconut and was draped with red tapa cloth. Shortly afterwards, it was also the site of the first Christian service on the islands – the funeral of William Whatman, an elderly member of Cook's crew who died of a stroke. Visitors are not allowed onto the temple platform, and in any case nothing remains of its former structures. In fact, Cook may well have precipitated his death by dismantling the wooden palings that surrounded it for use as firewood. It is possible to clamber your way around the perimeter, to get a sense of its scale and atmosphere.

PU'UHONUA O HŌNAUNAU NATIONAL HISTORICAL PARK

Map 4, D6. Daily 7.30am–5.30pm; $2 per person; ☎328-2288, ⓦwww.nps.gov/puho. US National Park passes are both sold and valid.
A featureless one-lane road runs south from Nāpo'opo'o for four miles, across the scrubby coastal flatlands, before meeting another road down from the main highway. The two converge at the entrance to **PU'UHONUA O HŌNAUNAU**, the single most evocative historical site in all the Hawaiian islands.

This small peninsula of jagged black lava, jutting out into the Pacific, holds the preserved and restored remains of a ɔyal palace, complete with fishpond, beach, and private canoe landing, plus three *heiaus*, guarded by carved effigies of gods. However, it is most famous for the **puʻuhonua** sanctuary that lies firmly protected behind the mortarless masonry of its sixteenth-century Great Wall.

Visiting the park

Visits to Puʻuhonua O Hōnaunau start at the small information desk at the far end of the parking lot. A schedule of daily talks by rangers is posted here, while immediately to the right is a sequence of large 3-D tiled murals, illustrating themes explained by brief taped messages.

Next you descend along paved walkways through the black lava field, into a grove of rustling giant palms. A couple of typical structures have been erected here on individual lava platforms – a small tent-like shelter used for storage, and a larger house, as used by the *aliʻi* (chiefs). To one side is a small but perfect sandy beach that once served as the royal canoe landing. Picnicking, sunbathing, and smoking are all forbidden here, but swimming and snorkeling are permitted. Away to the left is the King's Fishpond, as placid as a hotel swimming pool. Various lava boulders nearby were hollowed out by early Hawaiians to serve as bowls or salt pans; one was leveled to create a playing surface for *kōnane*, a game in which black and white pebbles were used as counters.

A simple A-frame thatched structure serves as a carving shed, and usually holds one or two idols on which work is still in progress. Master craftsmen also fashion outrigger canoes here, from mighty trunks of beautiful dark *koa* wood.

Beyond the royal area, the L-shaped **Great Wall** – 10 feet high and up to 17 feet wide – runs across the tip of the promontory, sealing off the sanctuary itself. Its northern end is guarded by the **Hale O Keawe Heiau**, once used to house the bones of powerful chiefs, possibly including those of Captain Cook. When dismantled and stripped by Lord George Byron in July 1825, this was the last *heiau* in the islands to remain in perfect condition. Now, like the houses, it has been reconstructed. All the fearsome wooden idols

CITIES OF REFUGE

Pu'uhonuas used to be promoted to tourists under the name of "Cities of Refuge" because of their alleged parallels with the cities mentioned in the Bible. That term is now discouraged, as these ancient Hawaiian sites were not cities but sacred precincts which, unlike the Jewish model, served not to protect the innocent but to absolve the guilty. The idea was that any condemned criminal who succeeded in reaching a *pu'uhonua* would undergo a ritual lasting a few hours – at the very most, overnight – and then be free to leave. As *pu'uhonuas* always stood near strongly guarded royal enclaves, however, the condemned had first to run a gauntlet of armed warriors by land, or dodge canoeists and sharks by sea.

The survival of the fittest was a fundamental principle of ancient Hawaiian law, in which might was generally considered to be right. The laws were determined by gods, not men, and were concerned not with acts such as theft and murder but with infractions of the intricate system of *kapu* – for which the penalty was always death. *Pu'uhonuas* provided a sort of safety valve to spare prime citizens from summary execution. They served other purposes as well. In times of war, noncombatants, loaded with provisions, could go to the nearest one to sit out the conflict, while defeated armies might flee to a *pu'uhonua* to avoid death on the battlefield. Each island had at least one, and the Big Island is thought to have had six, with other sites included Waipi'o Valley and Coconut Island in Hilo. In addition, certain high chiefs, such as Kamehameha's wife Queen Ka'ahumanu, were considered to be living, breathing *pu'uhonuas*.

that surround it are modern reproductions, but they're still eerie in their original setting.

Few buildings now stand beyond the wall. Apart from a couple of bare *heiau* platforms, there's just a scattering of trees on the rippling *pāhoehoe* lava that runs into the ocean. One large gray stone, supposedly the favorite spot of the chief Keōua, is surrounded by six holes that may have held the wooden poles of a canopy. Black crabs scuttle across the waterfront rocks, and countless pools are alive with tiny, multicolored fish.

The tide at Hōnaunau generally fluctuates by two or three feet; in February, however, rough seas and flooding can cause closure of the park.

You can't linger on the beach in the main part of the park, but stretches of **public beach** lie both north and south. The northern section, within sight of the sanctuary, is a renowned **snorkeling** spot, while a short walk or drive south from the parking lot brings you to the more attractive southern section. Even here there's very little sand along the shoreline, which consists of a broad expanse of black lava, but the shady grove beneath the coconut palms makes a great spot for a picnic. Visitors who come for the beach alone are not obliged to pay the *pu'uhonua* admission fee.

In ancient times, the coastal flatlands to the south were densely populated, and traces remain everywhere of housesites and other structures. Schemes are afoot to expand the existing park to incorporate trails through the most rewarding archeological areas.

St Benedict's Painted Church

Map 4, D6.

When you visit the *pu'uhonua*, be sure also to make the

slight detour north from Hwy-160, the spur road to Hwy-11, to see **St Benedict's Painted Church**. This small wooden church, an intriguing hybrid of medieval Europe and Hawaii, was decorated between 1899 and 1904 by a Belgian priest, Father John Velge, with brightly colored biblical and allegorical scenes. Columns with Hawaiian texts erupt into palm leaves on a vaulted ceiling depicting a tropical sky, and the walls behind the altar are painted with a trompe l'oeil Gothic cathedral modeled on that in Burgos, Spain. Orchids and *leis* festoon the altar and statuary within, while purple bougainvilleas fill the lush tropical gardens outside. The spectacular views down the hillside at sunset look out over the flat expanse of trees that line the coast between Hōnaunau and Nāpoʻopoʻo.

SOUTH KONA ACCOMMODATION

Low-key **accommodation** options are scattered throughout the various "coffee towns," ranging from simple traditional village **hotels** to luxurious purpose-built **B&Bs**. Not all are conspicuous from the main road; several of the most distinctive properties are hidden away from view on the lush South Kona slopes.

B&BS

A ʻHui ʻHou
PO Box 349, Hōlualoa, HI 96725 ☎ 324-0510 or 1-800/396-5369 (US & Can), ⓦ www.bbonline.com. Multilevel B&B set in a sprawling modern house on a three-acre coffee plantation a mile above Hōlualoa and a total of four miles from Kailua. Three guestrooms and two luxury suites share a common dining area, a huge veranda, and a hot tub. Rooms ❸, suites ❺.

Dragonfly Ranch
PO Box 675, Hōnaunau, HI 96726 ☎ 328-2159 or

1-800/487-2159 (US & Can),
ⓕ 328-9570,
ⓦ www.dragonflyranch.com.
Tropical retreat, just below the
Painted Church, that's geared
to New Age travelers. It's a bit
too "back to nature" for some
tastes, but does offer Hawaiian
massage, aromatherapy, and
other treatments. One of the
two rooms in the main house
has a bathroom, the other just
a shower, and there are three
separate suites with stereos,
TVs, and outdoor showers.
Rooms ❸, suites ❺.

Hale Aloha Guest Ranch

84-4780 Mamalahoa Hwy,
Captain Cook, HI 96704
ⓣ & ⓕ 328-8955 or 1-800/897-
3188 (US & Can),
ⓦ www.halealoha.com.
Comfortable guestrooms,
some en-suite and some not,
on a German-owned farm a
mile up from the highway.
There are tremendous views,
and rates include fresh fruits
and coffee, plus a
complimentary Hawaiian
massage. ❸–❹

Hōlualoa Inn B&B

PO Box 222, Hōlualoa, HI 96725

ⓣ 324-1121 or 1-800/392-1812
(US & Can), ⓕ 322-2472,
ⓦ www.konaweb.com/HINN.
Exquisite B&B, just below
the main road through
Hōlualoa, three miles and
1400 feet up the hill from
Kailua. Six tasteful en-suite
guestrooms arranged around a
Japanese-style open-plan
living room, plus a pool,
Jacuzzi, and homegrown
coffee. A crow's-nest seating
area on top of the small
central wooden tower looks
down on the rest of Kona,
enjoying incredible views.
Reservations essential, two-
night minimum stay, no
children under 13. ❺

Kalahiki Cottage

Reserve through Hawaii's Best
Bed & Breakfasts, PO Box 563,
Kamuela, HI 96743 ⓣ 885-4550
or 1-800/262-9912 (US & Can),
ⓕ 885-0559,
ⓦ www.bestbnb.com.
Secluded and colorful cattle
ranch, south of Hōnaunau,
has a superb one-bedroom
cottage as well as space for
additional guests in the main
house. The grounds feature a
large swimming pool. ❺

Rainbow Plantation

PO Box 122, Captain Cook, HI
96704 Ⓣ 323-2393 or
1-800/494-2829 (US & Can),
Ⓕ 323-9445, Ⓦwww.wwte.com
/hawaii/rainbow.
Appealing en-suite B&B
accommodation on a working
coffee plantation, off Hwy-11
a quarter of a mile north of
the top of Nāpo'opo'o Rd.
There are two guestrooms, a
separate cottage, and even a
converted fishing boat. ❸

HOTELS AND HOSTELS

Kona Hotel

76-5908 Māmalahoa Hwy,
Hōlualoa, HI 96725 Ⓣ 324-1156.
Extremely basic, very old-
fashioned (and very pink)
family-run hotel in the
attractive village of Hōlualoa,
three miles up-slope from
Kailua. Offers the plainest of
double rooms for under $30 a
night. ❶

Manago Hotel

PO Box 145, Captain Cook, HI
96704 Ⓣ 323-2642, Ⓕ 323-3451,
Ⓦ www.managohotel.com.

Century-old wooden hotel
in the center of Captain
Cook, offering some of the
best-value, most "Hawaiian"
lodging on the island.
Cheaper rooms, in the main
building, share bathrooms
and have minimal facilities,
but those in the newer three-
story wing at the back,
where the rates rise floor by
floor, enjoy magnificent
ocean views. Each of the
faintly musty conventional
suites has a small *lānai*, a
strong hot shower and a
period-piece radio, but no
phone; there's also one
special deluxe Japanese room,
costing $62 per night. The
Manago's paneled dining
room (daily except Mon
7–9am, 11am–2pm &
5–7.30pm) is cooled by
whirring fans and breezes
wafting up from the bay; full
breakfasts cost $5, while later
in the day a couple of lightly
breaded pork chops go for
$8. ❶–❷

Pineapple Park

Mailing address: PO Box 639,
Kurtistown, HI 96760
Ⓣ 323-2224 or 1-877/865-2266

(US), ⓦ www.pineapple-park.com. Clean, appealing budget hostel-cum-hotel, attached to a fruit stand on Hwy-11 in Kealakekua, halfway between mile posts 110 and 111. A bunk in one of the downstairs dorms costs just $17, while top-of-the-range en-suite rooms go for $65 per night. The nicer private rooms have far-reaching views. Airport pickup costs $15 per group. Dorms ❶, rooms ❷.

Pineapple Park runs another budget hotel/hostel near Hawaii Volcanoes National Park; see p.184.

HO'OKENA BEACH COUNTY PARK

Map 4, D7.

Continue south along Hwy-11 for just under three miles from the Hwy-160 turnoff, and another small road leads to the sea at **HO'OKENA BEACH COUNTY PARK**. The vegetation thins out as you drop the two miles down the hillside, but the park itself is pleasant enough. It consists of a genuine, if grayish, sandy beach, pressed against a small *pali* and shaded with coconut palms and other trees. Getting in and out of the water across the sharp lava can be a bit grueling if you don't have reef shoes, but the **snorkeling** is once again excellent.

This sheltered, south-facing bay was once a regular port of call for inter-island steamers, but it now houses very few buildings, although it does have toilets and a picnic area. It also allows **camping**; permission, as usual, must be obtained from the Department of Parks and Recreation in Hilo (☎ 961-8311) at a cost of $3 per day. *Neoki's Corner*, at the foot of the road, sells soft drinks and has public showers.

MILOLI'I

Map 4, D9.

The last point in South Kona at which access to the sea is practical is another twelve miles beyond Ho'okena, where a very tortuous five-mile single-lane road winds down the steep, exposed ridge of Mauna Loa. Having reached the sea at **Ho'opuloa** – no more than a few houses on bare rock – the road follows the coastline south, to drop to the small bay of **MILOLI'I**. The tiny stretches of beach here are mere indentations in the black lava along the shore, filled with a random scattering of white coral and black lava pebbles and backed by groves of coconut palms. The thick tongue of the most recent lava flow (in 1926) can be seen spilling over the sparse slopes above; it obliterated Ho'opuloa, and disputes over the allocation of land to rehouse the victims lasted for well over fifty years thereafter.

At the south end of the cove there's another county **beach park**, with a thatched picnic shelter and a restroom, near an especially sheltered pond that's a favorite with children. Camping is once again permitted, but this is too public a spot for that to hold much appeal, and most visitors content themselves with snorkeling around the rocks. A short way back from the sea, the Miloli'i Grocery Store sells snacks and sodas. The road ends next to the pastel-yellow, red-roofed **Hau'oli Kamana'o Church**.

North Kona

O n first impression, the coastal stretch of **North Kona**, immediately north of Kailua, conforms to few conventional ideas of beauty. When you arrive on this side of the island by air, as you drop towards Keāhole Airport, the gray tarmac runway appears as a tiny blemish on an unrelenting field of black lava, and the gap-toothed straggle of coconut palms at the edge of the ocean provides the only flash of color. Travelers eager for a glimpse of a Hawaiian volcano may find it hard to believe that the long low ridge ascending into the mists really is Hualālai, which, at just over eight thousand feet, is third in rank of the island's peaks. Scars from its most recent eruption, early in the nineteenth century, still trail down to the sea, though they're barely distinguishable from generations of earlier flows.

Until the 1970s, it was barely possible to travel overland along the coast **north of Kailua** – and few people had any reason to do so. Then **Queen Ka'ahumanu Highway**, Hwy-19, was laid across the lava, serving the new airport and granting access to previously remote beaches. Many of these were swiftly engulfed by plush resorts, but with the road running about a mile in from the ocean, the beaches remain occasional, distant bursts of greenery in an otherwise desolate landscape.

Despite the huge sums spent on all this construction, Big

Island tourism is not on the scale that was originally envisaged. As a result, the highway system here is unusual for Hawaii in being adequate to handle the volume of traffic. The one potential hazard for drivers is posed by the unpredictable "Kona Nightingales" (scrawny descendants of the donkeys that once hauled loads to and from the shoreline), which roam wild across the barren slopes.

HONOKŌHAU HARBOR

Map 4, B3.

A couple of miles north of Kailua, a short avenue leads down to narrow **HONOKŌHAU HARBOR**, which provides safe mooring for the town's pleasure boats and thereby leaves the jetty in Kailua free from congestion. This is a functional rather than a decorative place, and the only reason to come here is to take one of the many boat trips that leave from the far end of the quay. The most appealing spot to sit and watch the proceedings is the open-air deck of the *Harbor House* (Mon–Sat 11am–7pm, Sun 11am–5.30pm; ☎326-4166), a bar in the central Kona Marina complex that also offers a menu of reasonably priced snacks and sandwiches. To its left is a line of fishing charter vessels, together with an information kiosk on what they offer, the Charter Desk (☎329-5735, ⓦwww.charterdesk.com).

If you have an hour or two to kill before or after an excursion, a small, secluded and sandy beach, ideal for snorkelers, can be reached by hiking south for ten minutes across the lava, while a five-minute walk around to the north of the harbor brings you out at the southern access to the Kaloko-Honokōhau National Historic Park.

- -
Snorkel, dive, and fishing cruises leaving from
Honokōhau Harbor are detailed on p.46.
- -

HONOKŌHAU HARBOR

KALOKO-HONOKŌHAU NATIONAL HISTORIC PARK

Map 4, B3. Daily 8am–3.30pm; free; ☎ 329-6681.

The **KALOKO-HONOKŌHAU NATIONAL HISTORIC PARK**, north of the harbor and south of the airport, was established in 1978 to preserve one of the state's last surviving natural wetlands. Despite being administered by the National Park Service, it remains almost entirely undeveloped, and the goals of re-creating ancient techniques of aquaculture and farming, protecting endangered Hawaiian water birds, and returning the area to its pre-contact appearance seem as distant as ever. The few visitors the park attracts are usually – like the birds – here to fish, and it tends to disappoint anyone other than naturalists.

Even the entrance is almost impossible to find, via a scarcely discernible driveway *makai* of the highway, opposite Kaloko Industrial Park between mileposts 96 and 97. The bumpy lava track down, which is just barely passable in ordinary rental cars, ends after 0.7 miles beside the tranquil Kaloko Fishpond, sealed off from the ocean by a massive stone wall that has been extensively restored and rebuilt by the park authorities. The wetlands stretch away from the seafront picnic area, while a coastal footpath leads south to Honokōhau Harbor via the 'Aimakapa Fishpond.

Scattered across the mostly trackless expanse of the park are several *heiaus*, of which the least ruined is the Pu'uoina, as well as a *hōolua* ("land-surfing") slide and fields of petroglyphs. Descendants of Kamehameha the Great took pains to reserve this area for themselves, which suggests that one of its countless caves may still hold his bones.

KONA COAST STATE PARK

Map 4, B2. Daily except Wed 9am–8pm; free.

One of the Big Island's least known but most beautiful

EDMUND NÄGELE

Pu'uhonua O Hōnaunau

EDMUND NÄGELE

Miloli'i black-lava and white-coral beach

EDMUND NÄGELE

St Benedict's Painted Church

GREG WARD

Pu'ukoholā Heiau

EDMUND NÄGELE

The coast at Kailua

GREG WARD

Kīlauea eruption

Heliconas

Akaka Falls

beaches, designated as the **KONA COAST STATE PARK** and also known as **Kekaha Kai State Park**, lies a couple of miles north of Keāhole airport. Once again, you need to keep your eyes peeled to spot the driveway, and then be prepared to bump your vehicle for 1.5 miles over rippling *pāhoehoe* lava, on a virtually unsurfaced track.

At the bottom of the track, there's a parking lot; from its *mauka* end take the obvious path that sets off northwards across 200 yards of bare lava towards a dense grove of coconut palms. When you come to a single portable toilet, you can either cut in through the trees to reach the beach directly, or follow the path round until it emerges in the middle of a perfect horseshoe-shaped bay. All around you is an exquisite beach of coarse golden sand, lightly flecked with specks of black lava – what the locals call "salt and pepper" sand. Each of the headlands jutting to either side is a spur of rougher *'a'ā* lava, topped with its own clump of palms. Immediately behind the beach is the looming bulk of Hualālai, and at this point Mauna Kea becomes visible far inland, as does Haleakalā across the sea on Maui. The calm waters of the bay provide sheltered swimming; local surfers ride the tumbling waves offshore; and divers delve into submarine caves and tunnels.

Kona Coast State Park has no food and drink facilities for visitors.

KAʻŪPŪLEHU

Map 4, C1.

The area known as **KAʻŪPŪLEHU**, five miles north of the airport, consists of a forbidding expanse of rough, jet-black lava that was deposited by an eruption of the Hualālai volcano in 1801. Its utter inaccessibility led it to be chosen as the site of the *Kona Village Resort* in 1961 – at first, in the absence of a road, all guests and employees alike had to be flown in – though since the appearance of the *Four Seasons Resort* in the 1990s it has felt significantly less secluded.

Four Seasons Resort Hualalai

PO Box 1269, Kailua-Kona, HI 96745 Ⓣ 325-8000 or 1-888/340-5662 (US & Can), Ⓕ 325-8100, Ⓦ www.fourseasons.com.

The Big Island's newest resort, the sprawling *Four Seasons Resort* at Hualālai, was finally completed in 1996 after being delayed for several years by the discovery that its original site lay above an ancient Hawaiian burial ground. Plans for a conventional high-rise hotel were at that point abandoned in favor of a complex of smaller units, known as "bungalows" despite being two stories high. On first impression, they're not wildly prepossessing, but the individual rooms inside justify the minimum $450-per-night rate. Each holds a four-poster bed plus a bath and shower, and many have an additional outdoor, lava-lined shower. Set on an exposed headland, the *Four Seasons* stands a bit

too close to the ocean for comfort, and unlike the neighboring *Kona Village Resort* it lacks a proper beach – although high surf can unceremoniously dump sand into its three swimming pools. The real architectural success of the *Four Seasons* is its gorgeous *Pahui'a* restaurant, comprising several interlinked wooden pavilions laid open by sliding panels to the ocean. Sea breezes waft in, and spotlights play on the surf, while the food itself is excellent, with a wide range of Asian and American dishes. Appetizers such as a sashimi and *tako poke* combo cost $17, meat and fish entrees average around $30. Ⓥ

Kona Village Resort

PO Box 1299, Kailua-Kona, HI 96745 Ⓣ 325-5555 or 1-800/367-5290 (US & Can), Ⓕ 325-5124, Ⓦ www.konavillage.com.

If you cherish a fantasy of staying in a paradise where your every whim is anticipated – and you have unlimited funds – you could do no better than to stay at the *Kona Village Resort*, the oldest of the Big Island's luxury resorts. Supposedly it's a re-creation of the Polynesian past, but its main appeal lies in the very fact that it bears so little relation to reality of any kind. Set in the black Kona desertscape, the resort consists of 125 thatched South Pacific-style *hales*, or huts, most of which are surrounded by bright flowers. The huts have no phones, TVs, or radios, but each has a private *lānai*, a hammock and an alarm clock that wakes you by grinding fresh coffee beans. Beach gear, such as masks, fins, and even kayaks, is provided free for guests, and scuba equipment and instruction are also available for a fee. The daily rates of $450–795 for two include all meals at the *Hale Moana* and *Hale Samoa* restaurants; for nonresidents, a five-course dinner at the *Hale Moana* costs $62 and consists of a seafood appetizer, soup, salad and fresh fish prepared to your exact specifications. Most outsiders visit on *lū'au* night – Friday – when $72 buys an atmospheric beachside feast plus Polynesian entertainment; advance reservations are essential. The resort sits on sandy Ka'ūpūlehu beach, which is superb for snorkeling; stately turtles cruise by and manta rays billow in at night. Anyone can visit this isolated beach, though the resort's security guards do their best to discourage nonresidents. There's also a self-guided petroglyph trail on the property. **9**

KĪHOLO BAY

Map 5, B7.

As Hwy-19 crests a small hill a short way south of mile marker 82, an overlook offers a tantalizing glimpse of the turquoise waters of **KĪHOLO BAY**. This crescent lagoon, dotted with black-lava islands, is in part artificial, having been reshaped by ancient Hawaiians to serve as a fishpond. Most of their work was destroyed by the 1801 eruption of Hualālai, and that lava flow unfortunately makes access difficult to this day. The only way to reach the bay is via a 1.5-mile hike on a rough path that leaves the highway a mile further on. If you do make the effort, it's a fabulous place for a swim, though there's no beach to speak of.

KĪHOLO BAY

South Kohala

Though the western seaboard of the Big Island tends to be referred to as the Kona coast, the most famous of its resorts are in fact situated in the district of **South Kohala**, which starts roughly 25 miles north of Kailua. To confuse matters further, **Kohala Mountain** itself, the oldest and now at around 5000 feet high also the smallest of the island's five volcanoes, forms only the northernmost spur of the island, known as North Kohala (see p.144). South Kohala as it exists today was created by lava flowing from the newer peaks of Mauna Kea and Hualālai; the only vestiges of the original mountain to survive here are the offshore **coral reefs** with which it was once ringed. Erosion from those reefs is the reason why this region boasts the finest of the Big Island's few **white-sand beaches**, and it also explains why this is now the Big Island's most prestigious resort destination.

Overlooked not only by Mauna Kea, Hualālai, and Kohala, but on clear days also by Mauna Loa to the south, and even Haleakalā on Maui, South Kohala was all but inaccessible by land until the 1960s. The only visitors to the inlets along the shore were local fishermen and the occasional intrepid hiker or surfer. The Hawaiian villages that had once flourished here were long gone, and only wealthy landowners maintained a few private enclaves.

In the forty years since Laurance Rockefeller realized the potential that lay in South Kohala's status as the sunniest area in all Hawaii, the landscape has undergone an amazing transformation. Holes large enough to hold giant hotels have been blasted into the rock, and turf laid on top of the lava to create lawns and golf courses. **Queen Ka'ahumanu Highway** (Hwy-19) pushed its way across the bare lava slopes, and multiproperty resorts appeared in quick succession at **Waikoloa** and then **Mauna Lani**, a couple of miles further north.

Many of South Kohala's **beaches** were probably destroyed by lava early in the 1800s – so the *Hilton*, for example, had to build its own beach from scratch – but as you head north towards Kawaihae you come to some of the finest expanses of sand on the island. These were prime targets for the developers: the first of the luxury hotels was the *Mauna Kea Beach Hotel*, which went up at Kauna'oa in 1960, while what may well be the last was the *Hapuna Beach Prince Hotel*, erected on beautiful Hāpuna Beach in 1994, despite strong local opposition.

Since it's illegal for anyone to deny access to the Hawaiian shoreline, local people, and visitors not staying at the Kohala resorts, are entitled to use all the beaches along the coast. Some hotels make things difficult by restricting the number of parking permits they issue to nonguests – to as few as ten per day – but so long as you can get to the sea, you're entitled to stay there.

For information on South Kohala as a whole, with an especial emphasis on accommodations, contact the **Kohala Coast Resort Association**, 69-275 Waikoloa Beach Drive, Kohala Coast (℡ 1-800/318-3637, Ⓦ www.kkra.org).

WAIKOLOA

Map 5, C7.

For the ancient Hawaiians, the fundamental division of land was the *ahupua'a*, a wedge-shaped "slice of cake" reaching from the top of the mountain down to a stretch of the sea. The name "Waikoloa" referred to such a division, which is why modern visitors are often confused as to where exactly **WAIKOLOA** is.

The community called Waikoloa, generally referred to as **Waikoloa Village**, lies six miles *mauka* of Queen Ka'ahumanu Highway, halfway up to the Belt Road, while the **Waikoloa Beach Resort** – reached by a mile-long approach road that leaves the highway a little way south of mile marker 76, 25 miles north of Kailua and a mile south of the turning up to Waikoloa Village – is, unsurprisingly, down by the sea. It holds little other than the *Hilton* and *Outrigger Waikoloa Beach* hotels and the King's Shops mall.

Accommodation

Hilton Waikoloa Village

425 Waikoloa Beach Drive, Waikoloa, HI 96738

☎ 886-1234 or 1-800/221-2424, Ⓕ 886-2900, Ⓦ www.hiltonwaikoloavillage.com.

The 1240-room *Hilton Waikoloa Village* is almost a miniature city. Guests travel between its three seven-story towers on a light railway system, a mile-long network of walkways, or in boats along the canals. It boasts a four-acre artificial lagoon complete with waterfalls, and a beach of imported sand lined by coconut palms, some of which were flown here by helicopter from Kalapana on the south coast, just before it was engulfed by lava (see p.212). This synthetic tropical paradise cost a fortune to build, but opened (as the *Hyatt Regency*) in 1988, just in time to be hit by the Gulf War economic downturn.

Hilton bought out the original developers in 1993, for a rumored 25¢ on the dollar, and it's now the most popular of the Kohala resorts. If you book through a package-tour operator, it can also work out to be one of the cheapest. However, it can feel a bit like staying in a theme park, and thus appeals most to families with young children, and those who are quite happy to see nothing of the rest of the island. One of the resort's highlights is its "swim with a dolphin" program; although an hour in the lagoon with your favorite sea mammal can cost as much as $150, the experience is so much in demand that a lottery is held to decide which guests can take part. You can also take a free guided tour through the network of underground tunnels, used by staff to ensure unobtrusiveness. Surprisingly, neither of the more formal of the *Hilton's* seven restaurants – the North Italian *Donatoni's*, and the Japanese sushi and teppanyaki specialists *Imari*, both of which serve dinner only – offer sea views, though their food is as good as you'd expect. The best casual alternative is the breezy *Palm Terrace*, which presents a different $32 dinner buffet every night. Garden view ❺, ocean view ❼.

Outrigger Waikoloa Beach

69-275 Waikoloa Beach Drive, Waikoloa, HI 96738-5711
ⓣ 886-6789 or 1-800/922-5533,
ⓕ 886-7852,
ⓦ www.outrigger.com.
In contrast to its showy neighbor, the *Outrigger Waikoloa Beach* is considerably more restrained and elegant. Until recently, as the *Royal Waikoloan*, it was also significantly cheaper, but in style and price it's now on a par with the Kohala resorts further north. The main attraction here is the close proximity of 'Anaeho'omalu beach (see opposite), where available watersports include snorkeling, kayaking, scuba diving, and excursions in glass-bottomed boats and catamarans. All the 500-plus

well-equipped rooms have private balconies, most with ocean views. The principal restaurant, *Hawaii Calls* (daily 6am–2pm & 5.30–9.30pm), overlooks a carp pond and is tastefully themed to the heyday of Hawaiian tourism. It offers fine Pacific Rim cuisine in the evenings; entrees are $25–30, with a $35 seafood buffet on Fridays. Beside the pool, *Nalu's Bar & Grill* serves alfresco sandwiches and salads, and there's a twice-weekly *lūʻau*, open to all (Wed & Sun 6pm; $64 adults, $32 under-12s). Garden view ❼, ocean view ❽.

ʻAnaehoʻomalu

The *Outrigger Waikoloa Beach* stands at the northern end of a sheltered white-sand beach, which shelves very gradually out to sea. This is a favorite spot with snorkelers and wind-surfers, and bathing is generally considered safe. To reach the beach, however, you first have to follow the landscaped walkways that skirt the two ancient fishponds to which this area owes its name. **ʻANAEHOʻOMALU** means "pro-tected mullet," in recognition of the fact that the mullet raised in its two fishponds were reserved for the use of chiefs alone – *aliʻi* voyaging around the island would stop here to pick up supplies. The beach itself also witnessed one moment of high drama, when an unpopular king of Hawaii, Kamaiole, was slain by his rival Kalapana. The ambushers took advantage of the tradition that when the king set off on an expedition, his canoe was always the last to leave the beach.

The King's Shops

As a shopping destination, the 40-store **King's Shops mall** (daily 9.30am–9.30pm), sited at the point where the approach road splits off to the different hotels, can't begin

WAIKOLOA SHUTTLE BUSES

Waikoloa is connected with Kailua to the south by the **Kona Town Express** shuttle buses; see p.67. The same company also runs the **Kohala Coast–Waikoloa Resort Express** (daily 6.50am–9.50pm; $5 one-way, $15 for a one-day systemwide pass; ☎331-1582), which makes eleven daily trips between the King's Shops and *Mauna Kea Beach Resort* to the north.

to compete with Kailua – let alone Honolulu. It is an attractive little spot, however, arrayed along one side of an artificial lagoon, and its open courtyard features interesting plaques explaining Big Island geology and history.

Though it also holds several upscale clothing stores, Chinese and Japanese restaurants, and a small food court with good juice and coffee bars, the mall is best known as the home of the Big Island's only outlet of *Roy's* gourmet **restaurant** chain (daily 11.30am–2pm & 5.30–9.30pm; ☎885-4321). Flamboyant Pacific Rim dinners – best enjoyed in the moonlight on the lakeside terrace – feature dim-sum-style appetizers priced individually at $7–9, and entrees like potato-and-spinach-crusted swordfish and candied macadamia nut rack of lamb at $23–29. The shorter and simpler lunch menu offers great value, with gourmet sandwiches and salads for around $10, and Roy's signature baby-back ribs for even less.

Waikoloa Village

Most visitors to the Waikoloa resorts never head the eight miles up to **WAIKOLOA VILLAGE** itself. Should you want to do so, take the road that leaves Queen Ka'ahumanu Highway a short distance north of the resort turnoff, halfway to Mauna Lani. A small lot at this otherwise desolate intersection is the base for **helicopter** trips (see p.26) run for resort guests by Kenai Helicopters (☎885–5833) and Blue Hawaiian (☎961–5600) among others.

There's nothing to the village apart from a supermarket, a gas station, a golf course, and the **Waikoloa Highlands Village** mall, which features a couple of snack places.

MAUNA LANI RESORT

Map 5, C6.

A mile or so north of the Waikoloa Village turnoff, another approach road *makai* of Queen Ka'ahumanu Highway heads through lurid green lawns down to the plush **Mauna Lani Resort**. This area once belonged to the Parker Ranch (see p.136); then for forty years it was the secluded oceanfront retreat of Francis Hyde I'i Brown (whose name lingers on in the resort's golf courses), before being snapped up by developers in the early 1970s.

Two major resorts now face the sea in splendid isolation, sharing the use of two golf courses. The name *Mauna Lani*, a modern coinage, means "mountains reaching heaven," and refers to the misty volcanoes that loom in the distance to the north, south, and east.

Accommodation

Mauna Lani Bay Hotel

68-1400 Mauna Lani Drive,
Kohala Coast, HI 96743
☎885-6622 or 1-800/367-2323,
Ⓕ885-6183,
Ⓦwww.maunalani.com.
The gleaming white *Mauna Lani Bay* is a classic, unabashed resort hotel, with its central building thrusting like an arrow into the Pacific, and an oceanfront golf course to either side. Lavish rooms are accessed via a waterfall- and lagoon-filled central atrium, and offer extensive ocean views. Traces of ancient occupation

are everywhere on the extensive grounds, though the Kalāhuipua'a Trail, which leads back from the beach and the shoreline fishponds, soon turns into a grueling two-mile walk across craggy 'a'ā lava. The *Bay Terrace* restaurant commands ocean views from its indoor and outdoor dining room; appetizers range $7–16, entrees like the seafood Thai curry and Kona-coffee-marinated lamb chops are more like $30. The flamboyant open-air Polynesian-style *Canoe House*, close to the sea and surrounded by fishponds, serves some of Hawaii's finest but most expensive Pacific Rim cuisine, while the *Gallery* (Tues–Sat), beside the golf course, is similarly superb. Fifth night free. Garden view ❽, ocean view ❾.

The Orchid at Mauna Lani

1 North Kanikū Drive, Kohala Coast, HI 96743
Ⓣ885-2000, 1-800/845-9905
(US & Can) or 0800/973119 (UK), Ⓕ885-5778,
Ⓦwww.orchid-maunalani.com.
What's now the *Orchid at Mauni Lani* was, until 1995, the *Ritz-Carlton Mauna Lani*. Under its new owners, Sheraton, it has shaken off some of the stuffiness of the *Ritz-Carlton* image, while remaining the most sophisticated and elegant of the Kohala giants. All 539 rooms in this spacious complex of six-story buildings have en-suite bathrooms with "twin marble vanities" and enjoy extensive views either over the sea, or up to the volcanoes across one of the two golf courses in the area. As well as a lovely seafront swimming pool and Jacuzzi, there's an open-air "spa without walls." Both the principal restaurants, the *Orchid Court* and the *Grill*, serve fine Pacific Rim dinners nightly, with a full meal at either costing around $50; the *Orchid Court* also offers buffet breakfasts and lighter lunches. ❾

Puakō

An impressive array of ancient **petroglyphs** is located between the *Orchid at Mauna Lani* and the small community of **PUAKŌ**. The mile-long Malama Trail to **Puakō Petroglyph Park** heads inland from the *mauka* end of the Holoholo Kai Beach Park parking lot. Though not a difficult walk, it does traverse some rough terrain, and there's no drinking water along the way.

The Big Island's most extensive petroglyph
field is at Pu'u Loa; see p.241.

For the first 150 yards, the trail is paved, crossing open lava to some replica petroglyphs set up so visitors can take rubbings. From these, you plunge into a tinderbox-dry *kiawe* forest. Five hundred yards in, a few petroglyphs can be discerned on nearby rocks. Many visitors turn back here under the impression that they've seen all there is to see, but you should continue another 250 yards and cross an unpaved track. A short way beyond, a fenced-off viewing area brings you to a halt in front of a slightly sloping expanse of flat, reddish rock. This is covered with simple stick figures, most a couple of feet tall, still lying where they were left to bake centuries ago. Laboriously etched into bare *pāhoehoe* lava, the petroglyphs range from matchstick warriors to abstract symbols and simple indentations where the umbilical cords of newborn babies were reverently buried. A total of three thousand designs have been identified; many of them, unfortunately, are in areas that remain closed to the public. Those on view are easiest to see early in the morning or late in the evening, when the sun creates shadows.

Holoholo Kai Beach Park is a mixture of black lava and white coral, not especially good for swimming. Puakō itself

PUAKŌ

is beyond it to the north, but there's no through road from here. It's more of an exclusive residential area than a town, and all you'll see if you turn onto Puakō Beach Drive from Hwy-19, three miles down the road, is a long succession of private villas. The occasional gap permits public access to the thin strip of sand beyond, where the tidepools are interrupted at one point by a small concrete jetty and boat landing.

WAIALEA, HĀPUNA, AND KAUNAʻOA BEACHES

The best of the natural white-sand beaches of South Kohala are along the coast just south of Kawaihae Harbor. Such beaches are formed from the skeletal remains of tiny coral-reef creatures, which explains why they're found in the most sheltered areas of the oldest part of the island. They're now at the foot of Mauna Kea rather than Kohala Mountain, because lava from Mauna Kea has progressively swamped its venerable neighbor.

Of the three best-known beaches, separated by short stretches of *kiawe* forest, only the southernmost one, **Waialea**, remains in anything approaching a pristine state. Comparatively small, and sheltered by jutting headlands, it's a perfect base for recreational sailing, while the gentle slope into the sea makes it popular with family groups. The magnificence of both **Hāpuna** and **Kaunaʻoa** to the north has been impaired by the addition of mighty resort hotels.

Hāpuna Beach

Map 5, C6.
With its gentle turquoise waters, swaying palm groves, and above all its broad expanse of white sand, **HĀPUNA BEACH** has often been called the most beautiful beach in the United States. Though in summer it's the widest beach on the Big Island, capable of accommodating large crowds

of day-trippers, it always seems to retain an intimate feel, thanks in part to the promontory of black lava that splits it down the middle. However, its northern end is dominated by the giant *Hapuna Beach Prince Hotel*, which opened in 1994 despite bitter opposition from campaigners who treasured Hāpuna's status as an unspoiled state recreation area. Although the hotel is forbidden to leave furniture on the beach, to serve food or alcohol there, or to discourage public access to any area below the tree line, hotel guests inevitably dominate the sands north of the promontory.

Nonetheless, Hāpuna Beach remains a delightful public park, well equipped with washrooms and pavilions. *Three Dog Cafe*, a kiosk adjoining the parking lot, sells snacks and rents beach equipment. In deference to the safety of body-surfers, who consider this the best spot on the island, surfboards are forbidden. There's always the chance of unruly weather between October and March, so look for the warning flags that fly outside the hotel before you enter the water.

Six simple A-frame **shelters**, set well back from the beach itself above the parking lot and capable of holding up to four people, can be rented for $20 per night through the state parks office in Hilo (☎974-6200). Tent camping is not permitted.

Accommodation

Hapuna Beach Prince Hotel

62-100 Kauna'oa Drive, Kohala Coast, HI 96743 ☎880-1111 or 1-800/882-6060, ⓕ880-3026, ⓦwww.hapunabeachprincehotel.com Standing roughly six miles north of Mauna Lani, the luxurious *Hapuna Beach Prince Hotel* has since 1994 occupied the northern flanks of Hāpuna Beach. Despite being molded to the contours of the hillside, it's inevitably somewhat intrusive. The prospect from the inside looking out is superb: the hotel's giant central lobby is open to cooling sea breezes,

123

while the turquoise pool is set flush with a broad patio, complete with whirlpool spa. Few resorts in the world can offer the same combination of opulent accommodation and idyllic situation. Of its two dinner-only gourmet restaurants, the circular *Coast Grille* occupies by far the better location, and specializes in adventurous Pacific Rim fish dishes such as *opah* in a ginger and pistachio crust, at around $30 per entree. At the elegant but viewless Japanese *Hakone* (closed Mon & Tues), you can get a full sashimi or chicken dinner for $30–40, or enjoy a copious buffet for $52. Limited view ❽, ocean view ❾.

Kauna'oa Beach

Map 5, C5.

A mile north of Hāpuna Beach, barely a hundred yards beyond the turning for the *Hapuna Beach Prince*, and a mile south of the point where Hwy-19 meets Hwy-270, a separate approach road cuts down to reach the ocean at Kauna'oa Beach. Like its neighbors, this offers superb conditions for much of the year, but is exposed to very strong winds and high surf in winter, when much of the sand is washed away and swimming becomes very hazardous. The construction here of the *Mauna Kea Beach Hotel*, which opened for business in 1965 as the first of the Kohala resorts, was almost as controversial as the more recent development on Hāpuna Beach. However, although local Hawaiians fought and won an eight-year legal battle to have their rights of access respected, Kauna'oa Beach is barely used these days by anyone other than guests at the hotel.

Accommodation

Mauna Kea Beach Hotel
62-100 Mauna Kea Beach Drive, Kohala Coast, HI 96743;
☎882-7222 or 1-800/882-6060,
🅕882-5748, Ⓦwww
.maunakeabeachhotel.com.

Although the *Mauna Kea Beach Hotel* has undergone an extensive overhaul, and its guestrooms are kitted out to the highest of standards, for all its landscaping and lagoons the building itself still looks its age. Its one great strength is its fabulous setting: effectively if not legally, Kauna'oa Beach serves as the *Mauna Kea*'s own exquisite private beach. The dinner-only *Batik* restaurant (closed Tues & Sat), unique on the Big Island in requiring male diners to wear jackets, serves a hybrid Mediterranean-Hawaiian cuisine; appetizers are $15–20, and entrees are $30–50. The *Pavilion* prepares breakfast buffets and conventional American dinners, while the lovely outdoor *Terrace* is a great spot for a buffet lunch. The weekly *lū'au* (Tues 6pm; $70) takes place well away from the ocean, but there is a $70 Saturday-night clambake at the *Hau Tree* beachfront bar. ❾.

KAWAIHAE

Map 5, C5.
For the ancient Hawaiians, the natural harbor at **KAWAI-HAE**, a couple of miles north of Hāpuna Beach, was one of the most important landing points along the coast of the Big Island. Over the last fifty years, massive earth-moving projects have destroyed any beauty that it once possessed, but in terms of population it remains no more than a tiny settlement. The entire area is still dominated, however, by a great **war temple**, built by Kamehameha to demonstrate that the gods looked with favor upon his plans for conquest.

Samuel M. Spencer Beach County Park

Map 5, C5.
The last significant beach along the Kohala coast, **'Ohai'ula Beach**, is one of the few still geared towards

low-tech, low-budget family fun. Better known as the **SPENCER BEACH PARK**, it offers the best oceanfront **campground** on the island, as well as full day-use facilities, but it can get very crowded, and with the access road extending along its full length, it's seldom peaceful either. No cabins are available: campers are expected to bring their own tents or trailers and to obtain permits in advance from the Hawaii County Parks office in Hilo (☎961-8311).

The beach itself, sheltered by a long reef, is popular with recreational swimmers as well as more serious snorkelers and scuba divers; it takes a major storm to render bathing unsafe.

Puʻukoholā Heiau National Historic Site

Map 5, C5. Daily except hols 7.30am–4pm; free; ☎882-7218, ⓦ www.nps.gov/puhe.

PUʻUKOHOLĀ HEIAU is the most dramatic and imposing Hawaiian temple still standing on any of the islands; its construction between 1790 and 1791 by the future Kamehameha I is one of the greatest – and most horrific – epics of Big Island history.

The story of this *luakini*, a "**war temple**" fed by human sacrifice, began in 1782, when the young warrior Kamehameha seized control of the northwest segment of the Big Island. Over the years that followed, he conquered Maui, Lanai, and Molokai, but failed to defeat his rivals on the rest of his home island of Hawaii. Eventually, when he heard that his cousin Keōua was planning to expand out from Kaʻū in the southwest of the Big Island, Kamehameha sent his aunt to consult the prophet Kapoukahi of Kauai. who suggested that building a *luakini* at Puʻukoholā and dedicating it to his personal war god Kūkāʻilimoku would guarantee success in the coming conflict.

Kapoukahi himself came to the Big Island to oversee the construction of the new temple, on the site of a ruined *heiau* erected two centuries before by the legendary Lonoikamakahiki. The process was accompanied throughout by precise, exacting ritual: in the words of an old Hawaiian proverb, "the work of the *luakini* is like hauling *ohia* timber, of all labor the most arduous." The entire island had to be purified, by means of clearing the circle road and erecting altars at regular intervals.

For Kamehameha's rivals, the start of work was a clear announcement of impending war. They set out to sabotage the project, knowing that its completion would give Kamehameha irresistible *mana*, or spiritual power. Not only Keōua, but also the defeated chiefs of Maui, Lanai and Molokai, and even the rulers of Kauai and Oahu, joined forces to attack, but Kamehameha managed to hold them all off and pressed on with construction.

When the *heiau* was completed, in the summer of 1791, the prophet ordained a great feast, involving the sacrifice of 400 pigs, 400 bushels of bananas, 400 coconuts, 400 red fish, 400 pieces of *oloa* cloth and plenty of human beings, preferably themselves possessing considerable *mana*. Kamehameha therefore invited Keōua to attend the dedication and make peace. Like a figure from Greek tragedy, Keōua accepted the invitation.

The moment Keōua stepped ashore on the beach, he was slain with a spear thrust by Kamehameha's trusted warrior Ke'eaumoku (the father of Ka'ahumanu). All his companions were also killed before Kamehameha, who later insisted that he had not sanctioned the slaughter, called a halt upon recognizing the commander of the second canoe as his own son Kaoleioku. Keōua's body was the main sacrifice offered, together with those of ten of his associates (the war god, who did not like blood on his altar, preferred his victims to have been killed elsewhere).

As sole ruler of the Big Island, Kamehameha went on to reconquer first Maui, Lanai, and Molokai, then Oahu, all of which had been recaptured by their original rulers during the building of the temple. Finally he exacted tribute from Kauai, whereupon the whole archipelago took on the name of Kamehameha's native island, and thus became known as Hawaii.

The altar and idols at Pu'ukoholā were destroyed in 1819 on the orders of Kamehameha's successor Liholiho, shortly after the breaking of the ancient *kapu* system (see p.273).

Visiting Pu'ukoholā Heiau

The parking lot for the *heiau* stands just off Hwy-19, at the start of the approach road to Spencer Beach Park and next to a small visitor center, which hands out informative Park Service brochures. The temple's three colossal tiers of black stone are not immediately visible from here, so follow the signed trail for a couple of hundred yards down towards the sea.

As the path rounds "the hill of the whale" after which the *heiau* was named, the vast platform of the temple – 224 feet long by 100 feet wide – looms above you, commanding a long stretch of coastline. Disappointingly, this is as close as you'll get; access is forbidden, in part because this remains a sacred site, but also because recent earthquake damage has rendered it unstable. No traces survive of the thatched houses and other structures that originally stood upon it – the *hale moi*, the smaller *hale kahuna nui* for the priest, the oracle tower and drum house, and the lava altar that once held the bones of human sacrifices are all gone.

A little further towards the sea stands the subsidiary **Mailekini Heiau**, narrower but longer, and much older than the main temple. It, too, is inaccessible to visitors. Both *heiau*s loom large above Pelekane Beach, which you are free to walk along, although nowadays it's not all that spectacular. In Kamehameha's era the beach was far longer, and there was a royal compound in the palm grove just back from the sea. The land that now lies

JOHN YOUNG AND ISAAC DAVIS

Just off Kawaihae, in 1790, the tiny six-man schooner *Fair American*, belonging to the trading ship *Eleanora*, was stormed and captured by Hawaiians. They had been angered by the *Eleanora*'s captain Stephen Metcalfe, whose recent exploits included the slaughter of one hundred Hawaiians in the 'Olowalu Massacre, near Lahaina in Maui. The islanders, exacted revenge by looting the *Fair American* for its valuable iron and killing all its crew except Isaac Davis, who was spared because he put up such valiant resistance; among the victims was Metcalfe's own son, Thomas.

Ignorant of what had happened, Captain Metcalfe set out to search for his missing boat and crew. In due course, the *Eleanora* arrived at Kawaihae and first mate John Young was sent ashore. Kamehameha himself prevented Young from re-joining his vessel with news of the murders, whereupon Captain Metcalfe concluded that his envoy had been killed and sailed away. Metcalfe himself died soon afterwards and never learned of the death of his son; both Davis and Young, how-ever, remained on the islands, taking Hawaiian names and becoming valued advisors to the king. They taught the Hawaiians to fight with muskets and cannon – the royal arsenal began with two guns seized from the *Fair American*.

Renamed Olohana ("all hands"), Young served between 1802 and 1812 as governor of the Big Island, during which time he fortified Mailekini Heiau. He made his home 500 yards inland from the beach at Pu'ukoholā, just across the modern highway beside Makeahua Gulch. A difficult trail still leads there, although the remains of his original building are long gone. Young continued to oversee activities at Kawaihae – including the first shipments of cattle – until his death at the age of ninety in 1835. Isaac Davis, meanwhile, was poisoned mysteriously in April 1810.

immediately to the north is infill created during the construction of Kawaihae Harbor, when the beach itself was largely obliterated.

Breeding sharks still circle the **Haleokapuni Heiau**, dedicated to the shark deities, which lies beneath the waves around 100 feet out. The voracious beasts would devour offerings beneath the watchful gaze of the king, who would stand beside the stone Leaning Post that's still visible – though now in a sorry state – above the shore. Swimming is neither permitted nor particularly desirable: if the sharks aren't enough to put you off, the water is also clogged with gritty silt, which has completely obscured, and probably damaged, the underwater *heiau*.

Kawaihae Harbor and Shopping Center

Despite remaining without a wharf until 1937, **KAWAIHAE HARBOR** has long been the most important anchorage on the leeward coast of Hawaii. It was always the major port for the cattle of the Parker Ranch (see p.137); in the old days, intrepid cowboys would swim both cows and horses from the beach out to sea, then lasso them in the water and lash a dozen of them to the outside of flimsy whaleboats, which in turn rowed them to larger vessels anchored offshore.

The bay was finally dredged by the military during the 1950s. Casualties of the process included an assortment of delightful, grassy islands, each of which held a thatched shack or two, and most of the Big Island's best coral reef. Nevertheless, the port remains relatively low-key, poorly protected from occasional violent storms, and with few services nearby. Its biggest flurry of activity for many years came with the much-troubled filming of the Kevin Costner blockbuster *Waterworld* in 1994–95, during which the movie's centerpiece, a floating "slave colony," sank at least once to the bottom of the harbor.

Kawaihae's only shops and restaurants are to be found in the **Kawaihae Shopping Center**, at the junction of Hwy-19 and Hwy-270. This small, two-story mall is more upmarket than the location might suggest. As well as a few clothes stores and the *Harbor Gallery* of fine arts, there's a *Café Pesto* (Mon–Thurs & Sun 11am–9pm, Fri & Sat 11am–10pm; ☎882-1071), serving the same menu of delicious calzones and pizzas as the branch in Hilo (see p.196). Upstairs and around the back, you'll find a Mexican bar/restaurant and the very "local" *Akizuki's Takeout* (Mon–Sat 6am–3pm; ☎882-7776), which in addition to cooked breakfasts and plate lunches sells espresso coffees and smoothies.

KAWAIHAE HARBOR AND SHOPPING CENTER

Waimea

For many of the visitors who climb inland from Kawaihae on Hwy-19, the cool green plains between Kohala Mountain and Mauna Kea come as a surprise. Even less expected is the fact that these rolling uplands are cowboy country, still roamed on horseback by the *paniolos* (cowhands) of what claims to be the United States' largest private cattle ranch, the Parker Ranch.

The only town of any significant size in Kohala, **WAIMEA**, a dozen miles up from the ocean, started out as very much a company town. These days, however, the Parker Ranch employs barely one hundred of its eight thousand inhabitants, and while still proud of its cowboy past, Waimea has redefined itself as an exclusive residential community. Affluent locals are moving to Waimea in ever-increasing numbers, partly to get away from the sprawling resort developments of the coast and partly to take advantage of the region's distinctly cooler temperatures. As a result, Waimea is now home to a diverse community that includes international astronomers from the Mauna Kea observatories and successful entrepreneurs from the mainland. Poised halfway between the contrasting Kohala and Hāmākua coasts, Waimea has "wet" and "dry" sides of its own; it's the drier Kohala side, not surprisingly, where real estate is at a premium.

There's not all that much to Waimea as a destination; visiting sun-worshippers tend to restrict themselves to a quick burst of shopping and sightseeing on a round-island tour rather than an overnight stay. What town there is consists of a series of low-slung shopping malls lining Hwy-19 to either side of the central intersection, where it meets Hwy-190 from Kailua and makes a sharp right-angle turn towards Honoka'a and Hilo.

The most interesting gift and souvenir shopping is to be had at little **Parker Square**, on the west side of town, which holds several intriguing specialty stores. The much larger **Parker Ranch Shopping Center** is home to the local post office and the visitor center for the ranch itself (see p.139\); as this book went to press, it was being greatly expanded, with the promise of incorporating a new bookstore and a "national brand coffeehouse." Head one quarter of a mile east from here to see an appealing little cluster of clapboard **churches**, set well back from the road.

To avoid confusion with other Waimeas on Kauai and Oahu, the post office calls Waimea "Kamuela." Neither older nor more authentic, this name is simply a nineteenth-century corruption of "Samuel," one of the many scions of the house of Parker. Confusion nonetheless reigns in Waimea; it's still at the size where formal street addresses are seldom used, and virtually everything includes the word "Parker" somewhere in its name.

ARRIVAL AND INFORMATION

Waimea does have its own tiny **airport**, in the rolling ranchlands just south of town, but it sees very little use. The only airline offering scheduled service is Pacific Wings (℡887-2104 or 1-888/575-4546, ⓦwww.pacificwings.com), which operates daily flights to Honolulu (Mon–Sat 8am, Sun 3.10pm) and Kahului on Maui (daily

6.10pm). The standard one-way fare of $93 is reduced to $49 for Hawaii residents.

The town has also recently acquired a helpful **visitor center**, behind the High Country Traders building and alongside Parker Square on Hwy-19 on the Kawaihae side of town (Mon–Sat 9.30am–4.30pm; ☎885-6707, ⓦ www.NorthHawaii.net). As well as brochures and maps, it holds current menus for all the local restaurants.

ACCOMMODATION

Few visitors spend the night in Waimea, although it's one of the most pleasant towns on the island; the chief drawback is that the nights here are significantly colder than down by the ocean. For Hawaiians, that's a plus point, and the attractive local B&Bs are often booked well in advance.

Kamuela Inn

PO Box 1994, Kamuela, HI 96743 ☎885-4243 or 1-800/555-8968, ⓕ885-8857, ⓦ www.hawaii-bnb.com /kamuela.html.

Former motel, set back from the road a half-mile west of the central intersection, within easy walking distance of several restaurants. Refurbished and given an extra wing, it now holds rooms of varying but generally high quality, all with private baths, and some "penthouse

ACCOMMODATION PRICE CODES

All accommodation options in this book have been graded with the following symbols; for a full explanation, see p.29.

❶ up to $40	❹ $100–150	❼ $250–300
❷ $40–70	❺ $150–200	❽ $300–400
❸ $70–100	❻ $200–250	❾ over $400

suites" with kitchenettes as well. Rates include basic continental breakfast. Rooms ②, suites ③.

Tina's Country Cottage

Reserve through Hawaii's Best Bed & Breakfast, PO Box 563, Kamuela, HI 96743 ☎ 885-4550 or 1-800/262-9912, ℹ 885-0559, ⓦ www.bestbnb.com. Two-bedroom, two-bathroom cottage, with kitchen, wood-burning stove and spacious gardens, overlooking the Parker Ranch. Two-night minimum stay; reservations essential. ④

Waimea Country Lodge

65-1210 Lindsey Rd, Kamuela, HI 96743 ☎ 885-4100; or reserve through Castle Resorts ☎ 1-800/367-5004 (US & Can) or 1-800/272-5275 (HI), ℹ 885-6711, ⓦ www.castle-group.com. Simple and predictable motel units backing onto the Kohala slopes, at the start of

the road to Kawaihae from the junction in the center of Waimea. There's also a run-of-the-mill steakhouse on site. ③

Waimea Gardens Cottage

PO Box 563, Kamuela, HI 96743 ☎ 885-4550 or 1-800/262-9912, ℹ 885-0559, ⓦ www.bestbnb.com. Upmarket and hospitable B&B, owned by Barbara Campbell of the Hawaii's Best Bed & Breakfast agency (see p.31). Two miles west of central Waimea, it has two large and comfortable guest cottages, one with kitchen facilities, and both with private bathrooms. Both furnished with antiques and a library of Hawaiiana, the cottages boast views towards the rolling Kohala hills. Three-night minimum stay; reservations essential. ④

Hotels and restaurants listed in this chapter are keyed on map 6.

WAIMEA: ACCOMMODATION

135

KAMUELA MUSEUM

Map 6, B2. Daily 8am–5pm; $5 adults, $2 under-12s; ☏ 885-4724.

For sheer entertainment value, the **Kamuela Museum** –
two miles west of the central Waimea intersection, almost
directly opposite the junction of Hwy-250 and Hwy-19 –
is the best museum on the island. Its most memorable spec-
imen is its owner and curator, Albert Solomon, who was in
charge of the Honolulu police force motorcycle escort team
when Franklin Roosevelt came to Hawaii in 1934 – and
can show you the great man's slippers to prove it. If you
have an hour or two to spare, both he and his wife, Harriet,
can tell some great tales; she is a direct Parker descendant,
and their family anecdotes cover the entire period since
Americans first arrived in Hawaii. However, as both are
nonagenarians, and they've been attempting to sell the
museum, which is also their home, for several years, it's
possible that they will no longer be here by the time you
visit.

For the moment, the museum spreads through several
rooms of the Solomons' bungalow. Each of the dozens of
display cases contains an unpredictable mixture of items and
hand-written labels, which categorize the objects from
"unique" (the rope used to haul the Apollo 11 astronauts
out of the Pacific), through "quite rare" (a desiccated
Hawaiian bat suspended by its feet), down to simply "old"
(a motley assortment of toothpick holders, Japanese noodle-
cutting machines, accordions, "historic reptile dung,"
chicken spectacles and can openers). An intriguing collection of Chinese and Japanese porcelain, costumes and
weaponry culminates with a gun retrieved from the wreck-
age of a *kamikaze* plane that attacked the USS *West Virginia*
in April 1945.

Most visitors are drawn by the unusual and extensive
range of ancient **Hawaiian artifacts**, among them sinister-

looking idols of wood and stone, rows of daggers, "death cups" used in magic rituals, and lava knuckle dusters worn by fistfighters. Laid out for your inspection are all the daily implements of a world without metal, including wooden hooks that were baited with human flesh and used to catch sharks, fishhooks made from human bone, *poi* pounders and *tapa* beaters, and colorful feather *leis* and helmets.

THE PARKER RANCH

At its largest, in the nineteenth century, the **Parker Ranch** spread across more than half a million acres of the Big Island. It still covers more than ten percent of the island, currently holding around sixty thousand cattle on over 200,000 acres. The bulk of the land is divided into three huge parcels: one takes up most of North Kohala, one curves around the higher Hāmākua reaches of Mauna Kea, and the main tranche runs for forty miles up the western slopes of Mauna Kea from the ocean at Kawaihae.

It all dates back to **John Palmer Parker**, a ship's clerk from Massachusetts, who jumped ship in Kawaihae Harbor in 1809 and soon came to the attention of King Kamehameha, who gave him the job of maintaining the fishponds at Hōnaunau (see p.97). After a brief fit of wanderlust, when he joined the crew of a merchant ship and was detained in Canton for two years during the War of 1812, Parker returned to Hawaii at the end of 1814 and convinced the king that this time he intended to stay.

He returned at a fortuitous moment. In February 1793, Captain George Vancouver of the *Discovery* had presented Kamehameha with six cows and a bull, and suggested that a *kapu* be placed on the cattle to allow a population to grow. By 1815, wild cattle had become a serious problem, destroying crops and terrorizing villages, and wild mustangs too were roaming unmolested. Kamehameha gave

Parker permission to shoot the cattle, and from a base near Pololū he set out to impose discipline on the unruly beasts. With the decline of the sandalwood trade, the supply of beef and hides to visiting whalers became crucial to the Hawaiian economy. Parker managed the business for the King, and by taking his pay in live animals built up his own herds. Marrying Kamehameha's granddaughter Kipikane, he soon integrated into local society and was one of only two foreigners present at the famous banquet in 1819 when Liholiho broke the age-old *kapu* on men and women dining together (see p.273). He moved to the village of Waimea in 1835, established his homestead at Mana, and built a separate house for his son, John Palmer Parker II.

The ponchos, bandanas, and rawhide lassos of the Mexican, Native American, and Spanish *vaqueros* who were brought to work on the ranch were adopted by the Hawaiian cowboys they recruited and trained. They called themselves *paniolos* (from *Españoles*, or Spaniards).

Like many outsiders, Parker seized his opportunity in the Great Mahele of 1847, when private land ownership was first allowed (see p.275). He was granted two acres, and his wife, Kipikane, received 640 more. Soon he was in a position to buy another thousand acres and to lease the entire *ahupua'a* (see p. 283) of Waikoloa.

After the ranch was divided among Parker's immediate heirs, and the high-living Samuel Parker then frittered much of it away, the property was reunified under Thelma Parker in 1906. Attempts to diversify into sugar production and beekeeping came to nothing, but the cattle ranch went from strength to strength for the rest of the twentieth century, albeit with imported pedigree animals rather than the original Hawaiian stock. When the last Parker to control the operation, the sixth-generation **Richard Smart**, died in November 1992, he chose to leave just one percent of his holdings to his family. The ranch now belongs to a charitable trust, with assorted schools and health-care facilities in the Waimea area among the beneficiaries of its profits.

Parker Ranch Visitor Center

Map 6, G3. ☎ 885-7655, ⓦ www.parkerranch.com.
The small **Parker Ranch Visitor Center**, in the Parker Ranch Shopping Center in central Waimea, provides an overview of Parker family history as well as the general history of Hawaii. Its primary focus is on displays of old ranching equipment, with a slightly scaled down but genuine hut from the ranch crammed with saddles, spurs, bottles, and cowboy paraphernalia. A short video evokes the atmosphere of ranch life, with vintage footage of cattle being swum out to waiting steamers, as well as modern action shots of a dawn round-up high on Mauna Kea.

Visitor Center daily except hols 9am–5pm, last entry 4pm; $6, under-12s $4.50. Historic Homes daily except hols 10am–5pm, last entry 4pm; $8.50/$6. Combined ticket, sold 9am–3pm only, $12/$9.50. Wagon Tours, hourly Tues–Sat 10am–2pm, $15/$12. Parker Ranch Experience, including wagon tour and lunch at *Koa House Grill*, $42/$35.

The Historic Homes

Map 6, D4.
You may find your interest in the Parker family starting to flag at the so-called **Historic Homes**, half a mile out of Waimea towards Kailua, on Hwy-190. Construction of the stately **Puʻuʻōpelu** started in 1863, but it was completely remodeled in 1969 and now lacks any apparent connection

with things Hawaiian. Its pastel yellow rooms are filled instead with minor European paintings, while the melodious tones of its last owner, Broadway musical star Richard Smart, waft through the air.

The **Mana House** alongside looks like an ordinary white-clapboard house, but the interior gleams with dark *koa* wood, the sheer weight of which groans under your every step. These timbers were the only components robust enough to be moved in 1970, when it was decided to reconstruct the house here, twelve miles from the site where it originally went up during the 1840s. The walls of the tiny building are packed with family documents and fading photographs.

Five hundred yards beyond the Historic Homes towards Kailua, and six miles before the Saddle Road turnoff (see p.142), **Paniolo Park** is the home each July 4 of the **Parker Ranch Rodeo** (for information, contact ☎885-7655 or ⓦ www.parkerranch.com).

EATING

As one of the Big Island's most exclusive residential areas, Waimea has finally acquired the **restaurants** to befit its status. In addition, a few old-style cowboy places are still piling up meaty mountains of ribs, while the Waimea Center mall, down the road towards Hilo, is the place to head for **fast food**, with *McDonalds*, *TCBY,* and *Subway* outlets.

Aioli's
Opelo Plaza, 65-1227A Opelo Rd
☎ 885-6325.
French bakery-cum-deli-cum-bistro, tucked away near the back of an unexciting mall. There are fresh breads and great sandwiches for lunch, and dinner entrees such as ratatouille crepes for $14, and rack of lamb with Asian mustard for $15. Tues 11am–4pm, Wed & Thurs 11am–8pm, Fri & Sat 11am–9pm, Sun 8am–2pm.

Daniel Thiebaut

65-1259 Kawaihae Rd
ⓣ 887-1200.
Classy Mediterranean/Pacific
restaurant in the attractive
timber-framed "Historic
Yellow Building," a short way
up from Parker Square,
specializing in Asian-style
searing and spicing but rich
European sauces. Appetizers
like Hilo sweetcorn
crabcakes, and chicken won
tons cost around $8; entrees
such as wok-fried scallops or
five spice-dusted duck breast
are $20–25. There are also
plenty of vegetarian entrees,
and a changing daily three-
course prix fix menu for $33.
Daily 5.30–9.30pm.

Great Wall Chop Sui

Waimea Center ⓣ 885-7252.
Extensive and inexpensive
Chinese menu in an
unatmospheric mall. Entrees
include *chop sui*, noodles, and
seafood for as little as $6, and
there are cheap buffets for
both lunch ($8) and dinner
($10). Mon, Tues, Thurs &
Fri 11am–8.30pm, Sat &
Sun 9am–8.30pm, closed
Wed.

Koa House Grill

Hwy-19 at Waimea Center
ⓣ 885-2088.
This large modern highway
diner is the best of the
chicken-and-ribs cowboy
places in Waimea, with a
menu that strays into Pacific
Rim territory as well with
seared *ahi* and Thai curries.
Lunch works out around $10,
dinner entrees range from
$15 to $25. Mon–Sat
11.30am–10pm, Sun
11am–2pm.

The Little Juice Shack

Parker Ranch Center
ⓣ 885-1686.
Clean, busy deli next to the
Parker Ranch Visitor Center,
serving not only $3–4 juices
and smoothies but also $5
salads and sandwiches, and
daily lunch specials such as
Thai curry. Mon–Fri
7am–4pm, Sat 9am–4pm.

Maha's

Waimea Center ⓣ 885-0693.
Friendly, pretty, antiques-
furnished café, in an unlikely
1852 clapboard house at the
front of an otherwise modern
mall. Breakfast features

WAIMEA: EATING

granola for $4 or eggs for $5; lunchtime offerings ($6–11) include top-quality fish or chicken sandwiches plus smoked *ahi* tortillas or fresh *ahi* salads. Daily except Tues 8am–4.30pm.

Merriman's

Opelo Plaza, 65-1227A Opelo Rd ☎ 885-6822.
Gourmet restaurant with an emphasis on organic produce. Lunches are simple, with a $12 grilled shrimp on linguini the most expensive dish. Dinner entrees, priced at $20–30, tend to be much richer, but the signature wok-charred *ahi* is irresistible. Mon–Fri 11.30am–1.30pm & 5.30–9pm, Sat & Sun 5.30–9pm.

Waimea Coffee Co

Parker Square; ☎ 885-4472.
Lively vegetarian café where the fresh coffee is complemented by a large array of very inexpensive soups, salads, and sandwiches, priced at well under $5. Mon–Fri 7am–5pm, Sat 8am–4pm.

ONWARDS FROM WAIMEA

Whichever direction you head from Waimea, spellbinding scenery lies just a few miles down the road. Heading east towards Hilo on Hwy-19 brings you to Honoka'a in less than twenty minutes, with Waipi'o Valley not far beyond (see p.161). From an intersection just six miles south of Waimea, the **Saddle Road** starts its dramatic climb across the heart of the island between Mauna Kea and Mauna Loa – a journey covered in detail on p.200. The most attractive drive of all is **Hwy-250** along Kohala Mountain to Hāwi, described on p.145 onwards. However, the transition from the dry to the wet side of the Big Island can be experienced at its most marked if you make a slight detour off Hwy-19 three miles east of Waimea, to follow the atmospheric and little-used **Old Māmalahoa Highway**.

Old Māmalahoa Highway

Once part of Kamehameha's round-island trail, the **Old Māmalahoa Highway** was known to the ancient Hawaiians as "mudlane" and was notorious as a site where *'oi 'o*, or processions of the souls of the dead, might be encountered at night as they headed for the underworld said to lie below Waipi'o Valley. Now it's a minor road, somewhat slow and sinuous, but not difficult, even for cyclists.

The road heads first through treeless volcanic uplands where the rolling meadows, misty when they're not windswept, are grazed by horse and cattle. After about eight miles, you abruptly plunge into a magnificent avenue of stately old ironwoods. Thereafter, the vegetation is tropical and colorful, and homes with glorious gardens dot the hillside. Soon after passing through the residential community of **Āhualoa**, you rejoin the Belt Road near Honoka'a.

North Kohala

The district of **North Kohala**, which officially starts four miles or so north of Kawaihae (see p.130), for all intents and purposes comprises the low-rise flanks of Kohala Mountain itself. Spreading across both sides of the mountain, it's a microcosm of the whole island, with its dry leeward side separated by rolling uplands from the precipitous wet valleys of the eastern coastline. Only when you look closely at the occasional rounded hills dotted across the landscape — resembling nothing so much as upside-down Jello-molds — do you spot signs of their volcanic origin. They are in fact eroded cinder cones, topped by smoothed-over craters.

The road that curves around the north comes to an end at **Pololū Valley**, the last of a chain of valleys that begins with Waipi'o (see p.161). Like Waipi'o, Pololū was home to generations of ancient *taro* farmers; in fact, two centuries ago this region was the original power base of Kamehameha the Great, and several sites associated with Hawaii's first monarch can still be seen. The traditional Hawaiian way of life came to an end in 1906, when the waters from Pololū were diverted for irrigation. However, the last of the sugar plantations closed down in 1975, and these days the area is relatively unpopulated, scattered with tiny and characterful communities that have diversified into coffee and macadamia nut production.

Though North Kohala holds some of the most beautiful of all the Big Island's scenery, few visitors take the time to explore it. Its major drawback is that access to the sea is restricted, on both the leeward side, which is almost entirely devoid of beaches, and on the rugged windward coast. While almost no overnight accommodation is available, several local businesses are encouraging day-trippers to take adventure expeditions up into the hills, and there are at least several appealing little restaurants and snack bars.

ACROSS THE MOUNTAIN: HWY-250

With a maximum elevation of 5408 feet, Kohala Mountain is considerably lower than its younger Big Island rivals. Its summit is always green, never covered by snow, and its smooth velvet knobs betray few traces of their violent volcanic past. This landscape might not conform with what's usually thought of as Hawaiian, but the varying views of it obtained from a trip along **Hwy-250** are among the most sublime in the entire state.

For the first four miles or so out of Waimea, as the highway climbs the west flank of Kohala Mountain, a panorama of the Kohala coast gradually unfolds. At first the rolling lava landscape is covered with wiry green turf. Then scattered trees start to appear, together with clumps of flat-bladed cactus, often growing straight out of bare outcrops of chunky black lava. Higher still you enter proper ranching country; for a while the road becomes an avenue lined with two rows of splendid ironwood trees, between which you catch glimpses of undulating pastureland grazed by sleek horses. At various points along the way, vivid green turf-covered cinder cones bulge from the meadows, which are dotted with black and brown cattle.

Unfortunately, you never get the chance to turn off the road and explore the magnificent scenery higher up the mountain. As well as large landholdings of the Parker Ranch, there are several other private estates and even one or two old-style cattle-ranching communities hidden away along the northern half. The top of the mountain is a surreal landscape of eroded hillocks, which across the watershed turn so thickly forested as to be almost impenetrable. Rudimentary trails lead down to valleys such as Waipi'o, and the rough terrain is still cut through in places by irrigation channels such as the famous **Kohala Ditch**, constructed in the early 1900s to service the sugar industry.

ALONG THE COAST: HWY-270

The only alternative to Hwy-250 if you want to see North Kohala is the coastal **Hwy-270**, which heads north from Kawaihae Harbor. Most visitors drive a circular route that takes in both; the shoreline road is not as immediately attractive, but it does offer a handful of interesting historic sites, the occasional beach park and, in winter, the possibility of spotting humpback whales in the waters of the 'Alenuihāhā Channel.

The first dozen miles of Hwy-270 has no access to the ocean; if you want to snorkel in the bays at the foot of the low cliffs, join a boat excursion with Red Sail Sports (☎885-2876, ⓦwww.redsail.com).

Lapakahi State Historical Park

Map 5, B2. Daily 8am–4pm; free.
Fourteen miles north of Kawaihae, the first turn *makai* of the highway leads a short way down to **LAPAKAHI STATE HISTORICAL PARK**. The ancient village of Koai'e here is thought to have been inhabited for more than five hundred years until it was abandoned during the nineteenth century.

A hot, exposed but fascinating one-mile-long trail leads through what appears to have been a sizeable subsistence-level community of ordinary Hawaiians. They probably chose this site because of its white-coral beach and lack of cliffs, which made it the safest year-round canoe landing for many miles. Sustaining a population on such barren land must always have been hard, and the struggle seems to have been defeated in the end by a combination of a drop in the water table and the economic changes taking place in the islands as a whole.

You pass the villagers' dwelling places – their low walls, not necessarily roofed, served primarily as windbreaks – as well as assorted traces of their day-to-day life. Most of these are simply hollowed-out rocks; some were used to hold lamps, others served as salt pans of varying depths, and there's even a little indented stone, holding scattered black and white pebbles, used to play the game *kōnane*. Beside a fish shrine, where offerings would have been left to ensure a successful catch, a carved decoy rests on a open net; the shy *ahu* fish was captured when it attempted to make friends with its wooden counterpart.

The **beach** at Lapakahi is composed of medium-sized boulders rather than fine sand. This is a marine conservation area and the water is very clear, with parrotfish and darting yellow shapes visible in its turquoise depths. Visitors are only allowed to swim or snorkel north of the ancient village, and even there the use of sunscreen and towels is forbidden. From the bluff near the end of the trail, you may well be able to see Maui's towering Haleakalā volcano.

Māhukona Beach County Park

Map 5, B2.

A mile north of Lapakahi, another spur road connects Hwy-270 with North Kohala's first beach park, **MĀHUKONA BEACH COUNTY PARK**. In fact,

ALONG THE COAST: HWY-270

there's no beach at all, just a nineteenth-century harbor hemmed in by yet more lava outcrops. The seawall is still shored up, a mess of rust-streaked concrete pilings and jetties built to service the Kohala Sugar Company mill, which opened in 1863. For almost a century this was the shipping center for raw sugar brought by train from the fields around Niuli'i near Pololū; it closed down in 1956, after a final flurry of activity when the Hāmākua railroad was destroyed by the *tsunami* of 1946 (see p.180). The mill itself ceased to operate in 1975.

Māhukona is no place to swim; local divers join the swarms of yellow fish to explore the old railroad machinery beneath the waves, but conditions can get very stormy indeed, especially in winter.

Kapa'a Beach County Park

Map 5, B2.

KAPA'A BEACH COUNTY PARK, reached from another spur road off Hwy-270, a mile farther on, is much the same as Māhukona. Once again there's no beach, and the rocky stretch of coastline is cluttered with overgrown ruins. All Kapa'a has to offer is a pavilion equipped with restrooms, a barbecue/picnic area and views across to Maui on clear days.

Mo'okini Heiau and the Kamehameha Birthplace

Map 5, C1.

At the northernmost tip of the Big Island, very close to mile marker 20 on Hwy-270, a long straight road drops down to halt abruptly at the perimeter fence of **'Upolu** airport, built by the military during the 1930s and now barely used. From there, an unpaved road winds west along the coastline, degenerating occasionally into pools of mud. Though quite rutted, in dry conditions it poses few problems for ordinary rental cars. There are no trees along this exposed and windy stretch, and the rolling meadows halt a few feet up from the black lava shoreline.

One of Hawaii's remotest but most significant ancient temples, **MO'OKINI HEIAU**, is roughly two miles from the airport. It's accessible from a rudimentary parking lot, via a footpath up a small bluff. Though the gate is usually locked, visitors can go through the gap in the low walls. The *heiau*, in the center of a large green lawn, is a ruined but impressive pile of lichen-covered rocks; you can enter the structure and discern the traces of separate rooms, as well as a boulder on which victims were prepared for sacrifice.

Two conflicting legends make the temple's origins obscure. Its current guardians state that it was built between sunset and sunrise on a single night in 480 AD by Kuamo'o Mo'okini, using water-worn basalt stones passed from hand to hand along a fourteen-mile human chain from Pololū Valley. Alternative sources suggest it was created by the Tahitian warrior-priest Pa'ao seven centuries later, as a temple to Kū, the god of battle. The most likely way to reconcile the two stories would seem that Pa'ao simply rededicated an existing temple to Kū; it may even have been the site where the practice of human sacrifice was first introduced to Hawaii. The *Kahuna Nui*, the hereditary priesthood of Kū, has maintained an unbroken descent; the traditional *kapu* barring female priests has long since been broken, however, and the current *Kahuna Nui*, Leimomi Mo'okini Lum, is the seventh woman to hold the position.

A few hundred yards further along, the **KAMEHAME-HA AKAHI AINA HANAU** is a low, double-walled enclosure that slopes down a little closer to the sea. Kamehameha the Great is said to have been born here in

ALONG THE COAST: HWY-270

1758 – the date is known thanks to the appearance of Halley's Comet – at a time when his parents were in the retinue of King Alapa'i, who was preparing to invade Maui. Whisked away in secret and brought up in Waipi'o Valley, he returned to live in Kohala in 1782 (see p.152). The entrance to the large compound is from the south, *mauka* side; you can't go into the central enclosure, which amounts to little more than a patch of scrubby soil scattered with a few boulders. One rock marks the precise birthsite; visitors still leave offerings to Hawaii's greatest ruler on the walls nearby.

HĀWĪ

Map 5, C1.

More than 25 years after the closure of its *raison d'être* – the Kohala Sugar Company mill – the tiny town of **HĀWĪ**, a mile on from the 'Upolu turnoff, is hanging on as one of the most delightful little communities in Hawaii. It's an attractive place, with its all-purpose stores and new galleries and snack outlets still connected by creaking boardwalks, and every yard bursting with bright flowers.

Once you've filled up with gas at the intersection of highways 250 and 270, there's nothing to see or do in Hāwī beyond strolling across the village green and along the hundred yards of its main street. However, the spacious *Bamboo Restaurant and Bar* (Tues–Sat 11.30am–2.30pm & 6–8.30pm, Sun 11am–2pm; ☎889-5555) is perhaps the Big Island's nicest **restaurant**, serving "island-style" cuisine in a dining room furnished with bamboo and rattan furniture and festooned with tropical plants. A lunchtime salad, burger, or plate of stir-fried noodles costs $5–8, while dinner entrees ($14–22) include fish cooked to your specification in a range of styles such as "Hawaii Thai," as well as chicken, beef, and lamb from local farms. There's live Hawaiian music on weekend evenings, and the attached store-cum-gallery sells attractive *koa*-wood gifts and other crafts. If you're just after a light snack, the *Kohala Coffee Mill* (☎889-5577), across the street, has fresh Kona coffee plus burgers, bagels, and ice cream.

KOHALA MOUNTAIN ADVENTURES

The only way to experience the unique backcountry of Kohala Mountain is on a guided **adventure tour**.

Flumin' Da Ditch (daily 8.15am & 12.15pm; adults $85, ages 5–18 $65; ☎889-6922 or 1-877/449-6922, ⓦwww.flumindaditch.com) drives groups from the town of Hāwī up to a remote spot in the hills. Here you're loaded into five-person kayaks and paddled on an extraordinary 3.5-mile ride along the narrow irrigation channel known as the Kohala Ditch. The trip involves plunging through the mountains along thousand-foot dank tunnels and crossing deep gorges on wooden flumes. Once you're in the ditch, there are no long-distance views, but you do see rainforest waterfalls close-up. All in all, it's a great, if very wet, wilderness trip.

As HMV Tours, the same company also runs daily 4WD **jeep tours** into the hills, as does ATV Outfitters (closed Sun; ☎889-6000) from its base in Kapaʻau; prices range from $90 upwards. Kohala Eco Adventure in Hāwī (☎327-1133) specialize in guided **mountain bike tours** in the region, starting at $89.

Finally, you can also see the mountain on **horseback**. Kohala Naʻalapa Trail Rides (PO Box 992, Honokaʻa, HI 96727; ☎889-0022) sets off daily into the uplands from the ironwoods of Kohala Ranch (2hr 30min ride at 9am, $75 per person; 1hr 30min ride at 1.30pm, $55). Paniolo Riding Adventures (☎889-5354), based at Ponoholo Ranch, offers slightly more expensive rides.

KOHALA MOUNTAIN ADVENTURES

KAPAʻAU

Map 5, D1.

The main feature in the even smaller hamlet of **KAPAʻAU**, a couple of miles east of Hāwī on Hwy-270, is its **statue** of King Kamehameha. The original of the one facing ʻIolani Palace in Honolulu, it was commissioned from an American sculptor in Florence for the coronation of King Kalākaua in 1883. En route to Hawaii, it was lost when the ship carrying it foundered off the Falkland Islands. A couple of years later, by which time the insurance money had paid for a replacement, a passing ship's captain recognized the missing statue in a Port Stanley antique store and bought it for $875. Kamehameha had established his headquarters in **Hālawa** in 1782, in order to prepare for the imminent contest over the right to succeed the ageing King Kalaniopuʻu. All traces of Hālawa were ploughed over to plant cane many years ago, but it was very close to where modern Kapaʻau now stands, and so this sleepy town seemed a reasonable alternative location for the surplus statue.

There are actually three copies of the Kamehameha statue; the third is in Statuary Hall, in Washington DC.

Immediately behind the statue, the former courthouse now serves as the **Kohala Information Center** (Mon–Fri 10am–4pm). Staffed by local senior citizens, it holds a few rudimentary exhibitions, but it's basically a place to hang out and "talk story." *Jen's Kohala Café*, opposite (daily 10am–6pm; ☎889-0099), serves sandwiches, salads, wraps, smoothies, and all sorts of ice cream. In the restored *Nanbu Hotel* building, just up the street, the smart little *Nanbu Courtyard* (Mon–Fri 6.30am–4pm, Sat & Sun 8am–4pm) sells espresso coffees and lunchtime deli sandwiches, while the well-stocked and very welcoming Kohala Book Shop

(Tues–Sat 11am–5pm; ☎889-6400) claims to be the largest used bookstore in Hawaii.

Not far east of town, a narrow road *mauka* of the highway leads through some verdant countryside to the picturesque **Kalāhikiola Church**, built in 1855. Its first preacher, Revd Elias Bond, established the adjoining Bond Estate, a complex including homes, farm buildings, and a school.

Kēōkea Beach County Park

Map 5, D2.

The road on from Kapaʻau runs past the site of Hālawa; a huge wayside boulder at this tight curve is known as **Kamehameha Rock**, as the future king is said to have demonstrated that he was fit to rule by having sufficient *mana*, or spiritual power, to raise it above his head.

Immediately beyond, a lane leads, via a Japanese cemetery dotted with small black steles, down to **KĒŌKEA BEACH COUNTY PARK**. In the center of a rocky bay, a small stream flows into the ocean, and the surrounding hillsides have been pounded to pieces by high surf. An open-sided lookout shelter, exposed to the winds on a small hillock, makes a nice picnic spot, but there is no beach.

A short way along the side road to the beach, *Kohala's Guest House* (PO Box 172, Hāwī, HI 96719; ☎889-5606, ⓕ889-5572, ⓦhome1.gte.net/svendsen/index.htm; ❷) is the best accommodation option in North Kohala, doubling both as a **B&B** for short visits and a longer-term vacation rental. Each of the two separate houses has three bedrooms, and there's also a separate studio with kitchenette. The rooms are clean, fresh and comfortable; the rates are excellent; fruit trees fill the yard; and owner Nani Svendsen delights in sharing her extensive knowledge of North Kohala with her guests.

POLOLŪ VALLEY

Map 5, E2.

As Hwy-270 reaches its dead-end at a tiny parking lot, you get a view over one final meadow to the open cliff face that abuts the sea. Stretching away into the distance, it's punctuated by a succession of valleys, only accessible to visitors on foot and each therefore progressively less frequented and wilder than the last. The last of these, not visible from here, is Waipi'o (see p.161); the first, spread out beneath you, is **POLOLŪ VALLEY**.

If not quite on the scale of Waipi'o, Pololū was also once heavily planted by *taro* farmers. Regular *tsunamis* did little to encourage a stable population, however, and the death knell came when completion of the Kohala Ditch in 1906 drained off the valley's previously plentiful water supply for use on the nearby sugar plantations.

Pololū Valley remains a magnificent spectacle, and nowhere more so than from the initial overlook. If you take the time to explore it close up you may well find the hike down less strenuous, and more private, than its better-known equivalent further east. The pedestrian-only trail from the end of the parking lot takes twenty minutes without ever being steep, but when it's wet – which is almost always – it's an absolute quagmire of gloopy brown mud. Conditions are at their worst at the very start of the trail, which drops immediately into dense, head-high grasses. From there you wind down the hillside among ironwood, guava, and *hala* trees. Occasionally the trees yield to stretches of loose lava pebbles, which come as a welcome relief from the prevailing mud and offer glimpses of the shore below.

Once on the valley floor, the trail remains thoroughly squelchy as it approaches the broad river-cum-lake that meanders across the terrain, surrounded by marshy reeds. Hikers who try to head inland are swiftly confronted by "Private Property" signs warning you to go no farther.

Though Pololū's **beach**, like the one at Waipi'o, is commonly referred to as being black sand, it's basically gray grit, littered with decaying detergent bottles and pulverized flotsam. More welcome touches of color are added by the yellow and purple blooms that back the black lava rocks. In winter, the shore is prone to strong winds and heavy surf; there's no question of swimming even at the best of times. Take care, too, as you wade across the shallow but fast-flowing stream to reach the longer segment of the beach; high water is capable of carrying hikers out to the sharks offshore. On the far side of the stream, the beach is lined by gentle woodlands of pine-needle-covered hillocks, grazed by mules and horses.

Onwards from Pololū

A conspicuous but virtually impossible to follow trail switchbacks eastwards from Pololū over to the next valley, **Honokāne Nui**, and on to **Honokāne Iki** beyond that. The track doesn't go all the way through to Waipi'o, so at some point the few suicidal hikers who attempt it have to double back. As a rule the path follows the contours of the hillsides and doesn't drop back down to the sea each time, but it's in roughly the same bedraggled condition as the trail down to Pololū and is certainly no easier. Only experienced wilderness backpackers should even consider an expedition into this remote and uninhabited terrain.

ONWARDS FROM POLOLŪ

The Hāmākua Coast

Visitors to the magnificent **Hāmākua coast**, which extends for fifty ravishing miles along the northeastern flank of the Big Island, are confronted by archetypal South Seas scenery. This spectacular landscape has been carved by the great torrents of rain unleashed when the trade winds hit Mauna Kea, the highest peak in the Pacific, after crossing two thousand miles of open ocean. Countless streams and waterfalls cascade down the cliffs and gullies, nourishing dense jungle-like vegetation that is alive with multicolored blossoms and iridescent orchids. If you arrive on the dry Kona side of the island and never cross over to this **windward** coast, you'll be left, literally, with a one-sided impression of Hawaii.

Hāmākua farms once fueled the economy of the Big Island. Now agribusiness has all but pulled out – the last sugar mill closed in 1994 – and no one knows quite what might take its place. The state government initially promoted a plan that would lease former sugar land at bargain rates to a Japanese conglomerate to cultivate fast-growing eucalyptus trees. Local farmers, angry that they weren't being offered any similarly sweet deal, managed to block the scheme, but in doing so they antagonized the authorities in Honolulu to such an extent that state funding in the future seems likely to be very hard to come by.

For most of this stretch of shoreline, the **Belt Road** (Hwy-19) follows the original route of the sugar-company railroad, which carried local produce to ships waiting in Hilo and other smaller harbors. Barely rising or falling, the highway clings to the hillsides, crossing a succession of ravines on slender bridges. Damage to these bridges in the 1946 *tsunami* put the railroad out of business, but they were sufficiently repaired to be able to carry the road instead.

The drive is neither difficult nor particularly tortuous, but it's so beautiful that you may find it impossible to exceed the posted minimum speed of 40mph. Each little bridge offers its own glimpse of the verdant scenery, sometimes close to the ocean but high above it, sometimes winding further in to follow the contours of the gorges and passing babbling streams and waterfalls.

From Waimea, the Belt Road runs due east, curving to meet the coastline just south of the old-fashioned sugar town of **Honoka'a**. Turning north here onto dead-end Hwy-240 brings you, after ten miles, to one of the most unforgettable viewpoints on all the islands – the **Waipi'o Valley overlook**.

Southeast of Honoka'a, on the other hand, the main highway heads for forty miles down towards Hilo. This northern stretch of the Hāmākua coast held its largest sugar plantations, especially in the area around **Laupāhoehoe**. Further on, the fields are crammed ever more tightly into narrow, stream-carved "gulches," and there are few places to stop and enjoy the views. The two most popular off-road sightseeing spots are the impressive **Akaka Falls**, twelve miles beyond Laupāhoehoe, where a short loop trail through the rainforest offers a rare view of the interior, and the **Hawaii Tropical Botanical Garden**, ten miles beyond and just a few miles north of Hilo. Otherwise, if you just want to pause and take a few photos along the way, look out for the bridge just north of mile marker 18 (and south of Nīnole), from which you can watch the Waihaumalo River crash into the sea amid dramatic orange-blossomed trees and giant fanning palms, and the deeply indented Maulua Gorge at mile marker 22.

HONOKA'A

Map 5, H4.

The largest and most characterful of the Hāmākua towns is rough-and-tumble **HONOKA'A**, fifteen miles east of Waimea where the Belt Road reaches the ocean. Consisting largely of a row of quaint timber-framed stores set on the wooden boardwalks of **Mamane Street**, the town itself stands a couple of miles back from the ocean and is surrounded by rolling meadows.

Just over two thousand people live in Honoka'a, whose economy depended on a mill belonging to the Hāmākua Sugar Company from 1873 until it finally shut down in 1994. Still, this is one of several Big Island communities to have been spruced up and revitalized by federal funding, and its historic downtown district makes it an appealing port of call.

The most conspicuous landmark along Mamane Street is the Art Deco **Honoka'a People's Theater**, built as a movie theater in 1930 by the Tanimoto family (who also built the Aloha Theater in Kainaliu; see p.90). Restored and repainted in the last decade, it is now in use once again for occasional movie screenings and musical performances, and each October hosts the Hāmākua Music Festival, featuring Hawaiian bands and singers.

If you're lucky enough to find it open – afternoons are a better bet than mornings, but that's as far as regular hours go – a visit to octogenarian James Rice's **Hawaiian Shop**, also on Mamane Street, is the most memorable experience Honoka'a has to offer. At first glance it looks like a typical junk shop, but many of the artifacts piled high on all sides, crammed into crates and poking out from beneath layers of old newspaper, are anthropological museum pieces. The place is heaving with Buddhas, bottles, Aladdin's lamps, stuffed hog's heads, carved-lava Hawaiian deities and packing cases that appear to hold swathed mummies, but most importantly with idols, fertility symbols, and masks from Papua New Guinea. Such items don't come cheap – the simplest mask is likely to cost something approaching $100 – but you're unlikely to find this sort of stuff anywhere else in Hawaii. The town's handful of other antique and junk stores, a couple hundred yards up the road to Hilo, pale by comparison.

A steep road drops straight down towards the sea from the center of Honoka'a. Despite the closure of the sugar mill that blocks the way, you can't get right to the ocean. However, the **Macadamia Nut Factory** (daily 9am–6pm; free; ☎775-7201), very near the bottom, is, for no very good reason, a stop on many bus tours of the Big Island. It basically consists of a gift shop selling cookies, coffees, and the oleaginous nuts themselves. A window runs along the interior wall, enabling you to see into the factory and affording an insight into the mundane world of mac-nut preparation.

Practicalities

The only **accommodation** in central Honoka'a is the *Hotel Honoka'a Club*, on Mamane Street at the Hilo end of town (PO Box 247, Honoka'a, HI 96727; ☎ & ☎775-0678 or 1-800/808-0678; ❶–❷). A rambling, thin-walled and quite spartan old wooden structure, it offers a wide range of rooms, including appealing antiques-furnished en-suite ones on the upper floor with sweeping ocean views, and much more basic alternatives downstairs, some of which serve as $15-per-bed hostel-style dorms.

Two miles out of Honoka'a towards Waipi'o, the *Waipi'o Wayside B&B* (PO Box 840, Honoka'a, HI 96727; ☎775-0275 or 1-800/833-8849, ⓦwww.waipiowayside.com; ❸–❹) has five themed en-suite rooms in an attractive old plantation house. In Pa'auilo, six miles southeast, *Suds' Acres* is an appealing and more economical rural B&B, with two en-suite rooms in the main house, plus a two-bedroom guest cottage (PO Box 277, Pa'auilo, HI 96776; ☎ & ⓕ776-1611 or 1-800/735-3262; ❸).

The best place to **eat** in Honoka'a is *Jolene's Kau Kau Korner* (Mon–Wed & Fri 10.30am–8pm, Thurs & Sat 10.30am–3pm; ☎775-9498), next to the Lehua–Mamane intersection in the center of town. A lunchtime burger or stir-fry in this clean, attractive Hawaiian-style diner will set you back $4–8; more substantial dinner entrees, such as the tasty seafood platter of breaded fish, cost $12–17. If you're looking for something a little lighter, the main alternatives are the *Mamane Street Bakery Café* next door (Mon 6.30am–5.30pm, Tues, Wed & Sat 6.30am–5pm, Thurs & Fri 6.30am–6pm; ☎775-9478), for its breads, sandwiches, croissants, and espresso coffee, or *Café Il Mondo* opposite (Mon–Sat 10.30am–8.30pm; ☎775-7711), which sells soup and focaccia for $3.25 and calzones for $8.

KUKUIHAELE

Map 5, G4.

Beyond Honoka'a, Mamane Street continues north as Hwy-240. Eight miles on, and less than a mile short of the Waipi'o overlook, a looping spur road leads through the village of **KUKUIHAELE**, the nearest community to the valley. Its name, meaning "traveling light," is a reference to the lights carried by the ghostly nocturnal processions that head for the underworld below Waipi'o (see p.163).

As well as the *Waipi'o Valley Art Works* (☎775-0958), the appealing crafts store and snack bar that serves as the base for the Waipi'o Valley Shuttle and other tours described on p.166, it's home to a delightful **B&B**, *Hale Kukui* (PO Box 5044, Kukuihaele, HI 96727; ☎775-7130 or 1-800/444-7130, ⓦwww.halekukui.com; ❸–❹). Set in lush gardens above the ocean, with views of the valley mouth, the guest cottage here stands a couple hundred yards off the loop road as you head towards Waipi'o. Accommodation is in a one-bedroom studio or a two-room unit; credit cards are not accepted.

WAIPI'O VALLEY

Map 5, G4.

Nine miles out of Honoka'a, Hwy-240 comes to an abrupt end at the edge of **WAIPI'O VALLEY**. The southernmost of a succession of deeply indented, sheer-walled valleys stretching away up the coast to Pololū (see p.154), Waipi'o is the only one accessible by road. It's as close as the Big Island gets to the classic South Seas image of an isolated and self-sufficient valley, sparkling with waterfalls, dense with fruit trees, and laced by footpaths leading down to the sea. More dramatic examples of this kind of scenery abound on older islands such as Kauai, but as the Big Island is the newest in the chain, it's only here on the flanks of Kohala – its oldest volcano – that rainwater has had the necessary aeons to gouge out such spectacular chasms.

Between its high walls, the floor of the valley is surprisingly broad, and filled with rich silt carried down from the Kohala slopes by the meandering Waipi'o Stream (also known as Wailoa Stream). Visitors unfamiliar with Hawaii might not appreciate quite how unusual such large areas of prime agricultural land are in the islands. This was probably the leading *taro*-farming valley of the entire archipelago; its produce alone could feed the whole population of the island in times of famine.

The valley is now far more overgrown than it was in its heyday, but a few hardy farmers still squelch their way across paddy-like *taro* fields (known as *lo'i*, these have a consistency that has been likened to a "semi-jelled chocolate pudding"). They've been joined by assorted get-away-from-it-all *haoles*, including a sizeable population of latter-day hippies in the remoter reaches.

Only a small proportion of the steady trickle of visitors who admire the view from the Waipi'o overlook make their way down into the valley itself. It's a very strenuous hike, so most people join a motorized or horseback tour (see p.166 for details). Facilities at the bottom are minimal; there's nowhere to eat and a very restricted choice of accommodation. However, it's a magical, irresistible spot, and one that deserves to be included on even the most breakneck Big Island itinerary.

The history of Waipi'o

Wai being Hawaiian for "water," and *pi'o* meaning "a loop, bow or thing bent on itself," Waipi'o Valley was named "curving water" to describe the sinuous course of the Waipi'o Stream across its floor. This beautiful and enormously productive location occupies a crucial place in Big Island history, and retains a great cultural significance.

The Hawaiian word for "law," *kanawai*, literally means "the equal sharing of water," and the system to which it refers is said to have been instigated in Waipi'o at some indeterminate time by **'Umi-a-Liloa**. The first ruler to unite the entire Big Island, as a *taro* farmer he was responsible for the development of the valley's highly complex network of irrigation channels. Many remain in use to this day. 'Umi also had his nastier side, as one of the first major practitioners of large-scale human sacrifice. Victims, such as his rival high chief and half-brother Hakua-a-Liloa, were baked in an *imu* pit and their remains placed on the altar of Waipi'o's Moa'ula Heiau.

Both 'Umi and Hakua were the sons of the previous chief, Liloa. 'Umi, the product of a secret liaison, was raised in obscurity near Laupāhoehoe. As an adult, he revealed himself to his father in Waipi'o by swimming across the stream and climbing the walls of his stockade – an offense that would have been punishable by death had he not been able to prove his birthright.

Another Waipi'o legend states that a pit at the mouth of the valley (now ploughed over) marked the entrance to the underworld known as Kapa'aheo, the Hawaiian equivalent of ancient Greece's Hades. This insubstantial and barren wasteland was said to be populated by famished ghosts gnawing on lizards and butterflies, and dead souls could occasionally be seen making their way to it at night, in stately processions along the Old Māmalahoa Highway (see p.143).

Waipi'o was also the boyhood home of **Kamehameha the Great**, another future chief brought up in secrecy for his own safety. It was here that chief Kalaniopu'u granted Kamehameha custody of the war god Kūkā'ilimoku in 1780, thereby sanctioning his ambitions to become ruler. Eleven years later, his warriors fought Kahekili of Maui just offshore in the inconclusive but bloody "Battle of the Red-Mouthed Gun," in which, for the first time, Hawaiian fleets were equipped with cannons, operated by foreign gunners.

All sorts of estimates have been made of the population of Waipi'o in different eras. In Kamehameha's day, there may have been as many as 7500 inhabitants; within a century that was down to 2000, but you may still meet people brought up in the valley who can point out overgrown

WAIPI'O VALLEY

spots where Catholic, Protestant, and Congregational churches, and a Chinese temple, were thriving as recently as the 1930s.

However, large-scale settlement of Waipi'o came to an end after the *tsunami* of April 1, 1946, which scoured the valley from end to end. No one died, but few felt much inclination to rebuild their devastated homes. The busiest Waipi'o has been since then was during the 1960s, when it was used by the Peace Corps to train volunteers heading to work in Asia.

These days, sixty percent of the land is owned by one landlord – the Bishop Estate – which leases it to private farmers. So far, all threats to "develop" Waipi'o have come to nothing – tourists, and golfers in particular, don't like the rain. The latest scheme is for a complex of tree houses to be erected near the valley rim; just possibly, they'll be in place by the time of your visit.

Exploring the valley

If you just want to say you've seen Waipi'o, the view from the overlook is more comprehensive than any you get down below. Assuming that you've driven here, you must in any case leave your vehicle at the top. A few yards down from the parking lot, a pavilion stands in a small grassy area on the very lip of the cliff, about 900 feet above the sea. Off to your left is the green floor of Waipi'o, with terraced fields but barely a building in sight as it reaches back towards misty Kohala mountain. As you look straight up the coast, across the beach at the mouth of the valley you should be able to make out three distinct headlands. The first, the opposite wall of Waipi'o, is etched with the zigzagging trail that climbs up towards Waimanu Valley (see p.168); thanks to a landslide, it reaches right to the edge of the *pali*. The second is Laupāhoehoe Iki, on the far side of Waimanu, while Kauhola, beyond that, is up in North Kohala, near the town of Kapa'au on the road route to Pololū (see p.152). Unless you are the hardiest of hikers or kayakers, or take a flight-seeing tour, you'll never see the hidden valleys that lie in between. On clear days, the island of Maui is visible in the far distance.

A rough paved track heads down the side of the *pali* from the parking lot, but don't try to drive it yourself. Without four-wheel-drive it's suicidal – as the rusting relics in the undergrowth at the foot of the slope attest. Even if you do have 4WD, you need to know exactly what you're doing.

That leaves you with the choice of either taking a tour (see box, overleaf) or **walking** down. It takes about fifteen minutes to reach the floor, but be warned: the 25 percent gradient makes the return trip heavy going. It's so steep that even standing still, bracing yourself against the slope, can be exhausting, and the presence of mosquitoes won't add to your enjoyment.

One thing the tour operators don't mention is that they're not allowed to take visitors to the seashore. On foot, however, you're free to make your own way there. As soon as you come to the yellow warning sign at the bottom of the slope, double back onto what swiftly becomes a muddy lane. Don't stray off this path; the *taro* fields to either side are strictly private.

After a walk of roughly five minutes, through a fine avenue of ironwood trees, you'll get to the flat **beach** of gray sand, fronted by small black lava boulders. You may have heard stories about the black-sand beaches of Hawaii, but whatever people say, this isn't one of them. The sand here is simply silt washed down the mountainside, whereas a true black-sand beach is absolutely jet black and composed of tiny glass-like fragments of freshly spewed lava. The wide mouth of Waipi'o Stream cuts the beach in two; usually it's not too difficult to wade across, but don't

WAIPI'O VALLEY

WAIPI'O TOURS

An ever-increasing range of **organized tours** around the floor of Waipi'o Valley (available in horse-drawn wagons, on horse-back, and in 4WD vans), which drive visitors down the access road, offer a chance to learn more about the valley from local people. Many of the guides were born in Waipi'o and are eager to share stories of the old days. However, regulations as to what each operator is allowed to do tend to change from year to year. The beach is off-limits and the waterfalls are too remote, so most tours consist of anecdotal rambles through the *taro* fields and along the riverbank.

The Waipi'o Valley Shuttle, which runs ninety-minute **van trips** from the overlook, is based at the *Waipi'o Valley Art Works* (see p.161) in Kukuihaele, a mile from the end of the road. They prefer that you call ahead to reserve a trip, but there's often a driver hanging around the overlook itself waiting to fill up his vehicle (Mon–Sat, departures usually at 9am, 11am, 1pm & 3pm; $40 per person; ☏775-7121).

The Last Chance Store, also in Kukuihaele, is the headquarters

attempt it if the water is any deeper than your thighs. Neither should you drink it, as it's liable to carry diseases from wild animals in the hills. Leptospirosis in particular is a major problem here, so don't let the water come into contact with the smallest open wound (see p.53). Finally, though surfers and boogie-boarders while away days on end playing in the white breakers, it's no place for a casual dip.

If, instead of heading for the beach, you keep going at the foot of the slope, towards the back of Waipi'o, you soon come within sight of the 1200-foot **Hi'ilawe waterfall**, with the parallel but slimmer **Nani** cascade plummeting to its left. Both feed Waipi'o Stream as it emerges into the heart of the valley. The waterfall is far-for Waipi'o Valley Wagon Tours, which takes groups of up to twelve people on two-hour **covered-wagon excursions** (Mon–Sat, up to four tours daily, usually at 9.30am, 11.30am, 1.30pm & 3.30pm; $40 per person; ☎775-9518), and for Waipi'o on Horseback (daily 9.30am & 1.30pm; ☎775-7291), which runs **horseback expeditions** that last a couple hours and cost around $75. Waipi'o Na'alapa Trail Rides (Mon–Sat 9.30am & 1pm; ☎775-0419) offer similar excursions at similar prices.

In addition, various tours explore the backcountry close to and along the upper rim of Waipi'o without making the descent into the valley itself. Waipi'o Ridge Stables (☎ 775-1007, ⓦ www.topofwaipio.com) offers both **horse** rides ($75 for 2hr 30min, $145 for 5hr), and, as Waipi'o Rim Adventures (same number and website), **off-road vehicle** tours, either in individual all-terrain buggies ($85 for 2hr) or in 4WD jeeps ($85 for 3hr). Hawaiian Walkways organizes none-too-strenuous guided **hikes** ($85 for 4–5hr; ☎775-0372 or 1-800/457-7759, ⓦ www.hawaiianwalkways.com).

ther away than it looks; walking to its base takes an hour and a half and involves scrambling up a channel of giant boulders. This spot was once the site of Nāpo'opo'o, Waipi'o's main village, which was said to have had several thousand inhabitants.

A disused, century-old trail runs on a ledge behind and halfway up Hi'ilawe, following the line of the aqueducts and tunnels that formerly carried water to the sugar farms. The square building to the left of the falls, conspicuous for its mirrored paneling, is also empty. It was built as a restaurant in the 1960s, but local protests at the developers' ever more grandiose plans, which included installing a cable-car ride to the top of the falls, led to the project being abandoned.

WAIPI'O VALLEY

Accommodation

Waipiʻo Valley has neither restaurant nor café, nor does it any longer hold hotels or hostels of any kind. However, permission for up to four-nights' free tent **camping** in the woodlands just inland from Waipiʻo Beach, on the near side of the stream, is granted by the Bishop Estate, whose office is in the Keauhou Shopping Center near Kailua (78-6831 Alii Drive, Kailua-Kona, HI 96740; ☎322-5300).

Hiking beyond Waipiʻo

The moment you arrive at Waipiʻo Overlook and look across to the trail that climbs the far wall of the valley, you'll probably start wondering what lies **beyond Waipiʻo**. Very few people ever find out – it's one of the most difficult hikes in all Hawaii, way beyond what it's possible to achieve in a single day. In addition, the trail only continues as far as **Waimanu Valley**, eleven miles away. The four more valleys before Pololū (see p.154) are inaccessible from this side; a trail from Pololū in theory gets to two of them, but that too is an extremely demanding undertaking.

Because it involves wading through at least two deep and fast-flowing streams, the trail to Waimanu is only passable between May and October. Only consider setting off from Waipiʻo if you're equipped with a camping permit (see opposite) and everything necessary for a backcountry expedition – most notably a rainproof tent and clothing, and some kind of water purification system.

Start by heading slightly inland from the far end of Waipiʻo beach, and you'll soon pick up the uphill path. For most of the way, it passes through thick woodlands, so there are virtually no views of either sea or valley. The trail doesn't drop to sea level again until Waimanu, but climbs up and down through what feels like an endless succession of gullies.

Waimanu itself is a sort of miniature Waipi'o, with even more waterfalls. It, too, was once densely populated by *taro*-farmers and only abandoned after the *tsunami* of 1946. The beach itself is made up of large boulders, which means that not only is it not safe for swimming, but you can hardly even walk along it.

The main **campground** is on the far side of Waimanu stream. **Camping** is free, but limited to nine sites, and you can stay a maximum of six nights. Obtain a permit from the Department of Forestry in Hilo (1643 Kīlauea Ave, Hilo, HI 96720; ☎933-4221).

Local experts say that the easiest way to get to Waimanu and beyond is not by hiking at all, but by **kayak**. Naturally, only experienced kayakers should attempt such an expedition.

KALŌPĀ FOREST STATE PARK

Map 1, G2.

As you head southeast from Honoka'a, the first opportunity to investigate the upland slopes of Mauna Kea comes after a couple of miles, in the **Kalōpā Forest State Park**, a mile *mauka* of Hwy-19.

The reserve covers 615 acres, including the deep and dramatic Hanaipoe Gulch, which holds its greatest concentration of indigenous vegetation. The gorge is pristine because animals find it impossible to graze on its steep sides, and it's similarly very difficult for humans to gain access. The trails that lead there are very muddy and overgrown and the rangers positively discourage casual visitors from attempting the hike.

Instead, you're, advised to follow the **Native Forest Nature Trail**, a loop of less than a mile that starts from the State Park parking lot and winds through variegated woodlands. Most of what you see is planted rather than natural, but it still provides an interesting introduction to the native flora of the Big Island. It's a peaceful stroll rather than a spectacular one, and in places it can be hard to find your way. By the end of the trail, however, you should be able to spot the difference between the 'ōhi'a and kopiko trees, be familiar with ferns such as the hāpu'u and the nianī'au, and be appalled by the evil ways of the aggressive strawberry guava plant. The 'io (Hawaiian hawk) and the tiny but melodious 'elepaio make their nests in this area, though it may turn out that you see no creatures larger than voracious mosquitoes.

Local wild-pigs hunters tend to be active in the reserve, especially on weekends; their role in keeping the pig population down is one of the factors that helps the forest to survive.

The park has a small, tent-only **campground**, charging $5 per night, as well as four eight-bunk cabins, each equipped with bath, bed linen, and blankets, and sharing the use of a central kitchen and communal area. The cabins are let for up to five nights, at $55 per night. Reserve on the spot by finding the caretaker before 4pm, or call the state parks office in Hilo (☎974-6200).

LAUPĀHOEHOE

Map 1, H3.

For most of the Hāmākua coast, the shoreline cliffs are too abrupt to leave room for settlements by the sea. Hence the significance of **LAUPĀHOEHOE**, seventeen miles along from Honoka'a, where a flow of lava extruding into the ocean has created a flat, fertile promontory (lau means leaf, and pāhoehoe is smooth lava).

As the best canoe landing between Hilo and Waipi'o, Laupāhoehoe has long been home to a small community. The location has its perils, however. On April 1, 1946, a

THE WRECK OF THE *HORNET*

It was at Laupāhoehoe, on June 15, 1866, that the appalling ordeal of fifteen shipwrecked sailors finally ended. Left to drift across the open Pacific in a badly damaged longboat after their clipper ship, *Hornet*, caught fire and sank, they somehow survived 43 days and four thousand miles, drinking a few drops of rainwater each day and eating whatever fish and seabirds they could capture with their bare hands, as well as even their own boots and clothes. When they were finally washed ashore, as the young Mark Twain reported, "a crowd of natives (who are the very incarnation of generosity, unselfishness and hospitality) were around the strangers dumping bananas, melons, taro, poi – anything and everything they could scrape together that could be eaten – on the ground by the cartload; and if Mr. Jones, of the station, had not hurried down with his stewards, they would soon have killed the starving men with kindness."

ferocious *tsunami* destroyed the school at the tip of the headland, killing 24 teachers and children; rescue attempts were delayed as all boats and canoes in the vicinity were wrecked by waves up to thirty feet high.

As the approach road to Laupāhoehoe rounds the first tight corner on its way to the sea, you're confronted by a stunning view of the green coastal cliffs stretching away to the south. After rain, countless small waterfalls cascade from crevices in the rock.

The narrow road winds down past the **Jodo Mission**, a temple built by Japanese immigrants in 1899, and arrives at a flat spit of land at the bottom of the cliffs. Most of the space here is taken up by a large lawn, fringed with tall coconut palms that have an alarming tendency to shed their fruit in high winds. A number of seafront parking lots are squeezed in before the forbidding black-lava coastline and

LAUPĀHOEHOE

its pounding surf, in which swimming is definitely not advisable. To the right is the small boat launching ramp of Laupāhoehoe Harbor, so dangerous that it's usually sealed off from public access, while round to the left an open-sided beach pavilion tends to be the preserve of locals around sunset.

Until the *tsunami* of 1946, the main coastal road passed through Laupāhoehoe at sea level. Part of the village had already relocated higher up the hillside in 1913, however, when the sugar company **railroad** reached this far up the Hāmākua coast. Both the lower road and the railroad were destroyed by the *tsunami* – the railroad lost not only much of its track and its trestle bridges, but also the actual engines. The whole community, including a new school built to replace the one lost in the storm, subsequently shifted to the top of the cliffs.

Since the last of the local sugar mills closed, Laupāhoehoe has been facing an uncertain future. A fair few people still live along the various backroads in the district, but there's no town for visitors to explore, and no accommodation is currently available. The one concession to tourism is the little **Laupāhoehoe Train Museum**, housed in the former ticket agent's home alongside the highway (Mon–Fri 9am–4.30pm, Sat & Sun 10am–2pm; donations). Enthusiastic volunteers explain the history of the railroad, aided by a plethora of photos and artifacts, and can tell you how far they've got with their schemes to restore some of the rusted-up old machinery.

UMAUMA FALLS

Map 1, H3. Mon–Sat 9am–5.30pm; $7. ☎ 963-5427.

Heading inland from Hwy-19 along any of the little access roads around mileposts 19 and 18, roughly five miles south of Laupāhoehoe, enables you to join the minor road, parallel to the main highway, that leads to **Umauma Falls**. These previously little-known falls have become more prominent on tourist itineraries since 1995, when the surrounding land was opened to the public as the **World Botanic Gardens**.

So far, the gardens themselves are small and unexciting, but visitors who drop in at their roadside headquarters and pay the high admission fee are furnished with directions for reaching an overlook beside the Umauma Stream that commands a superb prospect of the tripled-tiered falls themselves. They're not nearly as dramatic as Akaka Falls (see overleaf), which you can see for free, but that doesn't make them bad; if paying $7 to admire an attractive waterfall seems worth it to you, go right ahead. The whole experience may become a better value for the money if the owners' ambitious schemes to develop the gardens ever come to fruition; plans include the construction of a chocolate factory.

KOLEKOLE BEACH PARK

Map 1, I3.

The only sizeable seafront park between Laupāhoehoe and Hilo, **Kolekole Beach Park**, marks the spot where the Kolekole Stream – fresh from its awesome drop over Akaka Falls (see overleaf) – flows into the ocean. Look out for a small turning *mauka* (inland) of the highway, just after a tall narrow bridge twelve miles out from Laupāhoehoe.

The road down to the park, lush even by Hāmākua standards, doubles back to end at the foot of the bridge struts, far below the highway. On both sides, the gorge is thick green, half-swallowing the rusting tin-roofed pavilions of the park. There's no beach, however, and while local youths thrill to ride the breakers back into the mouth of the river, lesser mortals should be wary of submitting themselves to the high surf that lies just a few yards beyond the rounded black boulders of the shoreline.

AKAKA FALLS

Map 1, H3.

Three or four miles up Mauna Kea from the Belt Road, just beyond Kolekole and fifteen miles short of Hilo, **Akaka Falls** is one of the Big Island's most photogenic sights. Though not the highest waterfall on the island, its setting is unrivaled – a sheer drop through a chasm overrun by tropical vegetation and orchids. An easy and enjoyable mile-long trail leads visitors through a dense "jungle" and past other falls, culminating at a viewpoint looking upstream to Akaka itself. You don't get close to the riverbed, let alone the falls, so the only dangers to contend with are the steamy heat and persistent mosquitoes.

The trail starts from a parking lot that's reached by following a straightforward series of signs off the highway, through Hōnomu (see opposite), and up Hwy-220 via a small belt of meadowland. A narrow staircase leads down from the edge of the parking lot, plunging you into dense tropical foliage, with thickets of bamboo soaring from the gorge below to meet high above your head. Few of the plants lining the route are native to Hawaii, and the whole forest is a battleground of yellow, purple, and pink blossoms. Among the most lurid are the fiery red "lobster-claw" heliconia, and that colorful relative of the banana, the bird of paradise, bedecked either in orange and blue, or white.

Shortly after you cross a narrow stream, the overhead canopy opens up and you reach an overlook facing **Kapuna Falls**. Slightly retracing your steps, you then follow the path up to your right. The mighty trees alongside are festooned with thick green mosses, fern, and creepers, with all kinds of parasitic plants erupting from their branches and trunks. To the left, a vast banyan drips with tendrils; hundreds have rooted themselves, and it's impossible to tell which was the original trunk.

Immediately across the next bluff, you get your first view of Akaka Falls itself, foaming through a narrow channel to plunge around 450 feet down a mossy cliff face and disappear in a cloud of spray into the pool below. After leaving the viewing area, you recross the stream at a higher point, where a small waterfall bubbles beneath another overhanging bamboo grove.

Hōnomu

Map 1, I3.
Were it not for the steady flow of visitors to Akaka Falls, tiny **HŌNOMU**, on the *mauka* side of Hwy-19, a mile or so south of Kolekole Beach Park, would probably have been swallowed up by the rainforest by now. As it is, the village consists of a row of little timber-frame galleries and crafts stores, a couple of which sell sodas, juices, and snacks as well as run-of-the-mill souvenirs. To sample the flavor of the place, the best stop is Ishigo's General Store, an authentic plantation store that has been run by the same family since 1910.

PEPE'EKEO SCENIC DRIVE

Map 1, I4.
PEPE'EKEO SCENIC DRIVE, a small side road that drops towards the sea at Pepe'ekeo, a couple of miles on from Hōnomu, then curves for four miles before rejoining Hwy-19 four miles north of Hilo, makes a worthwhile detour from the Belt Road. Until the highway came through, this was

part of the Old Māmalahoa Highway that once encircled the island (see p.143). That explains why the trouble was taken to plant its most impressive stretch, a superb avenue of over-hanging Alexandra palms imported from Queensland, Australia. They make their appearance just beyond a delight-ful gorge that bursts with African tulip trees.

Close to the north end of the road, *What's Shakin* (daily 10am–5pm; ☎ 964-3080) serves the best **smoothies** on the island – succulent $4 concoctions of fresh tropical fruits – plus sandwiches for around $7, and has a nice veranda over-looking its own orchards.

Few visitors make it to the end of the Scenic Drive with-out indulging in a daydream or two about the various real-estate parcels on sale on its *makai* side. Rest assured, even if you could afford the asking price for a piece of land, the restrictions on development would ensure that you couldn't do much with it once you'd bought it.

Hawaii Tropical Botanical Garden

Map 1, I4. Daily 9am–5pm; adults $15, under-17s $5; ☎ 964-5233, ⓦ www.hawaiigarden.com or www.htbg.com.

Occupying almost the entirety of **Onomea Bay** – one of the lushest, prettiest bays of the Hāmākua coast – the **Hawaii Tropical Botanical Garden** is the Big Island's premier showcase for tropical trees, orchids, and flowering plants. This labor of love has been created by Californian retiree Dan Lutkenhouse, who, since 1978, has gathered specimens from as far afield as Brazil, Malaysia, Madagascar and Guatemala, alongside endemic Hawaiian species, and garnished the collection with a few flamingos and macaws. Though a major stop on the tour-bus circuit, with crowds and prices to match, it still comes closer than anywhere to matching the popular conception of what a tropical rainfor-est should look like.

The process of turning the valley into a landscaped garden has obliterated most traces of its past, though Isabella Bird described Onomea Bay as having a picturesque "native village" in the 1870s. A few years later it had become a fully fledged harbor serving the Hāmākua sugar plantations.

The garden's headquarters are located halfway along the Scenic Drive, where it crosses Onomea Stream well back from the shoreline. From there, a signposted self-guided trail, occasionally interspersed with large wooden stairways, drops around 500 feet down to the ocean. Insect repellent, drinking water and umbrellas are available at the starting point, and it takes roughly an hour to complete its full length.

Striking features during the descent include views of a tall waterfall, on the innermost wall of the valley, visible at the upper end of the "palm jungle" of Alexandra palms. A little lower, just above a lesser waterfall, stands a huge Cook pine – not in fact a true pine, but a Polynesian species brought to Hawaii from New Caledonia by Captain Cook. The tree is surrounded by spectacular heliconia and vast spreading "travelers' trees" – so named because they are said always to hold a little water at the base of their leaves – as well as indigenous species.

Most of the plants are labeled, and there's a heady succession of gingers, bromeliads, dramatic orange and yellow heliconia, coconut palms with their writhing worm-like roots, and *hala*, or pandanus trees, whose roots serve as stilts that seem to lift the trunk off the ground. Perhaps the most prominent of all is the red-leafed *obake*, which with its lurid white or yellow "prong" is something of an island trademark.

At three little inlets in Onomea Bay you can enjoy fine views of the verdant shoreline; the largest, Turtle Bay, has a small black-sand beach, but at none of them are visitors allowed to leave the paths and approach the water.

HAWAII TROPICAL BOTANICAL GARDEN

Hilo

Until recently, windward Hawaii's major city, **HILO**, was the economic and political powerhouse of the island. It's still the capital, and home to 45,000 people, but with the sugar mills gone and Kona-side tourism growing ever more significant, Hilo now feels more like a rather traditional small town. As a place to visit, it's relaxed and attractive, spread over a surprisingly large area but with an appealingly old-fashioned downtown district where you can stroll between friendly cafés, street markets, and historic sites.

In the early 1970s, Hilo made a bid to become a major tourist center, but mass tourism has never taken off here; quite simply, it rains too much. Hilo averages 130 inches of rainfall annually, with fewer than ninety rain-free days per year. Most mornings, however, start out clear and radiant; the rain falls in the afternoon or at night, and America's wettest city blazes with wild orchids and tropical plants.

As well as having the only **airport** along the Hāmākua coast, Hilo holds all its **hotels**. In the absence of sizeable sandy beaches, tourists who come here are drawn largely by the beauty of the nearby coast. The fifty-mile excursion up to Waipi'o Valley is irresistible, but nearer at hand you can enjoy the delightful Pepe'ekeo Scenic Drive or the mighty Akaka and Rainbow falls.

Hilo stands where the Wailuku and Wailoa rivers empty

into an enormous curving bay, named "Hilo" by ancient Hawaiians in honor of the first crescent of the new moon. In 1796, Kamehameha the Great chose the best natural harbor on the island to build his *peleleu*, a fleet of eight hundred war canoes for his campaigns against the other Hawaiian islands. Characterized by his enemies as "monstrosities," these hybrid Western-influenced vessels carried mighty armies of warriors; some say they were never destroyed and still lie hidden in caves along the Kona coast.

The port prospered in the nineteenth century, when its strong missionary influence enabled it to present itself as a clean-living alternative to dissolute Honolulu. In the words of the evangelist Titus Coan in 1848:

No man staggers, no man fights, none are noisy and boisterous. We have nothing here to inflame the blood, nothing to madden the brain. Our verdant landscapes, our peaceful streets, our pure cold water, and the absence of those inebriating vials of wrath which consume all good, induce wise commanders to visit this port in order to refresh and give liberty to their crews.

Hilo became the center of the Big Island's burgeoning sugar industry, shipping out raw cane and serving as the arrival point for immigrants from around the world, and in the process acquired an unusually radical labor force. From the 1930s onwards, local workers spearheaded successive campaigns against the "Big Five" companies that had long dominated the Hawaiian economy (see p.276). Fifty people were injured in the "Hilo Massacre" of August 1, 1938, when strikers were attacked by armed police, and strikes in 1946 and 1949 helped to end the long-term Republican domination of state politics.

The innermost segment of the bay, encompassing both port and town, is protected by a long breakwater. In principle, this is a very calm stretch of water, but its funnel shape means that during great storms it can channel huge waves directly into the center of town. Cataclysmic *tsunamis* killed 96 people in April 1946, and an additional 61 in May 1960. Lava flows have also repeatedly threatened to engulf Hilo; in 1881 Princess Ruth Keʻelikōlani summoned up all her spiritual power (see p.234) to halt one on the edge of town, while in 1984 another flow stopped eight miles short.

ARRIVAL AND INFORMATION

Compact and walkable, **downtown Hilo** focuses on the junction of seafront Kamehameha Avenue and Waianuenue Avenue, which heads towards the Saddle Road across the island. However, the urban area extends for several miles, and the **airport** at General Lyman Field (℡ 935-4782), on the eastern outskirts, is well beyond walking distance. If you're not renting a car at the airport, you'll need to take an $8 taxi ride into town.

Limited **bus** service is offered by the Hele On Bus Company (℡ 961-8744). Their base, **Mooheau Bus Terminal**, is an open-air bayfront pavilion on Kamehameha Avenue, between the two highways. In addition to city routes, scheduled for commuters and of little use to visitors, there are a few longer-distance services. On weekdays only, the "9 Pāhoa" leaves Hilo at 2.40pm and 4.45pm, to reach Pāhoa, twenty miles southeast of Hilo, at 3.45pm and 5.40pm respectively; the "7 Downtown Hilo" leaves Pāhoa at 6.05am and arrives in Hilo at 7.35am. Several daily buses also run from Hilo to Honokaʻa and Waimea, but almost all are extremely early in the morning. The bus to **Hawaii Volcanoes National Park** and Ocean View, which leaves Mooheau Bus Terminal at 2.40pm on Monday to Friday only, is detailed on p.222.

For a full timetable of the once-daily cross-island bus between Hilo and Kailua, see p.25.

Details of helicopter and fixed-wing **flight-seeing** operators based at General Lyman Field appear on p.26; Big Island boat trips are restricted to the Kona side of the island.

Information and services

The **Hawaii Visitors Bureau** is at 250 Keawe St, one block up from the bayfront in the center of downtown (Mon–Fri 8am–4.30pm; ☏961-5797, 🖷961-2126, ⓦwww.bigisland.org). Its helpful staff can advise on accommodation and tours, and have piles of brochures for you to take away.

Hilo's main **post office** (Mon–Fri 8.15am–4.45pm, Sat 8.30am–12.30pm) is on the approach road to the airport, but there's another one downtown in the Federal Building on Waianuenue Avenue (Mon–Fri 8am–4pm). **Banks** are dotted all over town and in the malls, with the most central branch of the Bank of Hawaii based at 117 Keawe St.

ACCOMMODATION

Although downtown Hilo is extremely short of **hotels**, several options line the oceanfront crescent of **Banyan Drive**, a mile or so southeast. Sadly, most of these have become rather run-down in recent years, but the state has stepped in to provide incentives for regeneration, and the situation should improve within the lifetime of this book. There are also a number of B&Bs in the vicinity, while a couple of welcoming and inexpensive inns can be found north of the Wailuku River, a short walk from downtown.

HILO: ACCOMMODATION

ACCOMMODATION PRICE CODES

All accommodation options in this book have been graded with the following symbols; for a full explanation, see p.29.

1 up to $40   **4** $100–150   **7** $250–300
2 $40–70   **5** $150–200   **8** $300–400
3 $70–100   **6** $200–250   **9** over $400

Room rates are lower on this side of the island, in part because hotel owners assume that you'll be out exploring the volcanoes or the Hāmākua coast during the day. If that *is* what you're going to be doing, there's no great reason to spend more than a couple of nights in Hilo; if you plan to spend most of your time on the beach, then it's probably the wrong side of the island for you altogether.

Hotels and restaurants listed in this chapter are keyed on maps 7 and 8.

Arnott's Lodge

98 Apapane Rd
Ⓣ 969-7097, Ⓕ 961-9638,
Ⓦ www.arnottslodge.com.
Laid-back but safe and clean budget accommodation in a two-story, motel-style lodge just off the road to Onekahakaha beach, a couple of miles southeast of downtown. The downstairs dorm rooms have twelve beds for $17 each, while the second floor is divided into two-bedroom units; a private double is $47, or $57 en suite. You can also camp in the grounds for $9. There's a tree house and bar, but no food except a twice-weekly barbecue. The management provides free airport pickup, a $2 shuttle service into Hilo, and assorted van day-trips; excursions to South Point, North Kohala, and Volcanoes

National Park cost $43 each, and a trip to the summit of Mauna Kea is $48. **①—②**

Dolphin Bay Hotel

333 Iliahi St ⓣ935-1466, ⓕ935-1523, ⓦwww .dolphinbayhilo.com.

Very nice, very friendly little hotel within walking distance of downtown across the Wailuku River. Spotlessly clean studios and one- and two-bedroom suites are fully equipped with TV, bathroom and kitchen. No pool or restaurant, but free papayas and bananas dangle around the building, and the owner is a mine of useful advice. **②—③**

Hale Kai Bjornen

111 Honoli'i Pali ⓣ935-6330, ⓕ935-8439, ⓦwww.interpac.net/~halekai. Small, comfortable B&B, perched on a magnificent vantage point above the ocean a couple of miles north of downtown. Each of the three rooms in the main building (two-day minimum stay) has its own bath and shares a living room; the adjacent guest cottage (five-day minimum) has a living room and kitchenette. All share use of the pool and Jacuzzi. No credit cards; reservations essential. **③—④**

Hawaii Naniloa Hotel

93 Banyan Drive ⓣ969-3333, 1-800/367-5360 (US & Can) or 1-800/442-5845 (HI), ⓕ969-6622, ⓦwww.naniloa.com. Hilo's principal high-rise hotel, built in the 1970s, is now seriously showing its age. The rooms are thin-walled, overpriced, and long overdue for refurbishment; the pool is good, though. Restaurants include the formal *Sandalwood* and the *Ting Hao*, while the *Crown Room* features popular local musicians. Rooms **④**, suites **⑤—⑥**.

Hilo Hawaiian Hotel

71 Banyan Drive ⓣ935-9361, or reserve through Castle Resorts ⓣ1-800/367-5004 (US & Can) or 1-800/272-5275 (HI), ⓕ961-9642, ⓦwww .castle-group.com. Upmarket, luxury hotel in a superb setting; the only Banyan Drive property still

maintaining the highest standards. The long white crescent of the 285-room building directly faces Coconut Island, a few yards out in the bay, but there's no beach. All rooms fall within our price code ❹, though those with the best ocean view cost $30 extra. The excellent *Queen's Court* restaurant is reviewed on p.198. ❹

Hilo Seaside Hotel

126 Banyan Drive
Ⓣ 935-0821 or 1-800/560-5557,
Ⓕ 922-0052,
Ⓦ www.sand-seaside.com.
Simple, not particularly well-priced rooms in low motel-style units near the intersection of Banyan Drive with Kamehameha Ave. Part of a small Hawaiian-owned chain, the hotel has a tiny pool and offers discounts for seniors and on car rental. ❹

Holmes' Sweet Home

107 Koula St
Ⓣ 961-9089, Ⓕ 934-0711,
Ⓦ www.stayhawaii.com/holmes .html.
Two comfortable en-suite B&B rooms in welcoming private home, a mile off the Saddle Rd and three miles up from downtown Hilo, with extensive views across the bay. ❷–❸

Pineapple Park

PO Box 639, Kurtistown, HI 96760 Ⓣ 323-2224 or 1-877/865-2266 (US),
Ⓦ www.pineapple-park.com.
Large, modern budget hostel, about fifteen miles out of town in a pretty remote area south of Hwy-11, halfway between Hilo and Volcano. For the moment it no longer boasts the nighttime views of the erupting volcano that accounted for its location, but so long as you have your own transport it's not a bad option. Bunks in its eighteen-person dorms cost $17 each, and it also offers comfortable en-suite private rooms and a couple of fully equipped two-

---

Unless otherwise stated, all the properties listed here share the zip code HI 96720.

---

bedroom bungalows. Dorms ❶, rooms ❷, bungalows ❹.

Shipman House B&B Inn

131 Kai'ulani St

Ⓣ & Ⓕ 934-8002 or 1-800/627-8447, Ⓦ www.hilo-hawaii.com. Magnificent, turreted Victorian mansion, which once hosted author Jack London and Hawaiian royalty, has been converted by descendants of its original owners into a plush B&B. There are three grand antiques-furnished en-suite rooms in the main house, which has a lovely *lānai*, and two more in a guest cottage. Rates include breakfast and afternoon tea. ❺

Uncle Billy's Hilo Bay Hotel

87 Banyan Drive Ⓣ 961-5818, 1-800/367-5102 (US & Can) or 1-800/442-5841 (HI), Ⓕ 935-7903, Ⓦ www.unclebilly.com. The oldest of the Banyan Drive hotels, run by Uncle Billy and his family. The thatched chandeliers in the lobby set the tone: everything is relentlessly, but enjoyably, Polynesian. Two wings of basic rooms, not particularly well priced considering their fading charms, spread to either side of a tropical garden that's filled at sunset with birdsong. There's a small pool near the ocean, and the restaurant has a free nightly *hula* show (see p.199). Very popular with visitors from the other Hawaiian islands, it also offers car-rental discounts. ❹

Wild Ginger Inn

100 Pu'u'eo St Ⓣ 935-5556 or 1-800/882-1887 (US & Can), Ⓦ www.wildgingerinn.com. Pink-painted, somewhat spruced-up inn, in a quiet residential area just across the Wailuku River from downtown. While second-best to the nearby *Dolphin Bay*, it remains an invaluable resource for budget travelers. About thirty basic-but-adequate en-suite rooms arranged around attractive gardens, plus a few slightly more secluded "deluxe" rooms with TVs. All rates include a simple breakfast buffet. ❷

THE CITY

There is a simple and tragic reason why **downtown Hilo** seems so low-key, with its modest streets and wooden stores: all the buildings that stood on the *makai* side of Kamehameha Avenue were destroyed by the *tsunamis* of 1946 and 1960. Furthermore, the large gap between downtown and Banyan Drive, now occupied by the Wailoa River State Park, is there because the city was literally cut in two by the inundation of 1946. After the waters returned in 1960, all hope was abandoned of rebuilding the "little Tokyo" of Japanese-owned family stores, which lined Kamehameha Avenue all the way to the Wailoa River. Instead, the destroyed area was cleared as a "buffer zone," creating a new administrative complex above the high-water mark.

Little in central Hilo bears witness to its long history, but it's a pleasant place to amble around. That's especially so on Wednesdays and Saturdays, when a colorful **open-air market** takes place on Mamo Street, across the highway from the open ocean. As you wander past stalls selling amazingly low-priced orchids, tropical fruits and coffee fresh from the farm, it's hard to believe you're still in the USA.

The Pacific Tsunami Museum

Map 8, E6. 130 Kamehameha Ave. Mon–Sat 10am–4pm; adults $5, under-18s $2; Ⓣ 935-0926, Ⓦ www.tsunami.org.

Downtown Hilo's latest attraction is the high-tech **Pacific Tsunami Museum**, housed in a former bank at the corner of Kamehameha Avenue and Kalākaua Street. Although its primary emphasis is on the causes and effects of the two lethal *tsunamis* of the last century, and of similar and potential events throughout the Pacific, it also documents the entire history of Hilo. A scale model, complete with a running train, shows how the city looked before the 1946 disaster; contemporary footage and personal letters bring home the full impact of the tragedy. The section devoted to the wave of 1960, which hit just 53 days after the official reopening of Hwy-19, is even more poignant. It was caused by an earthquake off Chile, so locals had several hours' warning that it was on its way. Amazingly enough, many flocked down to the seafront to watch the wave come in; photos show them waiting excitedly for the cataclysm that was about to engulf them.

The Lyman Museum and Mission House

Map 8, D1. 276 Haili St. Mon–Sat 9am–4.30pm; adults $7, children 6–18 $3; ☎935-5021.

The two-part **Lyman Museum**, a few blocks up from the ocean, doubles as both downtown's principal historic site and a good museum of general Big Island history. Its main focus is the original **Mission House** of Calvinist missionaries David and Sarah Lyman, built in 1839. Guided tours of the oldest surviving wooden house on the island start at regular intervals from the museum itself, alongside.

The Lymans had been in Hilo for several years before building the house. Their congregation numbered just twenty until the charismatic Titus Coan arrived in 1835. Aided by a fortuitous *tsunami* in 1837, Coan started a Revival – complete with speaking in tongues – that led to the baptism of thousands of ordinary Hawaiians, but antagonized his superiors. With Christianity firmly established, the Lymans constructed the finest home in the city, fit to welcome Hawaiian royalty and foreign dignitaries alike. It had neither kitchen – for fear of fire – nor bathroom, but stood three stories high, with a towering thatched roof, a roomy *lānai* encircling the first two levels, and a spacious attic. Its original position was in what is now the middle of the street; it was moved slightly and many of its interior walls were taken down shortly before it became a museum in 1932. Most of the furniture inside is made of dark *koa* wood, as are the floors, whose broad planks are up to nineteen inches wide.

For more about the Big Island's first missionaries, see p.77.

The modern museum alongside traces the history of Hawaii from its earliest settlers, with a map of the Pacific to show the routes they followed, as well as a relief model of the Big Island, complete with black lava flows. A thatched hut holds the basic utensils of the ancient Hawaiians, with stone tools and fishhooks, rounded calabashes of *kou* and *koa* wood, and ornaments of dogs' and whales' teeth and even human bone (believed to transmit the spiritual power of the original owner to the wearer).

After a history of the missions comes a fascinating section on Hilo's different ethnic groups. The Japanese are represented by an ornate wooden "wishing chair," the Chinese by a resplendent red and gilt Taoist shrine rescued from a temple destroyed by the *tsunami* of 1960, and the Portuguese by the little four-string *braginha* guitar that was to become the ukulele.

Most of the space upstairs is occupied by the **Earth Heritage Gallery**, focusing on the geology and astronomy of the island. A model of the summit of Mauna Kea shows the various international observatories – computer-literate visitors can tap into their latest discoveries – while a brief account of Polynesian techniques of stellar navigation mentions that the Ahua'umi Heiau on Mauna Kea, now badly damaged, was probably the first observatory to be built up there. A huge sonar map of the entire archipelago shows how alarmingly prone Hawaii is to massive landslides, and pinpoints the fiery submarine volcano of

Lōʻihi thrusting its way to the surface just off the southeast coast of the Big Island. Another collection contains corals, shells – including those of some unique indigenous land snails – a few stuffed birds and fossils, and colorful minerals from around the world, some of which glow in the dark. The small **Shipman Gallery of Chinese Art**, also upstairs, consists mostly of delicately painted but uninspiring porcelain.

Wailuku River and Rainbow Falls

The **Wailuku River**, which defines the western limit of downtown Hilo, is at eighteen miles the longest river in the Hawaiian archipelago. Now safely channeled and crossed by three road bridges, it once had a fearsome reputation; *wailuku* means "destroying water," as it was considered extremely dangerous during periods of high rain.

A large rocky outcrop in the riverbed, visible upstream from the bridge that connects Puʻuʻeo and Keawe streets, is known as **Maui's Canoe**. In legend, it was abandoned by the mighty warrior after he'd raced it back from Haleakalā on his namesake island (with just two paddle strokes). Maui was hurrying to rescue his mother Hina, who lived in a cave further up the river and had become trapped by rising waters engineered by a dragon.

Maui's route is now followed by Waiānuenue ("rainbow seen in the water") Avenue, while the site of Hina's cave, two miles out from downtown, is known as **Rainbow Falls**. Sightseers drive out to admire this broad waterfall from a safe distance; short trails lead to different viewpoints, but don't let you anywhere near the actual water. From the fenced-off viewing area to the right of the parapet wall of the parking lot, you can see the falls square-on as they shoot over a thick shelf of hard rock. In the pool down below, the water has progressively scooped out the hollow that was supposedly home to Maui's mother. Climb a small but often very muddy and slippery staircase off to the left to draw level with the streambed at the top of the falls, with the summit of Mauna Kea looming high in the distance.

Just over a mile on up the road, the **Boiling Pots** are a succession of churning, foaming pools in the river as it drops towards the ocean, with another, smaller, set of falls. A treacherous ungraded path to the right of the viewing area allows you to approach the maelstrom, but you'd be crazy to swim.

Wailoa River State Park

Map 7, E3.

Wailoa River State Park, created in the aftermath of the 1960 *tsunami* in what had been downtown Hilo, is a tranquil – if marshy – landscaped park of lawns, coconut palms and dazzling orange-blossomed *lehua* trees. It's a little hard to find your way in: turn down Pauahi Street, which runs between Kīlauea and Kamehameha avenues, and then take curving Piopio Street halfway along.

Paved footpaths cross the river and clear-watered lagoons on double- or even triple-humped footbridges, with one pair leading to and from a tiny island, and another one connecting with Kamehameha Avenue and the seafront. A moving memorial, dedicated to all victims of Big Island *tsunamis*, consists of two low, black-lava ridges that shield a central tiled design.

Banyan Drive

Map 7, F1.

Green, semi-rural **Banyan Drive**, a mile east of downtown Hilo and not far from the airport, has become the prime hotel district for the city since being spared by the *tsunamis*.

Though the hotels themselves are deteriorating, it's an attractive area, graced by curving rows of the eponymous giant drooping banyan trees. Incredibly, these magnificent specimens are barely seventy years old, having been planted in the 1930s by the celebrities after whom they're named – Franklin Roosevelt, Babe Ruth, and King George V among others.

Hotels on Banyan Drive are reviewed on p.183 onwards.

The best place for a stroll among the trees is **Liliuokalani Gardens**, an ornamental Japanese park built to honor Japanese migrants to Hawaii. A slender footbridge stretches out to **Coconut Island**, now just a green speck on the edge of the bay but once, as Mokuola ("healing island"), the site of a *pu'uhonua* or "place of refuge," like that at Hōnaunau (see p.97). There was also a *luakini*, where human offerings were killed by having a huge stone dropped on their chests while lying bound to a rock. When the temple was dismantled during the 1870s, its stones were used to build a quarantine hospital, but that was in turn destroyed almost immediately by a *tsunami*.

A small covered market area next to the quayside on Lihiwai Street, just off Kamehameha Avenue, is the site (daily except Sun) of the **Suisan Fish Auction**. You have to arrive at around 7am to be sure of seeing anything; a nearby coffee stall will help wake you up. Suisan is a large operation, and fishing vessels from all over the island come here to sell their catch. Most of the trays are packed with glistening tuna, but you can also see red snapper, parrotfish, squid, ripped-up multicolored reef fish speared by scuba divers, and the occasional unfortunate shark. Though it's a hectic and lively spectacle, there's no dramatic shouting: buyers simply inspect the shiny rows of fish and write down their bids.

BANYAN DRIVE

HILO'S GARDENS

Hilo is renowned for its **tropical gardens**, which include commercial orchid farms, public parks, and scientific research facilities. The best combination of a wide range of plants in a scenic setting is the Hawaii Tropical Botanical Garden (see p.176). However, within the city confines there are several alternatives, of which the following are just a selection:

Hilo Arboretum, **Map 7, E6**, Kīlauea Ave and Kawili St; Mon–Fri 8am–3pm; admission free.
Almost twenty acres of woodlands, just over a mile from downtown. This is one of Hilo's most peaceful spots, since it's primarily a research establishment, intended to include specimens of all trees that currently grow anywhere in Hawaii. Trails are virtually nonexistent, but the overgrown lawns present no challenge to walkers.

Hilo Tropical Gardens and Gallery, **Map 7, I1**, 1477 Kalaniana'ole Ave; daily 8.30am–5pm; adults $6, children 13–18 $3, under-12s free; ☎ 935-4957.
Two acres of colorful gardens laid out among tidepools just south of Onekahakaha Beach Park, on the *makai* side of the highway. In addition to an abundance of orchids and heliconia, there's a gift store and free coffee.

Nani Mau Gardens, **Map 9, F2**, 421 Makakila St; daily 8am–5pm; adults $10, children 6–18 $6; ☎ 959-3541, ⓦ www.nanimau.com.
Formal commercial gardens, between the three- and four-mile markers on Hwy-11, which can be explored on foot or, for $5 extra, on a narrated tram tour. There's also a butterfly house, costing another $3. Its main business, however, is as a stop for tour parties; there's a copious $14.50 lunch buffet (10.30am–1.30pm), while Sunday's spread, served in the gardens from 10am to 1pm, is more of a brunch.

Panaewa Rainforest Zoo

Map 9, F2. Mon–Fri 9am–4pm, Sat 11am–2pm; free; ☎959-7224.

The little-known **Panaewa Rainforest Zoo** holds a relatively small menagerie of animals, few of them all that unusual. The main pleasure of stopping here en route to the volcanoes is the chance to roam beneath the zoo's canopy of tropical vegetation. Coming south from Hilo on Hwy-11, turn right just after mile marker 4, along the signed turning a short way beyond Stainback Highway.

On weekdays you may find that you're the rarest species of all, and that the animals will go out of their way to have a closer look at you. Walkways through the dense, steamy undergrowth lead past various enclaves holding a pigmy hippo (with giant-sized teeth), a Shetland pony, an ominously rotund American alligator, iguanas from South America, giant land turtles from the Seychelles, and wide-eyed lemurs and bushy-tailed colobuses from Madagascar. Several impressive peacocks wander the grounds at will, displaying their plumage to all and sundry, while rare Hawaiian owls and hawks are confined in rusty cages. The largest, lushest enclosure holds Bengal tigers, though the vegetation is so thick that you may well not spot any unless you're prepared for a long wait by their watering hole.

Beaches

If you're not bothered by sharks or pollution, you could in theory swim out among the canoes and fishing boats from the **Hilo Bayfront Park**, across the highway from downtown Hilo. It's said that this was one of the finest black-sand beaches in all the islands, and also a great surfing location, until the construction of the breakwater in 1908 and the dredging of the harbor in 1913. Now it's a pleasant place for a picnic, but the only spot nearby where you might be tempted to swim is at Coconut Island, off Banyan Drive (see p.191).

All Hilo's **beach parks** lie southeast of downtown, facing Mauna Kea across the bay and reached by following Kalaniana'ole Avenue beyond Banyan Drive. As few have any sand – they consist of shallow pools in the black lava at the ocean margin, usually backed by small grass clearings ringed with coconut palms – they attract local families rather than tourists, and so are only crowded on weekends.

Kalaniana'ole Avenue is lined with blue signs indicating the "Evacuation Route" in the event of a *tsunami* – unsurprisingly, the idea is to get away from the sea as fast as possible.

Probably the best spot for family groups is **Onekahakaha Beach Park**, a mile and a half down Kalaniana'ole Avenue. Here a solid breakwater of boulders has created a safe, calm lagoon for swimming, while the spacious lawns alongside are good for picnics. The open ocean beyond the breakwater can, however, be extremely dangerous, while fifty yards or so back from the sea the park acquires from time to time a sizeable population of homeless people. That's the main reason why none of Hilo's beach parks currently allows camping.

Leleiwi Beach Park, a couple of miles further along, is a little more exposed, with no sandy beach and some dangerous currents. Away from the open sea, the lagoon is so supremely still and tranquil as to appeal primarily to anglers, who stand in quiet contemplation almost entirely undisturbed by bathers.

Just beyond Leleiwi, and four miles from downtown, Kalaniana'ole Avenue comes to a dead-end at **Richardson Ocean Park**, where a tiny black-sand beach among the coconut groves is very popular with young children. Some venture out to play in the surf as it sweeps into the bay,

THE MERRIE MONARCH FESTIVAL

Since 1963, the city of Hilo has celebrated the week-long **Merrie Monarch** *hula* festival during the third week of April. The festival's centerpiece is a royal parade down the main street in honor of the "Merrie Monarch" himself, Kiṅg David Kalākaua. He was largely responsible for the revival of *hula* following decades of missionary disapproval, when, at the time of his coronation in February 1883, he staged a performance of women dancers and male drummers on the lawns of Honolulu's ʻIolani Palace.

Performers from around thirty different *hula hālua* (schools) – of which eighteen tend to be female, and twelve male, and not all are necessarily from Hawaii – compete for awards in both *kahiko* (ancient) and ʻauana (modern) styles of *hula*. Official events take place in the evenings at the six-thousand-seat **Kanakaʻole Stadium**, named after Auntie Edith Kanakaʻole, one of the Big Island's best-loved twentieth-century *kumu hulas* (*hula* teachers). In addition, informal demonstrations and associated events are held during the daytime in the *Hilo Hawaiian* and *Hawaii Naniloa* hotels.

Full schedules are available from the Merrie Monarch office at the *Hawaii Naniloa Hotel*, 93 Banyan Drive, Hilo, HI 96720 (☏935-9168). Tickets go on sale each year on January 1 but sell out almost immediately.

beyond the snorkelers exploring the rock pools. Behind the sea wall there's a larger "beach" area – more of a sandpit, really – while the adjacent gardens are laid out around some ancient fishponds, with a few explanatory labels.

EATING

Hilo offers an unusually varied assortment of **restaurants**, most of which are aimed more at locals than at visitors, and thus tend to have more at stake in satisfying their customers

than some of the fly-by-night Kona-side joints.
Downtown is at its busiest during the working week,
however, and you may be surprised at how **quiet** things are
on weekends. If you're looking for crowds, you're probably
better off spending the evening along **Banyan Drive**.

As for **fast food**, a wide selection of outlets can be found
at malls such as the Prince Kūhiō Plaza (*KFC*, *Pizza Ala Slice*,
Woolworth and half a dozen others) and the Puainako Town
Center (*McDonald's*, *Pizza Hut*, *Taco Bell*, *Subway*); both *KFC*
and *McDonald's* have downtown restaurants as well.

**Hotels and restaurants listed in this
chapter are keyed on maps 7 and 8.**

Bears Coffee

110 Keawe St ☎ 935-0708.
Hilo's coolest breakfast
hangout, one block from the
ocean downtown. All kinds
of coffees are available, plus
bakery goodies, freshly
squeezed juices and a menu
of specials such as souffléed
eggs on muffin with spinach
for around $3. Lunch consists
of $5 sandwiches, salads, and
some Mexican specialties.
Mon–Sat 7am–5pm, Sun
8am–noon.

Café Pesto

S Hata Building,
130 Kamehameha Ave
☎ 969-6640.
Large, light, and modern,

Pacific-influenced Italian
restaurant, at the southern
end of downtown Hilo. For a
substantial snack, the $8–10
lunchtime sandwiches, such
as the Japanese eggplant
Sandalwood and the shrimp
Miloli'i, are excellent values.
There's a wide selection of
pizzas and calzones, with
tasty and inventive fillings
such as lime-marinated fish,
eggplant, and artichokes. The
dinner menu also features
fresh fish, and a risotto with
lobster, shrimp and scallops
for $25. There's another *Café
Pesto* at Kawaihae Harbor;
see p.131. Sun–Thurs
11am–9pm, Fri & Sat
11am–10pm.

Harrington's

135 Kalaniana'ole Ave
ⓣ 961-4966.
Popular, informal restaurant,
a mile out of downtown,
looking out over Reeds Bay
from a low timber building
makai of Kalaniana'ole Ave.
Lunchtime salads and
sandwiches cost under $10.
Dinner appetizers include
steamed clams and *escargots* at
around $9, and an
inexpensive seafood chowder,
while among the entrees are
steaks and some excellent
seafood dishes for $16–20.
There's live contemporary
Hawaiian music Fridays and
Saturdays. Mon–Fri
11am–2pm & 5.30–9.30pm,
Sat & Sun 5.30–9.30pm.

Honu's Nest

270 Kamehameha Ave
ⓣ 935-9321.
Very central Japanese diner,
with just a handful of tables
set out in front of the service
counter. An ample bowl of
noodle soup costs $6, tempura
chicken or shrimp are $10,
and a substantial portion of
ahi (tuna) sashimi is $10.50.
Mon–Sat 10am–4pm.

Ken's House of Pancakes

1730 Kamehameha Ave
ⓣ 935-8711.
A much-loved Hilo
landmark, near the
intersection of Kamehameha
Ave and Banyan Drive; open
24 hours for snacks,
sandwiches and pancakes
galore.

Nihon Cultural Center

123 Lihiwai St ⓣ 969-1133.
Just off Banyan Drive, this
Japanese restaurant has
exquisite fresh fish and
magnificent views. Lunch
specials cost under $10.
Reservations are required for
dinner, when full meals
starting at $15 are served until
9pm; the sushi bar remains
open later. Mon–Sat
11am–1.30pm & 5–10pm.

Ocean Sushi Deli

239 Keawe St ⓣ 961-6625.
Simple Japanese cafeteria,
serving good and inexpensive
sushi (from $2 for two pieces)
and bento meals to the
downtown crowd. All-you-
can-eat sushi costs $16 at
lunchtime, $20 in the

HILO: EATING

evening. Mon–Sat
10am–12.30pm & 4.30–9pm.

Pescatore

235 Keawe St ☎ 969-9090.
Formal Italian dining in a
pastel-yellow building
opposite the HVB.
Lunchtime pasta specials cost
$7–10, while pricier meat and
pasta entrees, such as the
anchovy-rich *pasta puttanesca*
($16), are served for dinner.
Try the delicious $25 *cioppino
classico*, a stew of lobster,
mussels, scallops, and clams,
with garlic bread. Sun–Thurs
11am–2pm & 5.30–9pm, Fri
& Sat 11am–2pm &
5.30–10pm.

Queen's Court

Hilo Hawaiian Hotel, 71 Banyan
Drive ☎ 935-9361.
With its panoramic views,
this huge dining room makes
a perfect setting for top-
quality buffets. In addition to
breakfast and lunch spreads, it
offers dinner buffets for
$24–27: *paniolo* (barbecue) on
Monday and Thursday, Italian
on Tuesday, Chinese on
Wednesday, seafood on
Friday, and seafood and

Hawaiian *lū'au* dishes on
Saturday and Sunday. Sunday
also sees a very reasonable
$23.50 champagne brunch.
Mon–Sat 6.30–9.30am,
11.15am–1.15pm &
5.30–9pm, Sun 6.30–9am,
10.30am–1.30pm &
5.30–9pm.

Reubens

336 Kamehameha Ave
☎ 961-2552.
Mexican restaurant just south
of *Café Pesto*, serving a
predictable menu of flautas
and chile rellenos beneath a
ceiling festooned with
Mexican flags. Entrees cost
$8–12 at night, more like $5
for lunch. Mon–Fri
11am–9pm, Sat noon–9pm.

The Seaside Restaurant

1790 Kalaniana'ole Ave
☎ 935-8825.
The full name of this lively
family restaurant continues
"and Aqua Farm," which has
to be a good sign. Located
just over two miles out of
town, beyond Onekahaka
Beach, it's almost entirely
surrounded by water, with its
thirty-acre fishponds full of

trout, mullet, and catfish. The dining room decor is pretty minimal, although there are a few outdoor tables. But the fish is great. Unless you want a steak with your mullet, or you opt for the more expensive imported specials, you'd be hard-pressed to spend $20 on a full fish supper. Daily except Tuesday–Fri 5–8.30pm.

Uncle Billy's
Hilo Bay Hotel, 87 Banyan Drive

T 935-0861.
Themed Polynesian restaurant, where most of the menu consists of steak and breaded fish entrees for $11–20; the $20 seafood platter is excellent. Free nightly Hawaiian music and *hula* dancing, often presided over by beaming Uncle Billy himself, and featuring members of his extensive family. Mon–Sat 7–10am & 5.30–9pm, Sun 7–11.30am & 5.30–9pm.

SHOPPING

Although **downtown Hilo** is an enjoyable district to walk around, few of its stores are worth going out of your way for. Those that there are are mainly concentrated along sea-facing Kamehameha Avenue, with assorted outlets selling clothes, T-shirts, souvenirs, and fairly undistinguished "crafts." The best times for a stroll are Wednesday and Saturday mornings, to coincide with the **market** on Mamo Street (see p.186).

Most locals do their shopping at the various **malls**, of which **Prince Kūhiō Plaza** (Mon–Fri 10am–9pm, Sat 9.30am–7pm, Sun 10am–6pm), just south of the airport on Hwy-11, is the most extensive. As well as Sears, Liberty House, J.C. Penney, and Woolworth department stores, it has its own movie theater (T 959-4955), two bookstores, and a music store. The **Waiakea Center**, across the street, holds a large Borders bookstore (T 933-1410). **Banyan Drive** has a very limited selection of convenience stores.

The Saddle Road

From a glance at the map, the **SADDLE ROAD** appears to be the quickest route from one side of the Big Island to the other. What no map can convey, however, is quite how high and remote it is, involving a long slow haul to an altitude of well over 6000 feet in order to cross the "saddle" of land that lies between **Mauna Kea** to the north and **Mauna Loa** to the south. The fifty-mile stretch from Hilo to the point where it rejoins the Belt Road – six miles south of Waimea, and more than thirty northeast of Kailua – is one of the bleakest stretches of road imaginable, utterly unlike anything you'd expect to encounter in the middle of the Pacific Ocean.

Even if the Saddle Road is not much use as a shortcut, it is an enjoyable adventure in its own right. Despite the elevation, it passes a long way below the summits of the two mountains, so you probably won't see the snowcaps, but there's some memorable scenery en route. The trouble is, all the car-rental chains forbid drivers to take their vehicles along the Saddle Road, on pain of forfeiting your insurance cover and all rights to emergency rescue. The only way around this is to rent a **four-wheel-drive** vehicle (see p.22).

The rental-car ban was originally imposed because the road was poorly surfaced and narrowed in several sections to a single lane. These days, the surface is always reasonable, and even at its narrowest cars traveling in opposite directions can pass each other comfortably. Certain dangers remain, however; the road was built to serve the military bases in the high stretches and still sees a lot of uncompromising military traffic, and also the weather is often atrocious, so visibility can be very bad. Above all, there are no facilities of any kind for the entire 85 miles from Hilo to Kailua, so if you do get stuck or break down, rescuing you is a difficult and expensive job. If you choose to risk it, take it slowly, and be sure to allow time to complete your journey in daylight.

Leaving Hilo, along first Waianuenue Avenue and then Kaūmana Drive, the Saddle Road seems to go on climbing forever, straight from the ocean. Beyond the suburbs with their tropical gardens, it heads up into the clouds, winding through a moist and misty heathland of spindly trees, then undulating across bare lava fields, until with any luck it emerges into the sun, on what feels like a wide grassy plain between Mauna Loa and Mauna Kea.

Gradually the road then curves to the north, circling Mauna Kea and bringing Hualālai into view. Various plans have been put forward over the years to cut a more direct course down to Kailua, saving perhaps twenty miles on the total distance; so far the presence of environmentally or archeologically important sites has prevented them from materializing.

MAUNA KEA

For the moment, **MAUNA KEA** is, at 13,796 feet, the highest mountain in the entire Pacific, let alone in Hawaii. Being extinct, however, and therefore already eroding away, it's steadily losing ground to still-active Mauna Loa, 25 miles southwest. Nonetheless its height and isolation make

MAUNA KEA

Mauna Kea one of the very best sites for **astronomical observatories** on earth. Its summit is an otherworldly place, not just because of the surreal ring of high-tech telescopes trained out into the universe, but because it's so devoid of life, its naked hillocks composed of multicolored minerals. A spur road ascends to the summit from the Saddle Road, though its last nine miles are restricted to four-wheel-drive vehicles only, and the observatories are seldom open to casual visitors.

**For an account of how Hawaii's
volcanoes were formed, see p.220.**

The ancient Hawaiians named Mauna Kea the "white mountain," as it is capped by snow for over half the year. That didn't deter them from climbing right to the top, however. Like Mauna Loa, Mauna Kea is a shield volcano, so most of its slope is very gentle, but it differs from its neighbor in having been here during the last Ice Age, making it the only spot in the central Pacific to have been covered by **glaciers**. The ice had the effect of chilling its molten lava to create the best basalt in the islands. Incredibly, there's an ancient **adze quarry** 12,400 feet up the mountain. Dating as far back as 1100 AD, it was probably the major source of the stone used for all the islanders' basic tools.

Ellison Onizuka Visitor Center

Map 1, F4. Mon–Fri 9am–noon & 1–5pm, Sat & Sun 9am–6pm; stargazing sessions daily 6–10pm; ☎ 961-2180, Ⓦ www.ifa.hawaii.edu/info/vis.

The turnoff to the summit of Mauna Kea comes at mile marker 28 on the Saddle Road. At first the road passes through grazing land, covered with wiry grass but devoid of trees. Most of this land is open cattle range – a broad swath of this flank of Mauna Kea, just like the northern side, belongs to the Parker Ranch (see p.137). The road surface is good for the nine miles to the **Ellison Onizuka Visitor Center**, a small facility that houses displays about the observatories and also has its own much more basic telescope, used for the daily after-dark **stargazing** sessions. On the first Saturday of each month, an astronomer gives a talk about some aspect of the observatories' work, while the third Saturday sees a Hawaiian cultural program.

Whether or not you plan to continue on to the summit, the eerie views from here, 9000 feet up, make it worth coming this far. Bizarre reddish cinder cones and other volcanic protrusions float in and out of the mists that swath the grasslands; in the afternoon, the clouds usually obscure Hilo and the coast altogether. In any case, to help prevent **altitude sickness** and related problems, you should remain for at least an hour at this level before going any higher. It's also important to drink as much water as possible – and not to come this high within 24 hours of **scuba diving**.

The road to the summit

Map 1, F4.

The road on from the Visitor Center is kept in reasonably good condition – the astronomers who work at the top have to commute this way – but it's only safe to attempt it in a **four-wheel-drive** vehicle. In anything else, you'd quickly burn out your brakes coming down. The surface is unpaved for the first five miles, largely to deter visitors; for its final four miles, the road is paved once more, in order to avoid churning up dust that might interfere with the telescopes.

Locals from the Hilo side of the island in particular delight in driving to the top of Mauna Kea to fill their pickup trucks with snow. Most tourists, however, are keen to see the inside of the observatories. If that's your goal, the best day to come is either Saturday or Sunday, when staff members at the visitor center co-ordinate **free summit tours**. Participants are required to bring their own 4WD vehicles. If you don't have one, you could try to hitch a ride, but you can't arrange this in advance, and it's a big favor to ask, as you'll be dependent on your new friend for several hours. The tour parties assemble at 1pm to watch a very dated video presentation about the observatories, and then set off in convoy at around 2pm.

Three operators run guided tours to the summit of Mauna Kea; Paradise Safaris ($144; ☏ 322-2366), Hawaiian Eyes ($99; ☏ 937-2530), and the more perfunctory Waipi'o Valley Shuttle ($85; ☏ 775-7121).

Alternatively, if you're feeling energetic, you can also **hike** up. This involves a grueling haul up six miles of exposed road, with an elevation increase of 4000 feet, before you're rewarded with your first glimpse of the summit.

Weather conditions at and near the summit can be absolutely atrocious. Wind speeds of over 170 mph have been measured (at which point the anemometer snapped), twelve feet of snow has fallen in a single night, and visibility is always liable to drop to zero. It's essential to bring very warm, windproof clothing, sunscreen, and sunglasses.

The observatories

Map 1, F4.

When you finally reach the top of Mauna Kea, it's far from obvious which of the many rusty red and gold cinder cones in the vicinity is the actual summit. In fact, out of deference to Hawaiian sensibilities, all the gleaming golf-ball-shaped **observatories** are clustered on slightly lesser eminences; the highest mound of all is topped only by a small Hawaiian shrine.

Mauna Kea was first opened up to astronomical use in the 1960s and now holds a total of thirteen observatories. Each is leased to a different academic institution or consortium, but the site as a whole remains under the general auspices of the University of Hawaii. No further telescopes will be built, though the existing ones can be replaced as they become outdated.

Currently the most technologically advanced facilities are the two identical domes of the **Keck** observatories, which function in tandem, and the giant **Subaru Observatory**, which boasts the largest glass mirror in the world, at 8.3 meters (about 27ft 5in) across. (The observatory is not sponsored by the car company – Subaru is also the Japanese name for the Pleiades, or "Seven Sisters" stars.) When the mirror was installed in 1999, it took three days to drive it up here from the harbor at Kawaihae, at a top speed of two miles per hour. That sort of equipment is capable of detecting warm toast on the moon, but so far they haven't spotted any.

Some of the observatories, such as the Keck pair, are remote-controlled by technicians in Waimea and Hilo, while others do require human operators to be on hand. Working at this altitude brings unique problems; however often you come here, the thin air is liable to render you light-headed, and greatly affects your ability to concentrate. As a result, the weekend guided tours (see opposite) tend to be rather surreal, with guides and visitors alike unable to string coherent thoughts together. Those tours take you into three or four different observatories; if you arrive here alone, the original Keck installation, Keck I, is the only one with a visitor gallery (Mon–Fri 10am–4pm; free).

THE OBSERVATORIES

Don't expect to able to peer through the eyepieces of the telescopes; all information is digitally processed and can only be seen on computer screens. Astronomers from all over the world, including amateur hobbyists, can however submit proposals to use the telescopes for their pet projects. Typical usage fees run at around $1 per second; an academic would expect a single night's viewing to provide the basis for a year's research.

The summit of Mauna Kea

Map 1, F4.

The summit of Mauna Kea, the cinder cone officially known as **Pu'u Wēkiu**, stands off to the right of the observatory access road. It can only be reached via a short, steep hike up the crumbling slope. Alongside the geodesic plate at the top you'll find a simple cairn of rocks, erected as a Hawaiian shrine. The view, of course, is awesome, with assorted natural cones and craters nearby, and the mighty shapes of Mauna Loa and Haleakalā on the horizon.

If there's any snow on the ground, you may well find yourself sharing this magnificent spot with groups of teenagers, rendered imbecilic by the altitude, who come up here to **snowboard** down the rough surrounding slopes.

Mauna Kea holds one last surprise. Reached by a ten-minute hiking trail that leaves the main road at a hairpin bend just below the summit, **Lake Wai'au** is a permanent lake set in a cinder cone 13,020 feet above sea level. Some visitors swim in its icy waters, which are replenished by thawing permafrost. It makes more sense to wander over to the brass plaque by the shore, which marks where the ashes of Ikua Purdy, the 1908 World Rodeo champion, were scattered. He and his fellow Parker Ranch cowboys (see p.138) would come all the way up here when roping wild horses.

Mauna Kea State Park

Map 1, F4.

Once past the summit approach road, the Saddle Road starts to head slightly north, and views begin to open up of the whole Kona coast. Very near mile marker 35, a short, but very tiring two-mile hike in **MAUNA KEA STATE PARK** brings you to superb views of the island's three largest volcanoes.

From the parking lot, head past the wooden cabins – available for rent through the state parks office in Hilo ($45 per night; ☎974-6200) – and follow a jeep track towards Mauna Kea. Having made your way as far as three pale-blue water towers, continue along the track until just before you reach an older and rustier tower. So far the trail has all been flat, but now a footpath leads straight up a small-looking mound to the right. The next few hundred yards are chest-thumpingly steep. Climbing across a loose surface of powdery brown dust, you pass a wide range of brittle high-altitude plants, including desiccated shrubs and a few native silverswords. Though far below the top of Mauna Kea, the crest of the mound makes a perfect vantage point for views of the entire slope of Mauna Loa across the saddle, Hualālai away to the east, and the sprawling army camp below.

MAUNA KEA STATE PARK

Puna

With the compelling attractions of Hawaii
Volcanoes National Park just further on, few
tourists bother to leave the highway as they pass
through the district of **PUNA**, which takes up the south-
eastern corner of the Big Island. The county government
too seems to see it as a land apart, a quirky enclave that
doesn't quite fit in with the rest of the island. In the 1960s
and 1970s, large portions of the region were rezoned for
residential development, but it still lacks the infrastructure
that you – and the twenty-five thousand people who live
here – would expect. The volcanoes haven't helped matters
either, incinerating newly built homes and cutting the
coastal road to leave poor, traffic-ridden **Keaʻau** as the only
point of access to the whole region.

Although the eleven-mile stretch of oceanfront highway
that has so far survived the volcanoes makes an attractive
drive, there's no great reason to spend more than a couple of
hours in Puna. Stop for lunch in the self-consciously outlaw
town of **Pāhoa**, dominated by latter-day hippies and back-
to-the-landers, but don't expect to swim from any of Puna's
photogenic but dangerous beaches. If you're on your way to
the National Park, save your volcano-watching for there;
lava trails from Kīlauea are visible throughout Puna, but
nowhere are they as dramatic or accessible as in the park.

Puna has long had the reputation of being the Big Island's main center for the illegal growing of *pakololo* ("crazy weed"), also known as **marijuana**. Recent police crackdowns have put an end to most large-scale cultivation, but if you ever get the feeling of being made unwelcome as you explore the backwoods areas, the chances are that you're close to some clandestine activity.

KEA'AU

Map 9, F2.

The town of **KEA'AU** lies just south of Hwy-11 as it climbs towards the volcanoes, little more than three miles beyond the city limits of Hilo. As a dormitory community for Hilo's labor force, and the gateway to the rest of Puna, it's choked morning and evening by huge traffic jams.

Kea'au consists of little more than the large parking lot for the **Kea'au Shopping Center**. This low-key wooden shopping mall holds the Sure-Save supermarket and its funkier rival, Kea'au Natural Foods, as well as a laundry, a raucous sports bar and a couple of small Asian fast-food diners.

PĀHOA

Map 9, G4.

With its false-front stores and rudimentary timber boardwalks, tiny **PĀHOA**, a dozen miles southwest of Kea'au, is a distinctive blend of Wild West cowboy town and Shangri-la. Life here moves so slowly that it hasn't quite kept up with the rest of America; the streets seem to be filled with refugees from the 1960s – even if most of them were born a decade or two later. Just as incongruous are the occasional groups of *aloha*-shirted tourists, who regard the locals with much the same bemusement as did the coach parties that flocked to San Francisco to see the world's first hippies.

THE PUNA GEOTHERMAL VENTURE

If you were responsible for trying to reduce the cost of generating electricity in Hawaii, you might well find it frustrating to be confronted every day by the apparently limitless power of the volcanoes. But when the **Puna Geothermal Venture** (PGV) set out during the early 1980s to harness that power, many people in Puna were more distressed than pleased.

Based just outside Pāhoa at Pohoiki, the operation consists of a power plant that stands above three 3000-feet-deep wells. Superheated water is pumped to the surface and used to turn electrical turbines, and then fluids and steam alike are returned back underground. While its promoters see volcanic steam as a clean, renewable source of energy, protesters, who include Greenpeace and assorted rock stars, depict it as a dangerous desecration. Native Hawaiian campaigners argue that the very concept of geothermal development is offensive to Pele.

Lengthy legal challenges from local residents, who blamed the plant for symptoms such as nausea, migraine, sore throats, chronic colds, and severe fatigue, have resulted in tight restrictions on its emissions. The project as a whole however is now officially seen as a success. The PGV currently produces 25 percent of all the electrical energy used on the Big Island, and was granted permission by the Environmental Protection Agency in the summer of 2000 to double its capacity to sixty megawatts.

The only building of any size in Pāhoa is the venerable **Akebono Theater**, founded in 1917, where the parking lot is the scene of a lively Sunday-morning flea market. Fifty yards away on the boardwalk, the Hawaiian Hemp Co serves as headquarters for a campaign to legalize marijuana, and sells hemp (*cannabis sativa*) products of all kinds, including textiles from China and paintings.

PĀHOA

Practicalities

Although Pāhoa no longer offers any **accommodation** for visitors, it holds several reasonable **restaurants**, plus an ever-changing cast of coffeehouse hangouts filled with barefoot, tie-dyed locals. At the bottom end of the village, beyond the boardwalk and boasting a spacious wooden *lānai*, the *Godmother* (daily 7.30am–9pm; ☎965-0055) is the most upmarket option. It specializes in Italian cuisine, with pasta entrees costing around $8 at lunchtime and up to $16 at dinner. More adventurous alternatives include *Sawasdee*, a small Thai diner on the boardwalk (daily except Wed noon–8.30pm; ☎965-8186). It features the same delicious menu at both lunch and dinner, with *tom yum* soup ($7–11) in vegetarian or seafood versions, and red, green, and yellow curries for around $9.

Lava Tree State Monument

Map 9, H4. Daily dawn–dusk; free.

Set back in the rainforest just off Hwy-132, almost three miles out of Pāhoa, **LAVA TREE STATE MONUMENT** preserves the petrified record of a double catastrophe that took place two centuries ago. First there was a fast-flowing lava stream that destroyed the underbrush and lapped against the *'ō'hia* trees of the forest, clinging to their trunks and cooling as it met resistance. Then came an earthquake, which opened fissures in the ground into which the liquid rock quickly drained. They left the landscape scattered with upright columns of lava, hollow inside where the trees themselves had burned away.

It takes around half an hour to walk the level, paved trail that now loops around the finest specimens. With the exception of the mosquitoes, this is a tame and relatively clear section of the rainforest. Until recently, it echoed with the song of multicolored birds, but a recent infestation of Caribbean frogs has meant they now have to compete with incessant guttural croaking. The lava trees themselves look like black termite mounds, or gnarled old candle drippings. While this landscape is undoubtedly unusual and striking, if your time is limited it's best to push on to the main attractions of the national park.

THE PUNA COAST

Hwy-130 continues for just under ten miles from Pāhoa before its luck finally runs out a few hundred yards up from the sea. Halfway down, the "scenic point" to the left of the road at mile marker 15 marks the start of a short trail to a cluster of natural **steam vents**. Locals climb into these small cones to use them as steam baths, but you'd be crazy to follow suit; see p.226 for a salutary warning.

A thick layer of shiny black lava, unceremoniously dumped by Kīlauea in 1988, brings the highway to a halt close to mile marker 21. Some trees are still visible beyond, and new plant growth is starting to appear, but barely a trace survives of the extensive Royal Gardens residential area that once stood here.

Almost all the village of **Kalapana**, down below, has also been destroyed, though the timber-framed **Star of the Sea** church was hauled a few miles up the slopes to safety and now serves as a makeshift community center. Fortunately, however, it's still possible to join up with the coast road, Hwy-137, at this point, allowing you to complete an enjoyable loop drive back to Pāhoa that takes you about as far off the usual tourist track as you can hope to get on the Big Island.

Kaimū

Map 9, G6.

The spot where Hwy-130 reaches the ocean stands slightly

to the east of the former site of **Kaimū** black-sand beach. Until it was obliterated by lava flows in 1990, the beach was one of the most photographed spots on the island. Only the adjacent restaurant, now closed, was spared by the lava, but some of the coconut palms from the beach were rescued and airlifted to the *Hilton Waikoloa* hotel in Kohala (see p.115).

It is in theory possible to walk out across the lava field from beside the abandoned restaurant. At those times when the active flow from Kīlauea is entering the ocean, the plume of steam where it hits the water is often just as visible from this end as it is from the bottom of Chain of Craters Road (see p.242). However, only owners of the few Royal Gardens homes that still survive – now without road access – are allowed to set out into the wilderness. Unless you know exactly where you're going, which in this ever-changing topography is all but impossible, you could easily get yourself into very serious danger.

Kehena Beach

Map 9, G6.

Driving east from Kaimū along Hwy-137 takes you through a landscape that varies from one minute to the next, depending on the age of the lava flow you're crossing. In places the undergrowth thins out to bare black rock, but most of the route is dripping with tropical vegetation. From time to time you get glimpses of the ocean and successive palm-bedecked headlands, but only rarely is it possible to get down to the seashore.

The best spot to do so is **Kehena Beach**, close to the 19-mile marker, where a cluster of parked cars usually betrays the presence of a small path down the cliffs. At the bottom you'll find an absolutely stupendous little **black-sand beach**, backed by coconut palms that are home to a colony of wild parrots, and forever battered by spectacular crashing surf. Boogie-boarding and body-surfing can only be recommended if you know exactly what you're doing – locals do both naked – but from the jet-black shoreline it's often possible to watch dolphins at play in the water.

For more about black-sand beaches, see Punalu'u, p.256.

'Opihikao

Map 9, H5.

Just a mile beyond Kehena, as the road approaches the tiny community of **'OPIHIKAO**, it burrows its way beneath a dense canopy of trees outside the *Kalani Honua Culture Center and Retreat* (PO Box 4500, Pāhoa, HI 96778; ☎965-7828 or 1-800/800-6886, ⓦwww.kalani.com; ❷–❻). Part New Age teaching center, with courses in yoga, hula, massage therapy, and the like, and part B&B, the *Kalani Honua* offers an idyllic situation for long-stay visitors. It holds three lodges, ten cottages, and three tree houses, and offers guest-rooms with and without en-suite facilities, plus camping at $30 per site or $20 per person. There's also a small evening-only café.

Mackenzie State Recreation Area

Map 9, H5.

Another three miles on, **Mackenzie State Recreation Area** is a large, level picnic ground in a grove of ironwood on the oceanfront cliffs, where the earth underfoot is crisp with shed needles. Access to the seashore here is all but impossible: high surf scoops inexorably at the shallow cliff faces, hollowing them out to the extent that even walking to the edge is foolhardy. This tranquil forest glade is popular with locals, though tourists may feel it's not quite "Hawaiian" enough to be worth a stop.

Isaac Hale Beach Park

Map 9, I4.

Another two miles beyond the Mackenzie State Recreation Area, a short way oceanwards from the point where Hwy-137 meets a minor road from Pāhoa, **Isaac Hale Beach Park** finally enables you to get back down to the sea. Set in **Pohoiki Bay**, with a small beach of black and white pebbles, overhanging green vegetation and high surf, the park is popular with surfers, anglers, and picnickers, though it's not a place for family bathing or for anyone inexperienced in the ways of the rough Hawaiian seas. A small boat ramp, protected by an army-built breakwater, is used by local vessels; surfers occasionally hitch rides out into the breakers.

Not far from Pohoiki Bay, the *Pamalu Hawaiian Country House* (PO Box 4023, Pāhoa, HI 96778; ☎965-0830, ⓕ965-6198; three-night minimum stay; ❹–❺) is a gay-friendly **B&B**. The five-acre property offers four en-suite guest rooms and has its own swimming pool.

Ahalanui Beach Park

Map 9, I4. Daily 7am–7pm; free.

A mile further on from Isaac Hale Park, **Ahalanui Beach Park** is a much safer proposition for families. On paper, it can sound virtually irresistible – it's a sheltered oceanfront lagoon, filled with water that's naturally heated by volcanic action to 90°F, and surrounded by coconut palms. In reality, it feels more like an open-air swimming pool, having been shaped into a neat rectangle and surrounded by walls of cemented black lava boulders, complete with several small staircases into the water and attendant lifeguards. At weekends, it gets very crowded with local families.

At present, the park remains unmarked on most island maps, which label this spot **Pū'āla'a**. It's likely to become much better known in the near future, however, as Japanese developers have announced plans to build a 500-acre resort alongside, including a golf course, two small hotels, and an enclave of upmarket homes.

Cape Kumukahi

Map 9, 14.

As a paved road, Hwy-137 comes to an end four miles on from Pohoiki Bay, where it meets Hwy-132 from Pāhoa. To reach this spot, you pass over the site of **Kapoho**, yet another town swallowed up by the lava, this time in January 1960. A dirt road east from the intersection leads in just over a mile to the rudimentary **lighthouse** at **Cape Kumukahi**, which is closed to visitors. Much of the land in this area is entirely new, though at the edge of the vegetated zone you may spot an old Japanese cemetery and a *heiau* platform.

Hawaii Volcanoes National Park

Nothing you've ever seen could prepare you for the south coast of the Big Island, where the world's most active volcanoes are still at work building the youngest and largest member of the Hawaiian chain. In this extraordinary, exhilarating landscape, the earth itself ebbs and flows, prey to the changing moods of **Mauna Loa** and **Kīlauea**. Houses, roads, beaches, and even towns are liable to stop existing at any moment, and as rivers of molten rock steam their way into the ocean, they create a new coastline by the day.

Tourists have been marveling at this spectacle since the early nineteenth century. Mauna Loa and Kīlauea now constitute perhaps America's most dramatic national park – **HAWAII VOLCANOES NATIONAL PARK**. Apart from the two volcanic calderas, it ranges from arctic tundra and sulphurous desert to lowland rainforest and remote Pacific beaches.

The raw power of an active volcano is not something that can be tamed and labeled to suit those who like their scenery to stay still and their sightseeing to run to schedule.

Hawaii Volcanoes National Park may well be the most dynamic, unpredictable place you'll ever visit, and it's one where normal rules just don't seem to apply. What you see, and how long it takes to see it, is beyond all human control. Kīlauea, at the heart of the park, is often called the "drive-in volcano"; it's said to be the only volcano in the world where news of a fresh eruption brings people flocking *towards* the lava flows. Only very rarely does the lava claim lives, but much of the excitement of coming here stems from the ever-present whiff of danger.

The park is open 24 hours daily, 365 days a year; $10 per vehicle, $5 for cyclists, motorcyclists, and hikers (valid for seven consecutive days). An annual Hawaii Volcanoes Pass costs $20, and systemwide national parks passes are both sold and valid; eruption information ⓣ 985-6000; visitor center ⓣ 967-7311, ⓦ www.nps.gov/havo.

The park entrance is roughly a hundred miles southeast of Kailua, thirty miles southwest of Hilo, and ten miles (as the crow flies) from the ocean. Driving from the west of the island takes at least two hours, with the last thirty miles or so spent ascending through barren lava landscape similar to that in the Kona airport region. The road from Hilo, on the other hand, climbs more steeply through thick, wet rainforest.

Unexpectedly, you arrive at the park headquarters, beside the **caldera** (summit crater) of Kīlauea, with no real sense of being on top of a mountain. That's because Kīlauea, at only four thousand feet high, is a mere pimple on the flanks of **Mauna Loa**, which, despite its deceptively gentle incline, stands almost ten thousand feet taller. Furthermore, for all its trails and overlooks, the crater area is far from the park's most compelling attraction. Somewhere down the side of the mountain, molten lava is bursting out of the ground and cascading down towards the sea – assuming that the

HIKES IN THE PARK

eruption that has been going nonstop ever since 1983 has not died down by the time you visit.

In total, the irregular boundaries of the National Park take in 377 square miles. At the beginning of the twentieth century, it only occupied the Kīlauea Caldera area. Now it incorporates the summit craters and most of the eruption-prone rift zones of both volcanoes, an area that is largely desert but includes scattered pockets of rainforest and even one or two beaches. Although the most recent flows have been beyond the official boundaries of the park, its rangers still control public access to the danger spots. From being a solely geological park, its brief has expanded to cover responsibility for preserving the vestiges of pre-contact occupation in the region and protecting indigenous wildlife such as the Hawaiian goose, the *nēnē*.

Ever since the early missionaries, with their images of the fires of hell, Western visitors have tended to see the volca-noes as purely destructive. The ancient Hawaiians, whose islands would never have existed without the volcanoes, were much more aware of their generative role, embodied in the goddess **Pele**. It may take longer to create than it does to destroy, but fresh lava is rich in nutrients, and life soon regenerates on the new land. On a single visit to the park, it's impossible to appreciate the sheer rapidity of change. What is a crackling, flaming, unstoppable river of molten lava one day may well be a busy hiking trail the next. Come back twenty years later, and you could find a rich, living forest.

THE SHIELD VOLCANOES OF HAWAII

According to the classic popular image, a volcano is a cone-shaped mountain, with a neat round crater at the top that's filled with bubbling lava and spouts columns of liquid fire.

Hawaiian volcanoes aren't like that. Although you may be lured to the park by photos of pillars of incandescent lava, you're unlikely to see any such thing. These are **shield volcanoes**, which grow slowly and steadily rather than violently, adding layer upon layer as lava seeps out of fissures and vents all along the "**rift zones**" that cover their sides. The result is a long, low profile, supposedly resembling a warrior's shield laid on the ground.

Mauna Loa and Kīlauea are simply the latest in the series of volcanoes responsible for creating the entire Hawaiian chain. Like all the rest, they are fueled by a "**hot spot**" in the earth's crust, way below the sea floor, which has been channeling magma upwards for seventy million years. As the continental plates drift northwest, at around three inches per year, that magma has found its way to the surface in one volcano after another. Each island in turn has clawed its way up from the depths, emerged above the waves, and then ceased to grow as its volcanoes became ever farther removed from the life-giving source. In time, erosion by rain and sea wears away the rock, sculpting the fabulous formations seen at their most dramatic on Kauai, and eventually the ocean washes over it once more, perhaps leaving a ring of coral – an **atoll** – to bear witness. Though Kauai is the oldest Hawaiian island of any size, the oldest of all are by now 3500 miles away, mere specks in the Emperor chain, off the coast of Japan.

Look at the gentle slope of **Mauna Loa**, project that gradient down through almost 20,000 feet of ocean, and you'll see why its Hawaiian name, "long mountain," is so appropriate. It's the most massive single object on earth; its summit is, at 13,677 feet, very slightly lower than Mauna Kea (13,796 feet), but its volume of 10,000 cubic miles makes it a hundred times larger than Washington's Mount Rainier. It took two million years for Mauna Loa to swell from the bed of the Pacific into the air, and for another million years it has continued to climb. In the last 150 years, the world's highest active volcano has erupted every three or four years – in a single hour in 1984, it let forth enough lava to pave a highway from Honolulu to New York. Geologists predict that every spot on its surface will receive at least one more coating of fresh lava before the fires die down.

- -
For an explanation of the difference between
'a'ā and *pāhoehoe* lava, see p.227.
- -

Only about once a century does Mauna Loa erupt simultaneously with **Kīlauea**, however. Of late the younger upstart – its name meaning "much spewing" – has been grabbing the attention, having been in a record-breaking continuous state of eruption since 1983. Although fed by a separate conduit from the fires below, Kīlauea emerged as a lump on the side of Mauna Loa, so you can hardly tell it's a separate mountain. Its lava tends to flow consistently in the same direction, down towards the ocean. Since 1983, it has added well over 500 acres of new land to a nine-mile stretch of the Puna coastline.

Meanwhile the next volcano is on its way. Scientists are monitoring the submarine "seamount" of **Lōʻihi**, 20 miles southeast of the Kaʻū coast. Were you to stay around for

THE SHIELD VOLCANOES OF HAWAII

three thousand years, you might see it poke its head out for the first time. One day it may seem no more than a blemish on the vast bulk of Mauna Loa – or it may be destined to overrun its older sisters altogether.

PLANNING A VISIT

Broadly speaking, visiting Hawaii Volcanoes National Park involves some combination of three principal elements. First of all, there's the eleven-mile loop tour around Kīlauea Caldera from the visitor center, on **Crater Rim Drive**; second, you may choose to **hike** into or near the caldera, from one or more points along the way; and finally comes the fifty-mile round-trip down the **Chain of Craters Road** to the ocean, ending at the site of the current eruption. If you have the time, two further areas are open to exploration. Getting right to the **summit of Mauna Loa** involves a four-day hike, but it's possible to drive the first 3000 feet of the route to gain a different perspective on the region. Away to the west, the **Ka'ū desert** offers more trails into a harshly beautiful moonscape.

Few people allow enough time to see the park properly. In a single day you'd be hard-pressed to drive the two main roads, let alone hike any trails. Worse still, you'll probably miss the most spectacular experience of all – watching the eruption after dark.

Much the best option is to **spend the night** nearby, either in the park itself, at the *Volcano House* hotel (see p.225), at the campgrounds (p.227 and p.239), or in a B&B in the village of Volcano (p.249). Failing that, at least base yourself in Hilo, thirty miles away, rather than the distant Kona or Kohala coasts.

Although the best way to explore the park is in your own vehicle, you can at least get there by **public bus** from Hilo. On Monday through Friday only, the Hele On Bus

Company (☎935-8241) runs a service that leaves Hilo's Mooheau Bus Terminal at 2.40pm and calls at both Volcano village and the park visitor center around an hour later. The return ride is in the morning, leaving the visitor center at 8.10am. Buses continue beyond the park as far as Ocean View (see p.262), but not all the way to Kailua. Alternatively, you could opt for an organized **bus tour** (some are listed such as the *Roberts* tour mentioned on p.26), but generally these are not a good idea. They'll show you Kīlauea Caldera from above, but are unlikely to give you the flexibility to approach the eruption.

For details of helicopter tours of the park, see p.26.

Inevitably, what you do will depend on conditions on the day you arrive. The active lava flow might be right there at the end of the road, it might be an hour's hike away, it might be somewhere else entirely or it might have stopped altogether. If it *is* flowing, then seeing it should be your top priority. Why linger over photos in a museum when you can see the real thing?

CRATER RIM DRIVE AND THE PARK HEADQUARTERS

The **park entrance** is just off Hwy-11, the Belt Road, about a mile west of the village of **Volcano** (see p.249). If you're coming from the Kona side you can visit the park without ever passing through Volcano, but since it holds the only gas stations for miles you may well have to anyway. Within a few yards of the main gate, before you get a sight of the volcano, you'll come to the **Visitor Center**, on the right. From this point, **Crater Rim Drive** takes eleven miles to loop around the summit crater ("caldera") of Kīlauea – for safety reasons, not always in sight of the edge.

The major hiking trails in the caldera area are
described in a separate section, starting on p.231.

Looking from a distance like a large oval of predominantly gray lava, roughly three miles long by two miles wide, **Kīlauea Caldera** is ringed on two sides by a steep *pali*, around 400 feet high. On those sides, and in places down below the wall as well, patches of rainforest have escaped the fires; off to the south and east, however, the cliff dwindles to almost nothing, and strong-smelling sulphur drifts across the plains to ensure that nothing living can find a foothold. It's possible to walk right to the edge of the main center of activity within the caldera, **Halemaʻumaʻu Crater**, either from a parking lot on Crater Rim Drive or all the way across from *Volcano House*, on a trail that passes over the site of the last eruption up here, in 1982.

Kīlauea Visitor Center

Map 11, F2. Daily 7.45am–5pm; ☏ 967-7311,
ⓦ www.nps.gov/havo.

Though **KĪLAUEA VISITOR CENTER** does not overlook the crater of Kīlauea, it's worth calling in as soon as you arrive to pick up the latest information on the eruption and advice on hiking trails (if you plan to camp in the backcountry, you must register here). The center has a bookstore and a small museum and provides lots of excellent free literature. Every hour on the hour, from 9am to 4pm, it also shows a ten-minute video that's packed with eruption footage. Frequent lectures explain aspects of local geology, botany and environmental issues; at 7pm on most Tuesdays, the center reopens for a series of talks called "After Dark in the Park." Rangers also lead a changing daily program of free **guided hikes**.

Just beyond the visitor center, set a little way back from the road, the **Volcano Art Center** (daily 9am–5pm; ⊕967-7565), is a nonprofit gallery and crafts store that sells the work of local artists. Prices are slightly higher than elsewhere, but the standard of the artwork on offer tends to be *much* higher.

Volcano House

Map 11, F2.
Pride of place on the lip of Kīlauea Caldera belongs to the **Volcano House** hotel, which has in various incarnations stood near this spot since 1846. When Mark Twain was a guest, in 1866, it was a four-roomed thatched cottage; now it consists of two separate motel-style buildings, the main one of which stretches for over a hundred yards just a few feet back from the abyss. The Crater Rim Trail squeezes its way along the edge, commanding views over the *pali*, beyond the rainforest below and across the caldera. Halema'uma'u Crater should be visible, three miles out, but clouds and/or sulphurous mist usually obscure Mauna Loa on the far side.

During the day, *Volcano House* fills with day-trippers, attracted in part by the hurried and, frankly, dismal $12.50 lunch buffet (daily 11am–2pm). An equally unexciting breakfast buffet is served in the morning (7–10.30am; $9.50). But at night, *Volcano House* reverts to something like its old self, and the dining room serves decent pasta and meat entrees ($14–22) in formal surroundings.

Volcano House
PO Box 53, Hawaii Volcanoes National Park, HI 96718
⊕967-7321, ⑤967-8429.
The guestrooms in the *Volcano House* are simple and slightly faded, and not all of those in the main building face the volcano; the twelve that don't are significantly

cheaper, while ten more in the separate *Ohia Wing* are cheaper still. The same management is also responsible for renting the cabins in the *Nāmakani Paio* campground (see opposite). ❸–❺

Sulphur Banks and Steam Vents

Map 11, E2.

The first two stops on the Crater Rim Drive, on opposite sides of the road a few hundred yards and a mile respectively beyond the visitor center, are natural phenomena with the self-explanatory names of **Sulphur Banks** and **Steam Vents**. Both these unspectacular spots are characterized by white fumes that emerge from cracks in the ground to drift across open meadows; the difference is that the Sulphur Banks stink to high heaven, while the vapor from the Steam Vents is, once it condenses, in theory pure enough to drink. Unbelievably, two people have died in recent years after getting stuck when they've climbed into similar steam vents nearby in the hope of experiencing a "natural sauna"; instead, they've been poached alive.

Jaggar Museum

Map 11, C3. Daily 8.30am–5pm; ☏967-7643, ⓦwww.hvo.wr.usgs.gov.

A little less than three miles from the visitor center, and sited here for the good reason that it has the clearest, highest view of the caldera, is the fascinating **THOMAS A. JAGGAR MUSEUM**. Its primary aim is to explain the work of the adjacent **Hawaiian Volcano Observatory**, which is not open to the public. The staff can provide detailed updates on the current state of the eruption, while constantly wobbling seismographs linked to various spots in the park display every little tremor as it happens. You can also watch videos of previous activity, and there are panel displays illustrating Hawaiian mythology and historical observations by travelers.

This is the place to get the distinction clear between the kinds of lava known as 'a'ā and pāhoehoe (used by geologists throughout the world, these are among the very few Hawaiian words to have been adopted into other languages). Chemically the two forms are exactly the same, but they differ due to the temperature at which they are ejected from the volcano. Hotter, runnier pāhoehoe is wrinkled and ropy, like the sludgy skin of custard pushed with your finger, but with a sandpaper finish; cooler 'a'ā does not flow so much as spatter, creating a sharp, jagged clinker. Other volcanic by-products on display in the museum include what's known as **Pele's hair** – very fine filaments made of glass that really do look like hair – and the shiny droplets called **Pele's tears**.

Outside, a viewing area looks down into Kīlauea, and Halema'uma'u Crater in particular, which is 360 feet deep at this point. By now you're on the fringes of the Ka'ū Desert, so there are no trees to block the view. The trade winds have for millennia blown the noxious emissions from the crater southwest, so despite receiving large quantities of rainfall the land supports no growth.

Nāmakani Paio

Map 11, A3.

A ten-minute walk from the Jaggar Museum parking lot, away from the caldera, brings you to the only **campground** in the main area of the park, **NĀMAKANI PAIO**. It's actually just across the Belt Road, so if you're driving to it you don't enter the park proper. The pleasant wooded sites are **free** and available on a first-come, first-served basis for maximum stays of seven nights (in any one year).

CONTROLLING THE FLOW

When ancient Hawaiians found their homes threatened by approaching lava, they attempted to propitiate Pele with offerings (see box, p.234), but if they had to move away they were not greatly inconvenienced. Unlike their modern counterparts, they did not own the land on which they lived, and could simply rebuild elsewhere. They could also load their possessions into canoes and paddle out of harm's way.

A full-scale emergency in Puna today would be very different, with hundreds of vehicles attempting to flee along the one road out. What's more, anyone unfortunate enough to lose their home may face economic ruin.

That sort of scenario loomed in the mind of Thomas Jaggar, when he founded the **Hawaiian Volcano Observatory** in 1911. Its Latin motto means "no more swallowed up or buried cities," and one of its main goals was to understand the behavior of the volcanoes enough to control them.

In both 1935 and 1942, when Hilo appeared to be under threat from eruptions of Mauna Loa, attempts were made to **bomb** the lava flow. Angled walls have also been constructed at strategic points on the slopes, in the hope of channeling the stream away from specific targets. A military installation high on Mauna Loa seems to have been spared as a result, though a similar scheme in the Kapoho district (see p.216) could not prevent the town's destruction.

These days the emphasis is much more on prediction than containment; the emergency services are briefed to stop fires but not to try to divert the flow. Only partly is that out of respect for Pele – more important is the fear of **litigation**. Directing lava away from one site might have the effect of "aiming" it at another; aggrieved homeowners who lost their property could then blame – and sue – the authorities responsible.

Basic **cabins**, sharing use of the campground's restrooms and showers, can be rented for $40 per night through *Volcano House* (see p.225; ☎967-7321; ❷). Each holds one double bed and two bunk beds, and has a picnic table and barbecue area. Bed linen is provided, but there's no heating, so bring a sleeping bag or extra blanket as it can be very cold at night.

Halema'uma'u Crater

Kīlauea may be extremely active, but currently it's unusual for eruptions to take place up here at the summit. Since 1980, it's happened only twice, both times for less than a day. Such eruptions can create smaller craters within the caldera; the most conspicuous of these, **HALEMA'UMA'U CRATER**, is just over a mile from the museum.

Although you can see the crater from the roadside parking lot, you'll get a better idea of it by walking a couple of hundred yards across the caldera floor. The trail is clearly marked, and there's a handrail, but with gusts of white mist spouting from crevices in the rock you feel as if you're taking your life in your hands.

As you look from the rim into a steaming abyss heavy with the stench of white and yellow sulphur, it's easy to see where sections of the wall have collapsed, and the yawning cracks where they will do so in future. In the 1830s, Halema'uma'u was described as a dome rising out of the lava field; when Mark Twain saw it in 1866 it was a "heaving sea of molten fire," with walls a thousand feet high. Since a huge explosion in 1924, however, it's been shallower and quieter, and it's now a circular depression that drops about 400 feet below the rest of the caldera. If this walk whets your appetite, you might be tempted to brave the entire three-mile length of the **Halema'uma'u Trail**, right across the caldera from *Volcano House* (see p.225).

Keanakāko'i and Pu'u Pua'i

Map 11, E6.

From time to time, the route of the Crater Rim Drive has had to be redrawn, as fresh lava paves over the road and a new layer of tarmac is in turn laid down on top of the lava. The stretch immediately to the east of Halema'uma'u was cut in two in 1982 and now passes in between the sites of two recent eruptions.

Until it was filled almost to the brim by new outpourings, **KEANAKĀKO'I CRATER**, south of the road, was the site of an ancient adze quarry, a source of the hard stone used by Hawaiians to make tools and weapons. **PU'U PUA'I**, farther along, is a bare rust-colored cinder cone thrown up in 1959 and accessible along the Devastation Trail (see p.237).

Thurston Lava Tube

Map 11, I4.

Once past the Chain of Craters turnoff (see p.238), Crater Rim Drive plunges back into dense rainforest. This much less intimidating landscape is the location of the only short walk attempted by most tour groups, into the **THURSTON LAVA TUBE**.

As soon as you cross the road from the parking lot, a mile or so short of the visitor center, you're faced by a large natural basin bursting with huge 'ōhi'a trees. Beneath it is the tube itself, which was created when the surface of a lava stream hardened on exposure, enabling the lava below to keep flowing 28 miles to the sea with only a slight loss of temperature. When the lava eventually drained away, it left behind a damp, empty tunnel, an artificially lit portion of which is now open to the public. If you've ever descended into a subway system, the basic concept and appearance will be familiar.

It takes less than ten minutes to walk to and through the tube, which is remarkable only for the smoothness of its walls and its conveniently flat natural floor. Occasionally roots from the gigantic ferns that grow up above have worked their way through cracks in the rock to dangle from the ceiling. Back outside, the native red-billed *'i'iwi* bird can always be heard, if not seen.

HIKING IN KĪLAUEA CALDERA

Laying a road across the unstable surface of the caldera itself would be ludicrous even by the standards of this topsy-turvy park, so the only way to experience the crater floor is by **hiking**.

The only safe trails are those named and maintained by the park service and shown on their free handouts; venturing off these would be suicidal. To embark on even the most popular trails requires an act of faith verging on the superstitious: they're no more than ill-defined footpaths across the bare, steaming lava, guided only by makeshift rock cairns known as *ahus*. Frequent cracks reveal a crust that is on average around four inches thick – though considering the many such layers of lava piled up beneath you, that's not as alarming as it may sound. Geologists estimate that the molten lava here is two miles down. If you're nervous about setting off on your own, consider joining one of the many **ranger-led hikes** detailed each day at the visitor center.

There's no need to register for any of the caldera hikes. You must do so, however, if you're heading into the backcountry: see p.224.

The caldera is no place for agorraphobics; you can't assume that anyone will be on the same trail as you, so it's up to you to find your way and cope with the occasional burst of fear. Only two people in two centuries have been killed by eruptions, both photographers in search of the perfect shot. However, more mundane accidents happen frequently, and trying to hike at night is a very bad idea.

The longest trail in the caldera area, the 11.6-mile **Crater Rim Trail**, is not described in detail here because it so closely parallels the Crater Rim Drive, though it generally runs nearer the edge than the road. It is an exciting, dramatic walk, and a level and easy one too, but it shows you very little that you can't see from a car. All the trails in this section start from or cross the Crater Rim Trail, however, so you're likely to walk at least a short section of it.

The Halemaʻumaʻu and Byron Ledge trails

Map 11.

Two separate hiking trails – the **Halemaʻumaʻu** and the **Byron Ledge** – cross the main floor of Kīlauea Caldera. However, as they meet each other twice, it makes sense to combine the two into one single round-trip of roughly seven miles, which is likely to take around four hours.

The obvious place to start is along the Crater Rim Trail from *Volcano House*. Heading northwest (away from the park entrance), the path drops slightly for a hundred yards, until a signpost points to the left down the **HALEMAʻUMAʻU TRAIL**. From there, a clear, easy walkway descends through thick **rainforest**, with the bright orange heliconia growing to either side interspersed with delicate white-blossomed shrubs and green *hāpuʻu* ferns, capable of growing forty feet high. Except when the odd helicopter passes overhead, the only sounds are the chatter of the tiny bright birds that flit through the canopy, and the steady drip of rain falling from the highest branches. Every now and then, a glimpse of the steam vents on the crater floor far ahead reminds you that you're now inside an active volcano. Soon a sheer wall of rock to your left marks the abrupt fault line of the outermost crater rim. Less than half a mile down, from a small rain shelter, views open out across a small gorge filled with gently stirring jungle.

Not far beyond are the massive rock slides left by an earthquake in November 1983, which measured 6.7 on the Richter scale; the giant cubic boulders that tumbled down the cliff face now reach to the very edge of the path. Thereafter the vegetation thins out, and shortly after the first intersection with the Byron Ledge Trail, which you can ignore at this point, you come to the edge of the vast black expanse of the **crater floor**. The trail from here on is nowhere near as distinct as you might expect. At first the passage worn by the feet of previous hikers is clear enough, but before long you're gingerly picking your way from cairn to crude cairn, the schoolyard game of not treading on the cracks taking on a real urgency when you think of the lake of molten lava somewhere beneath your feet. The state of the trail depends on the age of the flow at each precise spot. Different vintages overlap in absurd profusion, and from time to time the path becomes a jumble of torn, cracked and uplifted slabs of rock.

For at least half an hour you cross a plain where tiny ferns have taken root in every fissure, creating a green latticework of fault lines. Here and there 'ōhelo bushes bearing the dew-glistening red berries sacred to Pele have established themselves. Then the ground begins to rise again, the cairns become harder to pick out against the general chaos, and wisps of sulphurous steam gust across the path with ever-greater regularity.

In due course you're confronted by what appears to be a low ridge of sharp, rough hills, like the battlements of some medieval castle, with no indication of what lies behind. A single clear footpath leads up to a gap; through that gap, a similar landscape opens up once again. If you don't know

PELE: THE VOLCANO GODDESS

Ancient Hawaiian chants relate that Pele, the "volcano goddess," made her first landfall in Hawaii on Kauai. Pursued from island to island by her vengeful older sister, the goddess of the sea, she finally made her home in the pit of Kīlauea. As well as manifesting herself as molten lava, she also appeared as a young woman or an elderly crone.

Imbued as they are with poetry, legend, history, and symbolism, it's now impossible to appreciate all that the tales of Pele meant to the ancient Hawaiians. Clearly they studied the volcanoes carefully; chants describe Pele's progress through the archipelago in the exact order of age agreed upon by modern experts. However, Pele's destructive power was just one small aspect of the goddess; she was also associated with the hula, fertility, and creation in general.

Talk of Hawaiian religion as a single system of belief ignores the fact that different groups once worshipped different gods. The god Kū, to whom human sacrifices were made in the luakinis (see p.287), was probably the chosen deity of the warrior elite; Pele may have been far more central to the lives of most islanders.

Christian missionaries found that belief in Pele endured even after the old ways were supposedly abandoned. They made great play of an incident in 1824, when Queen Kapi'olani, a Christian convert, defied the goddess by descending into the caldera while reading from her Bible and eating the kapu red 'ōhelo berries. Less fuss was made in 1881, when an eight-month flow from Mauna Loa had reached within a mile of Hilo, and Princess Ruth Ke'elikōlani was called in from Oahu to help. Watched by journalists and missionaries, she chanted to Pele at the edge of the molten rock, offering her red silk handkerchiefs and brandy. By the next morning, the flow had ceased.

what a **spatter cone** is yet, turn around; on this side the walls of most of the castellated hillocks are hollow, exposing fiery red interiors. They were created by the eruption of April 1982, when hikers in this lonely spot had to be evacuated immediately before a nineteen-hour onslaught. As you look back through the gap, the Jaggar Museum is perfectly framed high on the crater rim.

This spot is clearly marked as the intersection of the Halema'uma'u and Byron Ledge trails, which head on together for a couple hundred yards to the very lip of **Halema'uma'u Crater**. At this point you'll probably encounter other sightseers who have got here the easy way, via the short trail from the Crater Rim Drive; that walk, and the actual crater, is described on p.229. If you can arrange to be picked up at the parking lot, you can end your hike here. Alternatively, double back and take your choice as to your return route.

The Byron Ledge Trail

If you decide to head back along the **BYRON LEDGE TRAIL**, after the initial crossing of a rough *'a'ā* field, you'll find it generally easier to follow. It covers a shorter distance across the crater floor; the walk to the edge of the crater from the junction of the two trails takes around half an hour. This trail is more even underfoot, although once or twice it requires you to step across narrow (roughly nine inches) but alarmingly dark cracks in the ground, including one with a small tree in it.

The ascent to **Byron Ledge** (named after the cousin of the poet, who came here in 1825) is quite precipitous. The surface of the path is unstable gravel, of the same sharp shards of black glass as a new "black-sand" beach, and occasionally the scree slope plunges away below your feet. It can be very vertiginous; from this close, the black crater floor is so huge and featureless that the brain can't really take it in,

THE HALEMA'UMA'U AND BYRON LEDGE TRAILS

and it feels like a sheer wall rising up against you, or a bottomless pit. The rainforest at the top is gloomier and less lush than on the Halemaʻumaʻu Trail.

Heading back along the ledge, you pass two spur trails: one that connects to the Devastation Trail, and another that leads within minutes to the Kīlauea Iki Trail (see below). Sticking to the Byron Ledge Trail involves dropping right back down to cross a small segment of the caldera floor in order to rejoin the Halemaʻumaʻu Trail back to *Volcano House* at the spot where it reaches the basin.

The Kīlauea Iki trail

Map 11, H4.

Just east of Kīlauea Caldera proper, but still within the Crater Rim Drive, the subsidiary crater of **KĪLAUEA IKI** ("little Kīlauea") took on its current shape during a gigantic eruption in 1959. Prodigious quantities of lava, exploding in a vertical column that reached a record height of 1900 feet, raised the crater floor by around 350 feet; some of it is still thought to be red-hot a few hundred feet below the surface. Though Kīlauea Iki may not have quite the same sense of scale as the main caldera, it offers a similar and in some ways an even more spectacular assortment of terrain, which can be explored along the two-hour, four-mile **KĪLAUEA IKI TRAIL**.

The trail is most easily done as an anticlockwise hike from the **Thurston Lava Tube** (see p.230), a mile south of the visitor center. Start by following the Crater Rim Trail for about a mile, as it circles close to the lip of the gulf. At a three-way junction with the spur to Byron Ledge (see above), signs point left to the Kīlauea Iki Trail proper. Now the rainforest becomes especially dense, with ultra-dark, oily green leaves, startled wild game birds running along the path ahead, and songbirds overhead.

Soon you glimpse the far wall of Kīlauea Iki, tinged with pastel greens and yellows against the general darkness. Views of the crater floor thus far have made it appear smooth, but after a half-mile or so the path drops abruptly down steep steps cut into the rock to reach a primeval mess of jagged *'a'ā* lava. Follow the line of cairns for a few hundred yards before arriving at the vent where the 1959 eruption took place. This sudden, gaping maw in the hillside, filled like an hourglass with fine reddish-orange sand, is seen across an open scar in the lava; a barrier makes it clear that you should approach no closer.

The trail then descends slightly to a much more even, but no less alarming, expanse of undulating *pāhoehoe*, punctuated by white- and yellow-stained cracks that ooze stinking plumes of white vapor. You have to step across the odd fissure, and again it takes an act of faith to follow the scattered cairns that mark the way. It's easy to stray from the path and to succumb to a moment of panic at the thought that you're a mile from safety in a vague plain of swirling mists and splintered lava. Eventually, however, you pass through a final chaos of rocks into the dripping, dank bosom of the rainforest. The path then zigzags back up to the rim; the gradient is never steep, but it's a fair walk and can get pretty muddy.

Devastation Trail

Map 11, G5.
Much of the lighter debris from the 1959 Kīlauea Iki eruption (see opposite) was blown clear of the crater itself, then carried by the wind to pile up as a **cinder cone** near its southwestern edge. This is **Pu'u Pua'i**, which can be reached along the half-mile **DEVASTATION TRAIL** between two parking lots on Crater Rim Drive (see p.230).

If you set out from the Devastation parking area, opposite the top of Chain of Craters Road, you start by following the old route of Crater Rim Drive, which was severed at this point by the eruption. A paved pathway snakes from the end of the parking lot through low, light-pink undergrowth – a favorite haunt of the park's population of *nēnē* geese. Most of what you see is new growth, though a few older trees survived partial submersion in ash by developing "aerial roots" some way up their trunks. Pu'u Pua'i itself is just a heap of reddish ash, while the land around it is barren, scattered with bleached branches.

CHAIN OF CRATERS ROAD

CHAIN OF CRATERS ROAD winds down to the ocean from the south side of Crater Rim Drive, sweeping around successive cones and vents in an empty landscape where only the occasional dead, white tree trunk or flowering shrub pokes up. From high on the hillside, the lava flows look like streams of black tarmac, joining in an ever-widening highway down to the Pacific. Long **hiking trails** and the minor **Hilina Pali Road** lead to sites of geological and historic interest all the way down, but the real reason to head this way is to see what may be at the end – the ongoing **eruption of Kīlauea**.

Chain of Craters Road used to run all the way to Puna, then loop back up to the highway. The scale of the damage since 1983 has been too great to repair, however, so now it's a dead-end, and getting shorter year by year. One by one, the landmarks along its seafront stretch – such as **Waha'ula Heiau**, a temple believed by some to have been where human sacrifice was introduced to Hawaii, which was finally swallowed by the lava in 1997, and the gorgeous black-sand beach at **Kamoamoa**, whose short existence lasted only from 1988 until 1992 – have been destroyed, and before long the road may not follow the shoreline at all.

Check current conditions at the visitor center when you arrive and make sure you have enough gas. The end of the road is a fifty-mile round-trip from the park entrance, and there are no facilities of any kind along the way.

Hilina Pali Road

Map 10, E3.

Four miles down Chain of Craters Road, a sign to the right points out a detour along **HILINA PALI ROAD**. This crosses the bleak Ka'ū Desert for nine miles, to reach an overlook above the main 1200-foot drop of **Hilina Pali**. *Pali* is the Hawaiian word for cliff; you may be used to hearing it applied to the lush razorback hills of the Hāmākua coast, but Hilina is much starker and rawer than that, being the huge wall left behind when a piece of the island dropped into the sea. The views are immense, but desolate in the extreme. Infrequent clusters of battered palms in the distance show the locations of former coastal villages; the hillock of Pu'u Kapukapu, near the shore to the southeast, however, obscures the most popular of the park's backcountry campgrounds, at Halapē.

Halfway along the road, **Kulanaokuaiki** is one of the park's two fully equipped, drive-in **campgrounds**. Smaller and somewhat more basic than Nāmakani Paio (see p.227), it's free, and available on a first-come, first-served basis for up to seven nights in any one year. It opened in 1999 as a replacement for the nearby Kīpuka Nēnē campground, which has closed permanently in order to allow its resident population of *nēnē* geese to breed in peace.

Hiking in this area is never less than grueling, involving extended periods of walking across barren, exposed, and baking-hot lava flats. If you want to get to the shoreline, it makes more sense to hike the **Puna Coast Trail**

(see p.244) than to climb up and down the *pali* as well. However, gluttons for punishment have a choice of two trails to the sea. Both the **Hilina Pali** and **Ka'aha** trails start by zigzagging down the cliff along the same poorly maintained footpath; the Ka'aha leads for just under four miles to **Ka'aha Shelter** (see p.246), while the Hilina Pali covers the eight miles to the **Halapē Shelter**, joining the **Halapē Trail** from Kīpuka Nēnē. In addition, you can even walk to the Hilina Pali overlook from the Jaggar Museum, along the eighteen-mile **Ka'ū Desert Trail** (the "Footprints" section of which is detailed on p.248).

Mauna Ulu Trail and Pu'u Huluhulu

Map 10, F3.

Another three miles along Chain of Craters Road beyond the Hilina Pali turnoff, a small approach road on the left leads to the **MAUNA ULU TRAIL**. A couple of miles along, this becomes the **Nāpau Trail**, which runs for ten miles to the open **Pu'u 'Ō'ō** vent, far out along Kīlauea's East Rift Zone – the culprit responsible for most of the lava flows since 1983. At present, it's illegal to continue along the trail any further than the basic **campground** at Nāpau Crater, three miles short of the end. If you plan to spend the night here, you must register at the visitor center; see p.224.

Most hikers content themselves with the three-mile round-trip to **Pu'u Huluhulu**, an ancient cinder cone that has somehow escaped inundation for several millennia. It owes its name (*huluhulu* means "very hairy") to the dense coating of unspoilt, old-growth rainforest that surrounds it as a result. Following the footpath to the top of this small mound enables you to peer into its inaccessible hollow interior, circled by craggy red rocks and filled with primeval-looking green ferns and darting birds. The sensation of being in a real-life "Lost World" is enhanced by the wasteland visible all around.

Pu'u 'Ō'ō itself is extremely unstable; gaping holes regularly split its sides to release floods of liquid rock, and there have been several major collapses. You should be able to spot it from Pu'u Huluhulu, though when this book went to press it was no longer possible to see the "red glow" of the eruption. Views to the south are dominated by the miniature shield volcano of **Mauna Ulu**, created between 1971 and 1974 and already home to native trees and shrubs like the 'ōhi'a and 'ōhelo.

Pu'u Loa petroglyphs

Map 10, H6.

Ten miles beyond Mauna Ulu, and just after its descent of the 1000-foot Hōlei Pali, Chain of Craters Road passes within a mile of the most extensive field of **petroglyphs** – ancient rock carvings – on the island.

The level trail east to **PU'U LOA** ends at a circular raised boardwalk. Most of the petroglyphs visible from here are no more than crude holes in the lava, the kind you might make by rotating a coin against a brick. They only inspire any wonder if you're aware that each was probably carved to hold the umbilical cord of a newborn infant, carried here at a time when this spot was even more remote than it is today. *Pu'u loa* means "long hill," and by extension "long life," so this was considered a lucky spot for the traditional ceremony. The purpose of the boardwalk is not to display the most elaborate petroglyphs, but to discourage you from exploring further, for fear that you might damage such irreplaceable works of art as the images of pre-contact **surfers** said to lie somewhere in the area.

PU'U LOA PETROGLYPHS

Hōlei Sea Arch

Map 10, I6.

At the time of writing, Chain of Craters Road came to an end just beyond mile marker 20, with a small parking lot just beyond **HŌLEI SEA ARCH** used as a turnaround point for all vehicles. Less than two miles survive of the road's previous eleven-mile shoreline route to Kalapana, and soon it may not reach the coast at all.

Until recently, few visitors bothered to pause at the sea arch; now it's the only named feature left in what was once a very scenic area. From the parking lot, cross a few yards of sparsely grassed lava and you'll see a chunky pillar of basalt blocks to your right, tenuously connected to the rest of the island by the top slab. The thudding of the waves against the cliffs makes the ground reverberate beneath your feet – clear evidence of the fragility of this coastline, most of which is too dangerous to approach.

Approaching the eruption

It's impossible to do more than generalize as to what might lie beyond the end of Chain of Craters Road. Assuming that the eruption is still continuing, somewhere high on the hillside one or more fissures in the earth will be spilling out large quantities of molten lava, which then sets off towards the ocean. En route it may or may not have to pour over fault scarps (cliffs formed by minor earthquakes), and its surface may or may not harden to create an underground stream. You can only view the lava itself if the nearest active flow has reached a point you can walk to from the road; if it is flowing directly into the ocean, which is easy to spot because the contact produces great plumes of steam; or if it is crossing or flowing along the road itself.

Find out if any of these scenarios apply by calling the park's **Volcano Update line** (☎985-6000); its website (ⓦwww.nps.gov/havo) also carries up-to-date information. The Kīlauea visitor center (☎967-7311) can offer more detailed advice and implores all visitors to view a three-minute safety video. During the 1990s, five visitors died in separate incidents, including two fatalities at the eruption site, and many more people had to be rescued after becoming stranded out on the lava at night. The most dangerous situation occurs when lava flows directly into the **ocean**, when there's a risk of inhaling toxic fumes that contain not only acids but even tiny particles of glass. In addition, new land is extremely unstable; it may be no more than a thin layer of solidified lava resting on seawater – a "bench" – and thus liable to collapse at any moment. Swirling mists can make it hard to keep your bearings and can also mean that only occasionally do you see the actual lava. According to rangers, most problems arise when hikers attempt to approach the operation from the east, from the foot of Hwy-130, as described on p.213.

The park service maintains a wooden information shack (on wheels, for obvious reasons) at the end of the road, where they hand out alarming leaflets explaining that new lava is unstable and may collapse at any time, and that it's best to avoid clouds of hydrochloric acid. When safety permits, rangers lead **guided hikes** to the site of the eruption. A daily schedule is posted at the visitor center; as a rule they start in the early afternoon, in order to get back to the road before nightfall.

Walking across flaky, crumbling, new lava is an extraordinary experience. Every surface is like sandpaper, a fall can shred your skin, and even far from the apparent center of activity, the ground can be too hot to touch. Heavy rain dries off without penetrating your clothing. The sight of liquid rock oozing towards you, swirling with phlegmy gobbets and destroying all it touches; the crackle as it

APPROACHING THE ERUPTION

crunches across previous layers of lava; the sudden flash as a dried-out tree bursts into flame: all leave you with a disconcerting sense of the land itself as a living, moving organism.

After dark, the orange glow of the eruption becomes even more apparent. Pinpoint incandescent lights become visible all across the slopes and leave the mountain looking like the proverbial city on a hill. Without official sanction or approval, and heedless of the immense risks, many visitors stay out all night to marvel at the glowing rivers of molten rock. If you try it, be sure to carry a flashlight for the walk back across the lava.

Finally, it's only fair to warn you that when current activity is occurring several miles beyond the end of the road, as it has for much of the last three or four years, you may well feel a profound sense of **anticlimax** at the little you see. Children in particular, excited by photographs of lava fountains, are liable to be very disappointed by the reality. On the other hand, they may see something that one day they will tell their own kids about.

The Puna Coast Trail

The **southern coastline** of the Big Island is now very sparsely populated; the villages that once stood along its central section were abandoned around 150 years ago, following a succession of devastating *tsunami*. Underground upheavals make this region extremely prone to **earthquakes**; in 1960 the entire south coast dropped by three feet, and campers in backcountry sites were washed out to sea after another major landslide in 1975.

The only way to explore the area is on foot, by means of the **PUNA COAST TRAIL**. This starts roughly a mile up from the sea, at the Pu'u Loa parking lot (see p.241), and sets off west, away from the eruption area, towards the coastal campgrounds at **Keauhou** and **Halapē**.

Also known as the **Puna Ka'ū Trail**, it's a long and very challenging hike, and only worth attempting if you have several days to spare. It's possible to get to 'Āpua Point and back in a single day, but that's a thirteen-mile round-trip that still stops a long way short of the more interesting spots along the trail. If you plan to camp out, you must register at the visitor center in Kīlauea, as this area is prone to landslides and *tsunamis*. Collected rainwater is available at the campgrounds along the way, but carry plenty more yourself. All three campgrounds consist of three-walled shelters, so you'll need a tent as well.

From Chain of Craters Road, the trail makes its way across a patchwork of lava flows, the new ones glistening in the sun and crunchy underfoot, the older ones worn and smooth. Rock cairns help to plot a course in the vaguer patches, and here and there coarse weeds have managed to establish themselves. Roughly four miles along, you reach the low seafront cliffs, which you follow for a couple more miles to **'Āpua Point**. From a distance it's a welcome flash of green against the relentless grays and blacks of the lava; when you arrive it turns out to have just a few coconut palms emerging from a tangled carpet of the ivy-like native *naupaka* shrub.

With no water, shelter or other facilities at 'Āpua, you either have to turn back to the road, or continue along the coast. Heading west, you're faced by the massive fault scarp of Hilina Pali looming ever larger inland. As well as releasing cascades of rock and even lava towards the ocean, landslides like those that created the *pali* also produce *tsunamis* that flood the coastal plains, so little is left standing along this stretch of the shoreline. Both the **Keauhou** and **Halapē** campgrounds, three and five miles respectively from 'Āpua, remain visibly scarred by the battering they received in November 1975 (when two campers lost their lives at Halapē). However, the park service has been replanting coconut palms to restore their lost beauty, and Halapē still has the feel of a little oasis beside the sea. Unfortunately, so many campers trek out to its white-sand beach that the cabins at both sites are infested with ants and cockroaches. Snorkeling in the tidal pools is excellent, but the open sea can be very dangerous. In theory these are nesting grounds for endangered hawksbill turtles, though the regulations against disturbing them seem to be a case of too little too late, and hardly any seem to land here any more.

To get to the final oceanfront campground, at **Ka'aha**, requires a very difficult six-mile hike from Halapē, up and along the top of a lesser *pali*. You can also climb down, with equal effort, from Hilina Pali Road (see p.240). Either way, it too is riddled with insects and even more dangerous for swimming.

MAUNA LOA

If you're interested in seeing a bit more of **MAUNA LOA**, as opposed to Kīlauea, leave the caldera area by the main entrance and head west for a couple of miles. The third turn on the right, **Mauna Loa Road**, winds up towards the summit from there, although it stops a long way short and only very rarely allows you views either up the mountain or down towards Kīlauea and the sea.

Kīpuka Puaulu

Map 11, A1.

The great majority of those who come along Mauna Loa Road drive less than a mile of its fourteen-mile length to see the enchanting little forest sanctuary of **KĪPUKA PUAULU**. Known as the "bird park," this enclave is an utter contrast to the raw landscape elsewhere in the National Park. A *kīpuka* is a patch of land that has by chance been left untouched by lava, and thus forms a sort of natural island. Kīpuka Puaulu's well-preserved rainforest serves as a sanctuary for rare native birds such as the 'elepaio flycatcher and the 'amakahi honey-creeper.

A woodland stroll around the two-mile loop path takes you past some huge old *koa* trees and through sun-dappled clearings, with birds audible on all sides. However, unless you have a lot of patience – and binoculars – you may not manage to see more than the odd flash of color. Your best bet is to walk slowly and quietly and hope to surprise a group on the ground.

A covered picnic area makes this a popular lunchtime halt for park visitors.

The Mauna Loa Summit Trail

Map 1, E6.

Beyond Kīpuka Puaulu, Mauna Loa Road climbs through thick woodland virtually all the way to the end, fourteen miles up, crossing just one stray lava flow. Its width varies between one and two lanes, but it's driveable if not exactly conducive to a quick journey. The surrounding tree-cover gradually changes from tropical to high-altitude before the road finally stops in a small clearing, 6662 feet up.

The parking lot here is the trailhead for the **MAUNA LOA SUMMIT TRAIL**. As the very explicit signs in the small pavilion explain, this is no trail to attempt on a whim. The summit is a gradual but exhausting nineteen miles further on across bleak, barren lava, with a round-trip usually taking at least four days. There's no shelter along the way except for two crude cabins – check with the park service, with whom you must register anyway, to see whether they are stocked with water. Hypothermia is a very real threat, as the higher slopes are prone to abominable weather conditions. If you make it to the top, you're confronted by the **Moku'āweoweo Caldera**, similar to Kīlauea's, which last erupted in 1984.

THE MAUNA LOA SUMMIT TRAIL

In theory, it's also possible to hike to the summit from the **Mauna Loa Weather Observatory**, which stands at the end of a nineteen-mile spur road that leaves the Saddle Road close to the turnoff to the summit of Mauna Kea (see p.202). While the Observatory Trail is only six miles long, it's extremely steep and demanding, and the park service strongly advises against using it.

THE KA'Ū DESERT

All the land in the National Park that lies to the south and west of Kīlauea Caldera is officially known as the **KA'Ū DESERT**. By the conventional definition of a desert, it should therefore receive no rain: in fact it receives almost as much as the rainforest to the east, but here it falls as a natural acid rain, laden with chemicals from Kīlauea. Only a few desiccated plants ever managed to adapt to this uncompromising landscape, and most of those have in the last century been eaten away by ravenous wild goats.

Walking the eighteen-mile **Ka'ū Desert Trail** can bring you into close contact with this region if you so desire; there's one overnight shelter, the three-bed **Pepeiao Cabin**, about nine miles along the trail's great curve from the Jaggar Museum down to Hilina Pali Road. From the cabin you can choose instead to hike another six miles down to **Ka'aha Point** and connect with the Puna Coast Trail (see p.244).

The Footprints Trail

Map 10, A3.

Ten miles west of the park entrance on the Belt Road, an inconspicuous roadside halt marks the start of the **FOOTPRINTS TRAIL**, which leads due south for just under a mile across rough 'a'ā lava. A small shelter at what might seem like a random spot covers a bunch of depressions in the rock, which popular legend says are human footprints. Whether or not you agree, the factual basis for the story is bizarre.

In 1790, Keōua, a rival of Kamehameha, was returning to his own kingdom of Ka'ū after two major battles in Puna. As his armies, complete with attendant women and children, traversed this stretch of desert, he divided them into three groups. The first group got safely across; then Kīlauea erupted, and the third group found the members of the second strewn across the pathway. All were dead, poisoned by a cloud of gas from the volcano. Supposedly, their footprints in the falling ash solidified and can still be seen, alternately protected and exposed as sand blows across the desert. Keōua, who escaped unharmed, was to meet no less dramatic an end himself: see p.127.

VOLCANO VILLAGE

Map 10, E1.

Unless you stay in *Volcano House* (p.225) or the park-service campgrounds (pp.227 and 239), the village of **VOLCANO** offers the only **accommodation** in the vicinity of the park. Though it's just a mile or so east of the park entrance, towards Hilo, it would be easy to drive straight past it without realizing it's there. The main street runs parallel to the highway, on the *mauka* (uphill) side, but it's well hidden by a roadside fringe of trees. Along it you'll find nothing much of interest other than a small post office, a couple of general stores and the only gas station for miles.

Accommodation

The strange thing about staying in Volcano is that there's nothing to suggest you're anywhere near an active volcano

– only *Volcano House* in the park can offer crater views. Instead, the village's crop of small-scale **bed and breakfast** places are tucked away in odd little corners of a dense rainforest. Be warned, incidentally, that it rains a *lot* in Volcano.

- -
**The accommodation price codes
used here are explained on p.29.**
- -

Carson's Volcano Cottage

505 Sixth St, Volcano, HI 96785
ⓣ 967-7683 or 1-800/845-5282 (US), ⓕ 967-8094,
ⓦ www.carsonscottage.com.
A friendly, romantic little place, south of the highway, with three en-suite guestrooms and three private cottages in the garden, plus an open-air Jacuzzi. They also offer three separate rental cottages. ❸–❹

The Chalet Kīlauea Collection

PO Box 998, Volcano, HI 96785
ⓣ 967-7786 or 1-800/937-7786 (US), ⓕ 987-8660,
ⓦ www.volcano-hawaii.com.
This assortment of B&Bs and vacation rentals, all under the same management, offers accommodation for all budgets. The owners' original property, now known as the *Inn at Volcano* (❹–❽), is a very plush, lavishly furnished B&B, set well north of the highway on Wright Rd, with themed individual rooms in the main house and separate cottages, including a "tree house" on the grounds. Their cheapest alternative is the simple *Volcano B&B* (❷), where six rooms share bathrooms and use of a common lounge, while the luxurious *Castle Suites at Mauna Loa* (❺–❻), five miles west near the golf course, offers very quiet, secluded en-suite lodgings. ❷–❽

Hale Ohia

PO Box 758, Volcano, HI 96785
ⓣ 967-7986 or 1-800/455-3803, ⓕ 967-8610,
ⓦ www.haleohia.com.
Very attractive and tastefully furnished accommodation, ranging from studio

apartments in a lovely converted water tank (really) to a three-bedroom cottage. The buildings are scattered across the ravishing rainforest gardens of a former plantation estate, south of the highway across from the village. ❸–❺

Holo Holo Inn

19-4036 Kalani Honua Rd, Volcano, HI 96785 ⓣ967-7950, ⓕ967-8025, ⓦwww.enable.org/holoholo/. Volcano's cheapest option, this HI-AYH-affiliated hostel consists of a rambling rainforest home, half a mile up from the highway, that offers beds in rudimentary but adequate dorm rooms for $17, and private doubles for $40. ❶–❷

Kīlauea Lodge

PO Box 116, Volcano, HI 96785 ⓣ967-7366, ⓕ967-7367, ⓦwww.kilauealodge.com. Imposing former YMCA on the main street, which has been converted into a comfortable upmarket B&B, with some of its twelve en-suite bedrooms in secluded

chalets and cottages dotted across the grounds. The central lodge building holds a good restaurant (see overleaf. ❹

My Island

PO Box 100, Volcano, HI 96785 ⓣ967-7216, ⓕ967-7719, ⓦwww.myislandinnhawaii.com. Several different grades of accommodation in individual buildings set amidst dense tropical vegetation. The friendly owner lives in the central lodge; guests can use his library and a communal TV lounge. ❷–❹

Volcano Rainforest Retreat

Reserve through Hawaii's Best Bed & Breakfast; PO Box 563, Kamuela, HI 96743 ⓣ885-4550 or 1-800/262-9912; ⓕ885-0559, ⓦwww.bestbnb.com. Two striking, recently built en-suite B&B units set in a beautiful garden. There's a cottage with kitchen and living room, and a much smaller, hexagonal studio. ❹–❺

VOLCANO VILLAGE: ACCOMMODATION

Eating

Although *Volcano House* (see p.225) holds the only **restaurant** within the National Park itself, Volcano Village offers a good range of nearby alternatives. In addition to the upmarket restaurants listed below, it also has a couple of funky local **cafés** – the *Steam Vent* (daily 6.30am–4pm) behind *Surt's*, and the *Lava Rock Café* (Mon & Tues 7.30am–6pm, Wed–Sat 7.30am–9pm, Sun 7.30am–4pm) at the Aloha gas station. Both serve inexpensive snacks, plate lunches and espresso coffees.

Kīlauea Lodge

Volcano Village ☎967-7366. Large inn dining room, decorated with rich wooden furnishings and warmed by a blazing log fire, in the heart of Volcano Village. There's a full range of strong-flavored European-style meat and game entrees, including *hasenpfeffer*, a braised rabbit dish you won't find on many Big Island menus, plus house specialities such as Seafood Mauna Kea (seafood and mushrooms on pasta); most cost $20–25, and the wine list is expensive. Nonresidents should reserve well in advance. Daily 5.30–9pm.

Surt's

Volcano Village ☎985-6711. Friendly fine-dining restaurant, furnished in appealingly local style, with a menu of Asian-cum-European dishes. The daily fish specials, many in fiery Thai sauces and priced at $20 or more, are consistently excellent, while the less expensive salads and meat entrees are reliably good. Lunch offerings range from sandwiches for $6–7 to Thai curries for around $10 to pasta dishes for $11–15. Daily noon–9.30pm.

Thai Thai

Volcano Village ☎967-7969. Unassuming but high-quality and very popular dinner-only Thai place on the main village road. Almost all the entrees, which include salads as well

as green and yellow curries
and pad thai noodles, cost
well under $15. Daily
5–9pm.

Volcano Golf & Country Club

Hwy-11 ☎967-7331.
Up a sideroad two miles west
of the park entrance, this
daytime-only golf course
restaurant serves a
conventional but adequate
menu of steaks, fish and salad
at around $10 per entree. Its
large picture windows look
out across unlikely, but
boring, meadows. Mon–Fri
8am–3pm, Sat & Sun
6.30am–4pm.

Ka'ū

The district of **KA'Ū** occupies the southern tip of the Big Island, which is also the southernmost point of the United States. Stretching for roughly fifty miles along the southern side of the immense west flank of the "long mountain," Mauna Loa, it ranges from the bleak Ka'ū Desert area, now included in Volcanoes National Park, across fertile, well-watered hillsides, to the windswept promontory of **South Point** itself. Situated downwind of the acrid volcanic fumes emitted by both Mauna Loa and Kīlauea, it's far from being the most enticing area of the island. Nonetheless, it may well have been home to the first Polynesian settlers, and remains one of the last bastions in the state of anything approaching the traditional Hawaiian way of life.

Ka'ū was a separate kingdom right up to the moment of European contact. Its last independent ruler was Kamehameha the Great's arch-rival, **Keōua**, some of whose warriors met a bizarre end in the Ka'ū Desert (see p.249) and who was himself killed during the dedication of Pu'ukohola Heiau (see p.127).

The population today is very sparse, and it's likely to get sparser now that the sugar mill at **Pāhala**, the last working mill on the island, has closed. All the towns in the area are absolutely tiny; on the map the grid of streets at **Hawaiian Ocean View Estates** (usually abbreviated to either Ocean

View or H.O.V.E.) may look impressive, but this thirty-year-old residential development remains barely occupied, thanks to a lack of employment in the region.

In recent years, the state government has repeatedly come up with schemes to revitalize the local economy. After environmental campaigners managed to thwart proposals to develop a vast new luxury resort below Ocean View, the state vigorously promoted a plan to build a commercial **spaceport** at Pālima Point, just three miles outside the National Park, to launch satellites and the Space Shuttle. That would supposedly have created ten thousand jobs, but the concept of positioning such a facility on the *tsunami*-battered slopes of an active volcano attracted so much derision that it now seems to have been quietly abandoned. The spaceport was due to be named after the late *Challenger* astronaut and local hero Ellison Onizuka, who came from Ka'ū, until enterprising journalists uncovered remarks he made before his death opposing the plan. The most recent project to be considered by the authorities in Honolulu – the construction of a maximum-security prison in Ka'ū – has been revived several times in the past few years, though there's still no definite decision as to whether it will ever happen.

Although it has a handful of accommodation options, few people spend more than a day at most exploring Ka'ū. Access to the sea is limited, as the highway curves around the ridge of Mauna Loa roughly ten miles up from the shoreline. The two most obvious stops are **South Point**, to admire the crashing waves and perhaps hike to **Green Sand Beach**, and **Punalu'u**, which since the demise of Kalapana boasts the island's finest **black-sand beach**.

As you pass through Ka'ū, look out for the strange, eroded cinder cones that dot the landscape. Some of these craters are so steep-sided as to have been forever inaccessible to man or beast, and paleobotanists are intrigued by the pre-contact vegetation that is thought to survive within.

KA'Ū

PĀHALA AND WOOD VALLEY

Map 1, F7.

As the vegetation reasserts itself after the bleak Ka'ū Desert, 23 miles west of the National Park entrance, little **PĀHALA** stands just *mauka* of the highway. Apart from its tall-chimneyed sugar mill, a gas station, and a small shopping mall, there's nothing to catch the eye here, but a drive back up into the hills to the northwest takes you through some appealing agricultural scenery.

Just when you think the road is about to peter out altogether, it enters a grove of huge eucalyptus trees and you're confronted by one of the Big Island's least likely buildings: on top of a hill, and announced by streamers of colored prayer flags, stands a brightly painted **Tibetan temple**. Originally built by Japanese sugar laborers, the **Wood Valley Temple** (or Nechung Dryung Ling) was rededicated by the Dalai Lama in 1980 and now serves as a retreat for Tibetan Buddhists from around the world (PO Box 250, Pāhala, HI 96777 ☏928-8539, ⓦwww.planet-hawaii.com/nechung; ❶–❷). Priority is given to religious groups, but when there's room travelers can stay in the simple dormitory accommodation or private rooms at the temple.

PUNALU'U

Map 1, F8.

Five miles beyond Pāhala, at the point where the highway drops back down to sea level, **PUNALU'U** has been flattened by *tsunamis* so often that it's given up trying to be a town any more. A single road loops from the highway to the ocean and back, running briefly along what is now the largest **black-sand beach** on the island.

Black sand is a finite resource, as it's only created by molten lava exploding on contact with the sea, and at any one spot that happens very rarely. Even those beaches not destroyed by new lava usually erode away within a few years. Each time the coastline of Punalu'u Bay gets redrawn, however, its black sand washes in again, piling up to create a new beach. At the moment it's irresistible, a crescent of jet-black crystals surrounding a turquoise bay and framed by a fine stand of coconut palms.

On the north side of the bay, you can make out the remains of an old concrete **pier**. Until a century ago tourists used to disembark from their ships at Punalu'u for the ride up to the volcanoes by horse; later it became the terminus of a short railroad from Pāhala and was used for shipping sugar. In 1942, by which time it had fallen into disuse, the military destroyed it as a potential landing site for Japanese invaders.

Swimming in these rough waters is out of the question, but many people come to Punalu'u to **camp**. Hawksbill turtles drag themselves ashore on the main beach at night, so camping on the sand is forbidden, but there's a pleasant, if incredibly windy, campground tucked into the rolling meadows of Punalu'u Beach Park, immediately to the south. Permits can be obtained from the Department of Parks and Recreation in Hilo ($3 per day; ☎961-8341).

The dilapidated complex of pseudo-Polynesian buildings behind the palms in the center of the beach, facing the sea across its own private lagoon, holds a restaurant that has been closed ever since the Gulf War downturn in tourism.

Practicalities

The only **accommodation** nearby is in the *Sea Mountain at Punalu'u* condo complex, a few hundred yards from the beach on the southern segment of the loop road (PO Box 70, Pāhala, HI 96777 ☎928-8301 or 1-800/488-8301,

Ⓕ928-8008, Ⓦwww.seamtnhawaii.com; ❸—❺). It's an incredibly remote and often very windy place to stay, but most of its studios and one- and two-bedroom apartments, arrayed along what looks like a typical suburban residential street, are well equipped and comfortable. A two-night minimum stay is required. Alongside it, but a separate entity, is the Sea Mountain **golf course** (☎928-6222), where the $40 greens fees are among the lowest on the island. The name "Sea Mountain," incidentally, refers to the underwater volcano of Lōʻihi, here just twenty miles offshore (see p.221).

NĀʻĀLEHU

Map 1, E8.

You can't miss **NĀʻĀLEHU** as you drive through Kaʻū. Eight miles south of Punaluʻu, it lines each side of the highway for around half a mile, without stretching very far away from the central ribbon. Although it bills itself as "America's southernmost town," Nāʻālehu offers little to induce drivers to stop. **Whittington Beach Park**, a couple of miles outside it to the north, is not so much a beach as a picnic ground, and the only reason to call in at Nāʻālehu is for a quick lunch.

The town has a handful of **snack places**, which change names with monotonous regularity. The longest survivor, the *Nāʻālehu Fruit Stand* (☎929-9099), is a general store that sells sandwiches and drinks as well as lots of fresh island fruit. There's also an espresso café and a Japanese takeout counter.

WAIʻOHINU

Map 1, E8.

Having climbed away from the sea for two miles west of Nāʻālehu, the highway makes a sweeping curve around the small settlement of **WAIʻOHINU**. This held a dozen houses when Mark Twain passed through in 1866, and boasts barely more than that today. Twain planted a monkey-pod tree here, but even that has now been dead for forty years. Alongside what may or may not be its descendant, a few hundred yards east of the center, *Mark Twain Square* is a gift shop that also sells sandwiches, cakes, and coffee (T 929-7550). Nearby, the basic but appealing *Shirikawa Motel* (PO Box 467, Nā'ālehu, HI 96772 T 929-7462; ❶) is gradually being overwhelmed by trees, while just around the highway bend you pass a pretty chapel, the white-and-green clapboard 1841 **Kauahā'ao Church**.

Half a mile south of the church, *Macadamia Meadows* (94-6263 Kamaoa Rd; reserve through Hawaii's Best Bed & Breakfast, PO Box 563, Kamuela, HI 96743 T 885-4550 or 1-800/262-9912, F 885-0559, W www.bestbnb.com; ❸) is a large modern home that offers four comfortable, spacious B&B rooms. Guests have use of the on-site pool and tennis courts.

SOUTH POINT ROAD

Map 1, E8.

As you circle the southern extremity of the Big Island on the Belt Road, you're too far up from the ocean to see where the island comes to an end. It is possible, however, to drive right down to the tip along the eleven-mile **SOUTH POINT ROAD**, which leaves the highway six miles west of Wai'ohinu.

Car-rental agencies forbid drivers from heading to South Point because vehicle damage is more likely on poor road surfaces, and providing emergency recovery is inconvenient. Like the similarly proscribed Saddle Road (see p.200), however, it's not a difficult or dangerous drive. Most of the way it's a single-lane paved road, with enough room to either side for vehicles to pass comfortably.

The road heads almost exactly due south, passing at first through green cattle-ranching country. As it starts to drop, the landscape takes on a weather-beaten look, with pale grass billowing and the trees bent double by the trade winds. It comes as no surprise to encounter the giant propellers of the **Kamoa wind farm**, though you're unlikely to see many of them turning: the winds have proven too gusty and violent for the farm to be a commercial success.

Ka Lae

Map 1, E9.

After ten miles, the road forks 100 yards beyond a sign announcing the **KA LAE NATIONAL HISTORIC LANDMARK DISTRICT**. The right fork ends a mile later at a red-gravel parking lot perched above a thirty-foot cliff. Local people fish over the edge, and ladders drop down the cliff face to boats bobbing at a small mooring below.

Walk a couple of minutes south and you come to **Ka Lae**, or **South Point**, where you can reflect that everyone in the United States is to the north of you, and in much less danger of being blown to Antarctica. The earliest colonizers of Hawaii battled against the winds to reach this spot long before the Pilgrims crossed the Atlantic, and in doing so traveled a far greater distance from their homes in the distant South Seas. Abundant bone fishhooks found in the area are among the oldest artifacts unearthed in Hawaii, dating as far back as the third century AD. At the newly restored **Kalalea Heiau**, at the very tip, offerings wrapped in *ti* leaves are still left by native Hawaiians. Beyond that is a ledge of black lava, steadily pounded by high surf.

The deep waters offshore were renowned not only for holding vast quantities of fish, but also because they're prey to such fierce currents that it can take days on end for human- or sail-powered boats to negotiate the cape. An old legend tells of a king of Kaʻū who became deeply unpopular after stealing fish from fishermen and forcing his people to build heavy-walled fishponds for his benefit. He was finally abandoned by his warriors after he plundered a fleet of canoes near Ka Lae and stole so much fish that his own canoe began to founder. The currents swept him away to a lonely death.

Among the rocks at the headland, you can still see holes drilled for use as **canoe moorings**. In ancient times, fishermen would tie their canoes to these loops by long cords so that they could fish in the turbulent waters without having to fight the sea. Looking inland, you can follow the gray outline of Mauna Loa in the distance; on a cloudless day, you might even make out its snowcapped peak. Nearer at hand, across a foam-flecked sea to the northwest, is the stark shoreline cinder cone of **Puʻu Waimānalo**.

Green Sand Beach

Map 1, E9.

GREEN SAND BEACH, a couple of miles northeast of Ka Lae, doesn't live up to its name. It is a beach, and it is greenish in a rusty-olive sort of way, but if you're expecting a dazzling stretch of green sand backed by a coconut grove you'll be disappointed. The only reason to venture here is if you feel like a bracing, four-mile hike along the oceanfront, with a mild natural curiosity at the end. Without great expectations, and on a rain-free day, it's worth the effort.

If you want to try it, go back to the junction on South Point Road a mile short of Ka Lae, and drive down the left fork as far as you can go, which is a turnaround point just beyond some military housing. If conditions are dry enough, you might continue down to the boat landing below on any of the many rutted mud tracks that crisscross each other down the slope. However, you'd have to have a very-high-clearance four-wheel-drive vehicle to follow the two-mile track from there to the beach.

Apart from one or two heavily rutted sections, the walk itself is very easy, although on the way out you can expect to be pushing into a stiff trade-winds breeze. For most of the route you cross rolling, pastel-green meadows – an oddly pastoral landscape considering the mighty surf pummeling at the lava rocks alongside.

Your destination comes in sight after just over a mile – the crumbling **Pu'u O Mahana** cinder cone that forms the only significant bump on the line of the coast. As you approach you can see that half the cone has eroded away, and the resultant loose powder has slipped down the cliffs to form a long sloping beach. You can see all there is to see from up above, but with care it's possible to scramble down to the seashore and examine handfuls of the "green sand." Close inspection reveals shiny green-tinged crystals of various sizes – this is in fact a mineral called **olivine**, which once formed part of a lava flow. Green Sand Beach is, however, much too exposed for swimming – or even walking too close to the sea.

The huge **Kahuku Ranch,** which stretches inland from the Belt Road near South Point Road almost to the summit of Mauna Loa, is currently being considered for incorporation into Hawaii Volcanoes National Park, which may have the effect of opening this entire region up to hiking and backcountry exploration.

HAWAIIAN OCEAN VIEW ESTATES

Map 1, D8.

West of South Point Road, you can't get down to the sea again in the twelve miles before the Belt Road reaches South Kona. The road does, however, run past a few isolated buildings and communities where you can get a snack or fill up with gas.

For the views from its blue *lānai*, it's fun to stop for a meal or drink at the *South Point Bar & Restaurant*, raised above the highway at the 76-mile marker (Mon–Sat noon–8pm; Sun 8am–8pm; ☏929-9343). They try out a different menu every month, but don't bank on anything more exotic than burgers, grilled chicken, and steak. They occasionally offer live entertainment as well.

A little further on, you enter the residential zone of **HAWAIIAN OCEAN VIEW ESTATES**, also known as "Ocean View" or "H.O.V.E.," an area designated for development during the 1960s. Intricate grids of roads were planned, and some sites were sold that were no more than patches of bare lava. Only a tiny proportion of the lots have been built on and many of the roads still don't exist. Unless the plans to develop a megaresort at Pōhue Bay, a currently inaccessible white-sand beach directly below Ocean View, ever get off the drawing board, there's little prospect of the area acquiring a substantial population.

The center of Ocean View consists of two small malls: one has a Texaco gas station and the *Ohia Cafe* espresso bar, while the other is home to the friendly, clean little *Desert Rose* (daily 7am–7pm; ☏939-ROSE), which serves simple breakfasts and lunchtime sandwiches and salads. Just off the highway a couple hundred yards north, the takeout counter at *Mr Bell's* (daily 7am–9pm; ☏929-9291) offers breakfast for $5, and basic plate lunches taken on a shady *lānai*.

Accommodation

Convenient places to **stay** nearby include the four-roomed *Bougainvillea B&B* (PO Box 6045, Ocean View, HI 96737 ☏929-7089 or 1-800/688-1763; ❷), and the three-roomed *South Point B&B*, *mauka* of the highway on Ocean View's eastern fringes (92-1408 Donola Drive, Donola, HI 96704 ☏929-7466; ❷).

MANUKĀ STATE PARK

Map 1, D8.

Kaʻū comes to an end half a dozen miles west of Ocean View, as you cross the long ridge of Mauna Loa. The former royal lands on the border with Kona, once the *ahupuaʻa* of **MANUKĀ**, remain set aside to this day as the **Manukā Natural Area Reserve** – at 25,000 acres, the largest natural reserve in the state.

Only a small segment of the reserve is open to the public – **Manukā State Park**, three miles west of Ocean View on the *mauka* side of the highway. From its leafy roadside parking lot, equipped with a picnic pavilion, restrooms, benches, and rolling lawns, the one-hour, two-mile **Manukā Nature Trail** leads into peaceful woodlands. Almost all the terrain is *ʻaʻā* lava, and although there's no great climb, the path can be very rough underfoot. Humans aren't the only ones who find it hard to cross lava flows, so pigs and exotic plants alike are relatively scarce, and the area remains a haven for native plants. One of the main features of long-established native species tends to be that they've lost unnecessary defenses against predators; thus you'll see a mint with no smell and a nettle with no sting. The trail's only dramatic feature is a collapsed lava pit, whose sides are too steep to permit access to wild pigs (see p.292), and which gathers enough moisture to feed plants, such as the *ʻieʻie* vine, that normally only grow in much wetter areas.

Maps, free at the trailhead, explain how the vegetation varies with the age of the lava flow. Some of the ground is new and barren, and some is around two thousand years old, but those areas that date back four thousand years have managed to develop a thick coating of topsoil.

About eight miles beyond Manukā, as the road heads due north towards Kailua, you come to the turnoff down to **Miloliʻi Beach** – see p.105.

CONTEXTS

A brief history

Until less than two thousand years ago, the Big Island remained an unknown speck in the vast Pacific, populated by the mutated descendants of the few organisms that had been carried here by wind or wave (see p.289). Carbon dating of fishhooks and artifacts found at Ka Lae (South Point) suggests that Hawaii's earliest human settlers arrived during the second or third centuries AD. Except perhaps for their first chance landfall, they came equipped to colonize, carrying goats, dogs, pigs, coconut palms, bananas, and sugar cane among other essentials.

These first inhabitants were **Polynesians**, probably from the Marquesas Islands. Their ancestors spread from Asia to inhabit Indonesia and the Solomon Islands 30,000 years ago. Such migrations, across coastal waters shallower than they are today, involved hopping from island to island without crossing open ocean. There then followed a 25,000-year hiatus, while the techniques were acquired to venture farther. Just over three thousand years ago, the voyagers reached Fiji; and spread via Tahiti to populate the "Polynesian Triangle," extending from Easter Island in the east to Hawaii in the north and New Zealand in the south.

Recent archeological and scientific investigations have thrown a number of long-cherished beliefs about the ancient history of Hawaii into doubt, while confirming, thanks to DNA testing, that the Polynesians did indeed enter the Pacific from southeast Asia. Thor Heyerdahl's argument for a North American origin has thus been finally disproved. On the other hand, historians are no longer sure whether traditional accounts of Hawaii being settled by successive waves of migrants at widely spaced intervals are in fact true. According to that model, Marquesas Islanders continued to arrive until the eighth century and were followed by Tahitians between the eleventh and fourteenth centuries, with each new group violently supplanting its predecessors. One piece of evidence that does point to a Tahitian influx is the name "**Hawaii**" itself, which is known previously to have been an alternative, "poetic" name for the largest of the leeward Tahitian islands, Raiatea, the home of the voyaging temple of Taputapuatea. Whether or not Tahitians did reach Hawaii in significant numbers, it remains unquestioned that by the time the Europeans appeared, no two-way voyaging between Hawaii and the South Pacific had taken place for around five hundred years.

The coming of Captain Cook

No Western ship is known for certain to have chanced upon Hawaii before that of **Captain Cook**, in January 1778; the first European to sail across the Pacific, the Portuguese Ferdinand Magellan, did so without seeing a single island.

There is, however, considerable circumstantial evidence of pre-Cook contact between Hawaiians and Europeans. **Spanish** vessels disappeared in the northern Pacific from the 1520s onwards, while during the two centuries, starting in 1565, that the "Manila Galleons" made annual voyages across the Pacific between Mexico and the Philippines, at least nine such ships were lost. Cook observed that the first

Hawaiians he encountered were familiar with iron, and he even suggested that some bore European features. Hawaiian legends speak of what may have been Spanish mariners being shipwrecked on the north coast of Lanai during the sixteenth century, and again off Maui some time later, while the log of the Dutch ship *Lefda* in 1599 spoke of eight seamen deserting to an unknown island at this latitude.

Spanish influence might explain the similarity of the red and yellow feather headdresses of Hawaiian warriors – unknown elsewhere in Polynesia – to the helmets of Spanish soldiers, and account for what seemed the phenomenal speed with which syphilis spread through the islands after it was supposedly introduced by the Cook expedition. The skeleton of a young woman was recently unearthed on Oahu who appears to have died of syphilis in the mid-seventeenth century; other contemporary burials have been shown to contain small scraps of sailcloth.

Cook first encountered Hawaii on his way to the north Pacific in search of the (nonexistent) Northwest Passage. He initially sailed past the Big Island before stumbling upon Kauai. When he returned a year later, his ships, the *Discovery* and the *Resolution*, skirted Maui and, to the fury of their crews, cruised the coast of the Big Island for almost seven weeks before anchoring in Kealakekua Bay on January 17, 1779. The first European to set foot on land was William Bligh, later captain of the mutinous *Bounty*.

A vast crowd of Hawaiians had gathered to greet Cook. For three weeks, he was feasted by chief Kalaniopu'u and his priests, attending temple ceremonies and replenishing his supplies. The departure of the *Resolution*, amid declarations of friendship, might have been the end of things, had it not been forced to return just a week later, following a violent storm. This time the islanders were not so hospitable, and far from keen to part with further scarce resources. On February 14, Cook led a landing party of nine men in a bid to kidnap Kalaniopu'u and force the islanders to return a stolen small boat. In an undignified scuffle, surrounded by thousands of warriors, Cook was **stabbed** and died at the water's edge. His body was treated in the manner of a dead chief: the skull and leg bones were kept, and the rest cremated.

The **interpretation** of Cook's death has always been surrounded by controversy. It became widely believed by Europeans that the Hawaiians had taken Cook to be the great god Lono. The legend goes that, by chance, Cook had arrived at the temple of Lono at the height of the Makahiki festival, a major annual celebration in honor of Lono. The billowing sails of the *Resolution* were taken to be Lono's emblems, while the ship itself was believed to be the floating island of tall trees on which he was expected to voyage around Hawaii.

Some argue, however, that this story is based in part on a European view of Cook and of primitive people in general, rather than on Polynesian perceptions of the man. The European mentality of the time assumed that a noble figure of the Enlightenment such as Cook must appear god-like to the superstitious "natives." His voyage was perceived by the British as bringing civilization and order to heathen lands, while Cook saw himself as a stern father forever having to chastise the islanders, who were his "insolent" children. His last recorded words are "I am afraid that these people will oblige me to use some violent measures; for they must not be left to imagine that they have gained an advantage over us."

Cook may have wanted to be seen as the representative of a superior civilization and creed, but to Pacific islanders his superiority was largely a matter of **firepower**. A common theme in European contacts with the peoples of Polynesia is the attempt to draw well-armed foreigners into local military conflicts. It's impossible now to say whether the elaborate ceremonies at Hikiau Heiau, during which Cook was obliged to prostrate himself before an image of the god Kū, were designed to recognize him as Lono, or simply an attempt to incorporate him into the *kapu* system (see p.287) as a man of equal ranking with the high chiefs.

The major anomaly in the Cook-as-Lono legend is quite why the Hawaiians would have killed this "god." Some say it was a ritual sacrifice, while others argue that the man who struck the final blow had only just arrived from upcountry, and "didn't know" that Cook was a "god." The usual explanation, that it was simply an accident, serves both to perpetuate the idea of Hawaiians as "innocent" savages, and to absolve Cook himself of any responsibility for his fate. Though the British version of the dismantling of Hikiau Heiau has the priests eager to cooperate in return for iron trinkets, other sources, including Hawaiian tradition, have Cook's peremptory behavior seen as sacrilegious. That suggests that while Cook might have appeared a valuable potential ally to the chiefs, the priests and commoners viewed him as a blasphemer, and when he antagonized the chiefs by seizing Kalaniopu'u, deference gave way to defiance.

After Cook's death, news of the **"Sandwich Islands"** swiftly reached the rest of the world. Hawaii became a port of call for traders of all kinds, especially those carrying furs from the Pacific Northwest to China.

Kamehameha the Great

For a few brief years the Hawaiians remained masters of their own destiny, with the major beneficiary of the change in circumstances being the astute young warrior **Kamehameha** on the Big Island. Although he remains Hawaii's greatest hero, Kamehameha also played into the hands of the newcomers who flocked to the islands from all over the world.

The future Kamehameha the Great was born in northern Kohala in 1758, and raised in Waipi'o Valley. Both his mother, Kekuiapoiwa, and father, Kaūai, were of royal blood, as the niece and nephew either of the then ruler of the Big Island, Alapa'i, or of Kahekili, the ruler of Maui. Kahekili himself may even have been Kamehameha's true father.

When Kamehameha reached adulthood, Kalaniopu'u was high chief of the Big Island. Kamehameha became a valuable warrior, and was present at the death of Captain Cook. After Kalaniopu'u died in 1782, Kamehameha defeated his son Kiwalao in battle, and took control of Kona, Kohala and Hāmākua; however, Kiwalao's brother **Keōua** survived to establish his own power base in Ka'ū.

For more than a decade, a three-way struggle raged back and forth between Kamehameha, Keōua and Kahekili, ruler of Maui and Oahu. Kahekili's hopes of capturing the Big Island were dashed by the "Battle of the Red-Mouthed Gun" off Waipi'o Valley in 1791 – the first time Hawaiian fleets were equipped with cannons, operated by foreign gunners. The long campaign against Keōua finally ended at the dedication of the *heiau* at Pu'ukoholā, when Keōua himself was the chief sacrifice.

As sole ruler of the Big Island, Kamehameha reconquered first Maui, Lanai, and Molokai, then Oahu, and exacted tribute from Kauai. So eager was he to obtain military assistance from the Europeans that he briefly ceded the Big Island to Great Britain, though this was never made formal.

By now, many Europeans had settled permanently on the islands, bringing practical skills of all kinds. Kamehameha's most important foreign advisers were John Young and Isaac Davis (see p.129), who, in return for royal patronage, led his

armies into battle, personally gunning down enemy warriors in droves.

For some time Kamehameha had his capital in the fledg-
ling port of Lahaina on Maui. By the time he died in 1819,
however, he had returned to live in a palace on the Kona
Coast of the Big Island.

The end of the old order

Kamehameha's successor, his son Liholiho – a weak figure
also known as **Kamehameha II** – was dominated by the
regent **Queen Ka'ahumanu**. As a woman, excluded from
the *luakini heiaus* at the center of political power, she set out
to bring down the priesthood. Liholiho was plied with
drink and cajoled into dining with women in public; that
act ended the *kapu* system (see p.287) and precipitated a
civil war in which the upholders of the ancient religion
were defeated in battle near Hōnaunau. Altars and idols at
heiaus throughout Hawaii were destroyed.

Hawaii was thrown into moral anarchy just as the first
Puritan **missionaries** arrived. Inspired by the pious death
of Henry 'Opukaha'ia, a *kahuna* priest from Hikiau Heiau
who had converted to Christianity (see p.77), they were
determined to turn the islands into the Promised Land.
Their harsh strictures on the easygoing Hawaiian lifestyle
might have been calculated to compound the chaos, as they
set about obliging Hawaiian women to cover unseemly
flesh in billowing *mu'umu'u* "Mother Hubbard" dresses,
condemning the *hula* as lascivious and obscene, and dis-
couraging surfing as a waste of time, liable to promote
lewdness.

In general, the missionaries concentrated their attentions
on the ruling class, the *ali'i*, believing that they would bring
the commoners to the fold in their wake. The initial ten-
sions between missionaries and the new breed of foreign

entrepreneurs later disappeared as their offspring intermarried, acquired land and formed the backbone of a new middle class.

The foreigners take control

For ordinary Hawaiians, the sudden advent of capitalism was devastating. Any notion of Hawaiian self-sufficiency was abandoned in favor of selling out the islands' resources for cash returns.

Sandalwood: the first sell-out

Sandalwood logs were first picked up from Hawaii in 1791, scattered among a consignment of fuel. Traders had searched for years for a commodity that the Chinese would buy in return for tea to meet English demand. Once it became clear that the Chinese would pay enormous prices for the fragrant wood, the race was on.

Kamehameha had a monopoly on the sandalwood trade until his death, but thereafter individual chiefs out for profit forced all the commoners under their sway to abandon *taro* farming and fishing and become wage slaves. By the end of the 1820s, the forests were almost entirely denuded, and traditional agriculture had collapsed.

Whaling

The first whaling ships arrived in Hawaii in 1820, the same year as the missionaries – and had an equally dramatic impact. Modern visitors often assume that it was the humpback whales seen in Hawaiian waters that attracted the whaling fleet to the islands, but humpbacks were not hunted during the nineteenth century. Instead, the whalers would chase other species in the waters around Japan in winter and in the Arctic in summer, and then call at Hawaii each spring and fall to unload oil and baleen to be shipped home in other vessels, to stock up, and to change crew.

Any Pacific port would have seemed a godsend to the whalers, who were away from New England for three years at a time and paid so badly that most were either fugitives or plain mad. Hawaii was such a paradise that up to fifty percent of each crew would desert, to be replaced by Hawaiian *sailamokus*, born seafarers eager to see the world.

Whaling centered on the burgeoning ports of Honolulu on Oahu, and Lahaina on Maui, but it had huge implications for all the islands (and even brought Hawaii's first tourists). Provisioning whaling ships became the main activity on the Big Island, most conspicuously in the rapid growth of the **Parker Ranch**. The Hispanic cowboys imported to work there, known as *paniolos* (a corruption of *españoles*), were among the first of the many ethnic groups to make their homes on the Big Island.

By now the center of power had moved, for good, away from the Big Island to Oahu. While Honolulu had previously been a tiny village, Westerners recognized it as the finest deep-water harbor in the Pacific; it swiftly became the whalemen's favorite port.

The Great Mahele

By 1844, foreign-born fortune seekers dominated the Hawaiian government. As the foreign powers jostled for position, it was by no means inevitable that the islands would become American. As late as the 1840s, New Zealand was taken by the English and Tahiti by the French.

At first, foreigners could not legally own land. In the old Hawaii there was no private land; all was held in trust by the chief, who apportioned it to individuals at his continued pleasure only. The king was requested to "clarify" the situation. A land commission was set up, under the direction of a missionary, and its deliberations resulted in 1848 in the **Great Mahele**, or "Division of Lands." In theory all

land was parceled out to native Hawaiians, with 60 percent
going to the crown and the government, 39 percent to just
over two hundred chiefs, and less than one percent to
eleven thousand commoners. Within two years, however,
the *haole* (non-Hawaiians) were also permitted to buy and
sell land. The jibe that the missionaries "came to Hawaii to
do good – and they done good" stems from the speed with
which they amassed vast acreages; their children became
Hawaii's wealthiest and most powerful class.

The sugar industry and the US Civil War

At the height of the whaling boom, many entrepreneurs
began to put their money into **sugar**. It swiftly became
clear that this was an industry where large-scale operators
were the most efficient and profitable, and by 1847 the field
had narrowed to five main players. These **Big Five** were
Hackfield & Co (later to become Amfac), C. Brewer & Co,
Theo Davies Co, Castle & Cooke (later Dole), and
Alexander & Baldwin. Thereafter, they worked in close co-
operation with each other, united by common interests
and, often, family ties.

Hawaii was poised to take advantage of the impending
Civil War, when the markets of the northern US began to
cast about for an alternative source of sugar to the
Confederate South. The consequent boom in the Hawaiian
sugar industry, and the ever-increasing integration of
Hawaii into the American economic mainstream, was the
major single factor in the eventual loss of Hawaiian sovereignty.

Hawaii's first sugar plantation was started in 1835 in
Kōloa on Kauai, while the Big Island's first sugar mill
opened in Kohala in 1863, followed by plantations all along
the Hāmākua coast. The ethnic mixture of modern Hawaii
is largely the product of the search for laborers prepared to
submit to the draconian conditions on the plantations – first

the **Chinese**; then the **Portuguese**, brought from Madeira and the Azores; then the **Koreans**; **Japanese**; and **Filipinos**.

The end of the Kingdom of Hawaii

Hawaii is ours. As I look back upon the first steps in this miserable business, and as I contemplate the means used to complete the outrage, I am ashamed of the whole affair.

US President Grover Cleveland, 1893

When sugar prices dropped after the Civil War, the machinations of the sugar industry to get favorable prices on the mainland moved Hawaii inexorably towards **annexation** by the US. In 1876 all trade barriers and tariffs between the US and the Kingdom of Hawaii were abolished; within fifteen years sugar exports to the US had increased tenfold.

By now, the Kamehameha dynasty had come to an end, and the heir to the Hawaiian throne was chosen by the national legislature. The first such king, William Lunalilo, died in 1874, after a year in office. The second, **King David Kalākaua**, is now remembered as the "Merrie Monarch," who revived Hawaiian pursuits such as *hula* and surfing. However, at the time he was seen as being pro-American, and was to some extent the tool of the plantation owners. In 1887 an all-white group of "concerned businessmen" forced through the "Bayonet Constitution," in which he surrendered power to an assembly elected by property owners (of any nationality) as opposed to citizens. The US government was swiftly granted exclusive rights to what became Pearl Harbor.

Kalākaua died in San Francisco in 1891, and his sister **Liliʻuokalani** became queen. When she proclaimed her desire for a new constitution, the same group of business

THE HAWAIIAN MONARCHY

Kamehameha I	1791–1819
Kamehameha II (Liholiho)	1819–1824
Kamehameha III (Kauikeaouli)	1825–1854
Kamehameha IV (Alexander Liholiho)	1854–1863
Kamehameha V (Lot Kamehameha)	1863–1872
William C. Lunalilo	1873–1874
David Kalākaua	1874–1891
Liliʻuokalani	1891–1893

men, now known as the "**Annexation Club**," called in the US warship *Boston* and declared a provisional government. President Grover Cleveland (a Democrat) responded that "Hawaii was taken possession of by the United States forces without the consent or wish of the government of the islands… [It] was wholly without justification… not merely a wrong but a disgrace." With phenomenal cheek, the provisional government rejected his demand for the restoration of the monarchy, saying the US should not "interfere in the internal affairs of their sovereign nation." Finding defenders in the Republican US Congress, they declared themselves a **republic** on July 4, 1894.

Following an abortive coup attempt in 1895, Liliʻuokalani was charged with **treason**, and placed under house arrest. Though she lived until 1917, hopes of a restoration of Hawaiian independence were dashed in 1897, when a Republican president, McKinley, came to office claiming "annexation is not a change. It is a consummation." The strategic value of Pearl Harbor was emphasized by the Spanish–American War in the Philippines, and on August 12, 1898, Hawaii was formally **annexed** as a territory of the United States.

A territory and a state

At the moment of annexation there was no question of Hawaii becoming a state; the whites were outnumbered ten to one and had no desire to afford the rest of the islanders the protection of US labor laws, let alone to give them the vote. Furthermore, as the proportion of Hawaiians of Japanese descent (*nisei*) increased, Congress feared the prospect of a state of people who might consider their primary allegiance to be to Japan. Consequently, Hawaii remained for the first half of the twentieth century the virtual fiefdom of the Big Five, who, through their control of agriculture, dominated transport, utilities, insurance and government.

Things began to change during World War II. Hawaii was the only part of the United States to be attacked in the war, and it demonstrated just how crucial the islands were to the rest of America. On the Big Island, all ports except Hilo were closed after the Pearl Harbor attack, and most of the Waimea area became a military training camp.

The main trend in Hawaiian history since the war has been the slow decline of agriculture and the rise of tourism. Thanks to a series of strikes by plantation laborers, the long-term Republican domination of state politics ended, and Hawaii's agricultural workers became the highest paid in the world. Arguably, this led to the eventual disappearance of their jobs in the face of third-world competition. Big Island agriculture had already been dealt a severe blow by the *tsunami* of April 1, 1946, which devastated Hilo and destroyed the railroad along the Hāmākua coast; fifty years later, all the sugar mills have closed.

Hawaii finally became the fiftieth of the United States in 1959, after a plebiscite showed a 17-to-1 majority in favor, with the only opposition coming from the few remaining native Hawaiians. **Statehood** triggered a boom in tourism and also in migration from the mainland to Hawaii. On the Big Island the most obvious effect has been the growth of the Kona coast and the decline of Hilo. The seat of power on the island in the plantation years, Hilo now finds itself treated as a backwater by the entrepreneurs who have flooded into the sun spots of the western coast.

The major issue now facing the Big Island is the struggle to preserve its environment while creating new jobs to replace those lost by plantation closures. The island's economy seems fated to become ever more closely tied to the tourist industry. Fifty million dollars were invested to extend the runway at Kona's Keāhole Airport in order to accept direct flights from Asia, Europe, and the Midwest, but visitor numbers have yet to climb back to the levels reached prior to the Gulf War.

Official figures showing the growth of the Hawaiian economy since statehood conceal a decline in living standards for many Hawaiians. Rises in consumer prices in the state have consistently failed to match those in wages. Real estate prices in particular have skyrocketed, so that many islanders are obliged to work at two jobs, others end up sleeping on the beaches, and young Hawaiians emigrate in droves with no prospect of being able to afford to return.

The Sovereignty Movement

Since the late 1980s, support has mushroomed for the concept of **Hawaiian sovereignty**, meaning some form of restoration of the rights of native Hawaiians. Everyone now seems sure that sovereignty is coming, but no one knows what form it will take. Of the three most commonly advanced models, one sees Hawaii as an independent nation once again, with full citizenship perhaps restricted either to those born in Hawaii or prepared to pledge sole allegiance to Hawaii. Another possibility would be the granting to native Hawaiians of nation-within-a-nation status, as with

Native American groups on the mainland. Others argue that it would be more realistic to preserve the existing political framework within the context of full economic reparations to native Hawaiians.

Even the US government has formally acknowledged the illegality of the US overthrow of the Hawaiian monarchy with an official **Apology to Native Hawaiians**, signed by President Clinton in November 1993. A separate but related problem, indicative of the difficulties faced in resolving this issue, is the failure by both federal and state government to manage 200,000 acres set aside for the benefit of native Hawaiians in 1921. The state has now agreed to pay Hawaiians more than $100 million compensation, though disputes remain over where the money will come from and to whom it will go.

The sovereignty issue attained such a high profile in 1998, thanks to the centenary of annexation, that it provoked something of a backlash among elements of the state's non-native (in particular, Caucasian) population. The Office of Hawaiian Affairs, the body responsible for looking after the interests of native Hawaiians and, potentially, distributing compensation, had long been run by a board whose members were elected by native Hawaiians only. In a landmark ruling in February 2000, the US Supreme Court declared such race-based elections to be unconstitutional. New elections later that year were open to all state residents and produced one new non-native board member. Hawaiian activists fear that their movement is in jeopardy, with state programs liable to be dismantled by the courts. Nonetheless political support appears to remain strong for, at the very least, federal recognition of the status of native Hawaiians as being equivalent to that of native peoples elsewhere in the country, and veteran state senator Daniel Akaka has repeatedly introduced drafts of a bill to that end in Washington.

Ancient culture and society

No written record exists of the centuries between the arrival of the Polynesians and the first contact with Europeans. However, sacred chants, passed down through the generations, show a history packed with feuds and forays between the islands, and oral traditions provide a detailed picture of the day-to-day life of ordinary Hawaiians.

Developing a civilization on the most isolated islands in the world, without metals and workable clays, presented many challenges. Nevertheless, by the late eighteenth century, when the Europeans arrived, Hawaii was home to around a million people. Two hundred years later, the population has climbed back to a similar level. Now, however, virtually no pure-blooded Hawaiians remain, and the islands are not even close to being self-sufficient in terms of food. The distribution of the population has changed, too. In the past, the Big Island's population would have been far larger than the 130,000 it is today, and Oahu's population smaller, but no precise figures are known.

Daily life

In a sense, ancient Hawaii had no economy, not even barter. Although then, as now, most people lived close to the coast, each island was organized into wedge-shaped land divisions called **ahupua'a**, stretching from the ocean to the mountains. The abundant fruits of the earth and sea were simply shared among the inhabitants within each *ahupua'a*.

There's some truth in the idea of pre-contact Hawaii as a leisured paradise, but it had taken a lot of work to make it that way. Coconut palms had to be planted along the seashore to provide food, clothing and shade for coastal villages, and bananas and other food plants distributed inland. Crops such as sugar cane were cultivated with the aid of complex systems of terraces and irrigation channels. *Taro*, whose leaves were eaten as "greens" and whose roots were mashed to produce *poi*, was grown in the great valleys of Waipi'o and Pololū.

Most **fishing** took place in shallow inshore waters. At Ka Lae, you can still see holes drilled for use as **canoe moorings** – fishermen tied their canoes to these loops by long cords, enabling them to fish in the turbulent waters without having to fight the sea. Fishhooks made from human bone were believed to be especially effective; the most prized hooks of all were made from the bones of chiefs who had no body hair, so those unfortunate individuals were renowned for their low life expectancy. Nets were never cast from boats, but shallow bays might be dragged by communal groups of wading men drawing in *hukilau* nets (Elvis did it in *Blue Hawaii*, and you occasionally see people doing it today).

In addition, the art of **aquaculture** – fish-farming – was more highly developed in Hawaii than anywhere in Polynesia. It reached its most refined form in the extensive networks of fishponds that ring much of the coast, such as the royal fishpond at **'Anaeho'omalu** at Waikoloa, where the "protected mullet" were reserved for the sole use of high chiefs (see p.117).

Few people lived in the higher forested slopes, but these served as the source of vital raw materials such as *koa* wood for canoes and weapons. The ancients even ventured to the summit of Mauna Kea; as the only point in the Pacific to be glaciated during the last Ice Age, it has the hardest basalt on the islands. Stone from the **adze quarry**, 12,400 feet up, was used for all basic tools.

Ordinary commoners – the **maka'āinana** – lived in simple windowless huts known as *hales*. Most of these were thatched with *pili* grass, though in the driest areas they didn't bother with roofs. Buildings of all kinds were usually raised on platforms of stone, using rounded boulders taken from river beds. Matting covered the floor, while the pounded tree bark called *kapa* (known as *tapa* elsewhere in the Pacific, and decorated with patterns) served as clothing and bedding. Lacking pottery, households made abundant use of gourds, wooden dishes, and woven baskets.

The most popular pastime was **surfing**. There's a petroglyph of a surfer among the carvings at Pu'u Loa (see p.241), and there was even a surfing *heiau*, at Kahulu'u near Kailua. Ordinary people surfed on five- to seven-foot boards known as *alaia*, and also had *paipus*, the equivalent of the modern boogie board; only the *ali'i* used the thick sixteen-foot *olo* boards, made of dark oiled *wiliwili* wood. On land the *ali'i* raced narrow sleds on purpose-built, grass-covered *hōlua* slides and staged boxing tournaments.

The ali'i

The ruling class, the **ali'i**, stood at the apex of Hawaiian society. In theory, heredity counted for everything, and great chiefs demonstrated their fitness to rule by the length of their genealogies. In fact the *ali'i* were educated as equals, and chiefs won the very highest rank largely through physical prowess and force of personality. To hang on to power, the king had to be seen to be devoutly religious and to treat his people fairly.

For most of its history, the Big Island was divided among up to six separate chiefdoms, with major potential for intrigue, faction, and warfare. Canoes being the basic means of transportation, it was also feasible for chiefs to launch inter-island campaigns, and the north of the island in particular was prone to fall under the control of the kings of Maui.

Complex genealogies of the great *ali'i* still survive, but little is recorded other than their names. The first ruler to unite the entire island – **'Umi-a-Liloa**, who ruled from the *taro* fields of Waipi'o Valley – is listed as representing the sixtieth generation after the sky god Wākea. He was responsible for Hawaii's first legal code, the *kanawai*, which concerned itself with sharing the water from Waipi'o's irrigation ditches, and was among the first to make human sacrifice an instrument of state policy.

Other names to have been preserved include the six or seven Big Island chiefs said to have been either banished or killed by popular revolt, and the enigmatic ruler **Lono**, who may have been Umi's grandson. Legends suggest that he lost his throne after quarreling with, or even murdering, his wife, and left the island in a half-crazed fit of self-loathing. Some say that he regained his sanity, returned to unite the island, and was deified as Lonoikamakahiki, patron of the annual *makahiki* festival. Others claim that the Hawaiians predicted his return for centuries and believed these prophecies to be fulfilled by the arrival of Captain Cook (see p.270).

THE ALI'I

285

Religion

It's all but impossible now to grasp the subtleties of ancient Hawaiian **religion**. So much depends on how the chants and texts are translated; if the word *akua* is interpreted as meaning "god," for example, historians can draw analogies with Greek or Hindu legends by speaking of a pantheon of battling, squabbling "gods" and "goddesses" with magic powers. Some scholars, however, prefer to translate *akua* as "spirit consciousness," which might correspond to the soul of an ancestor, and argue that the antics of such figures are peripheral to a more fundamental set of attitudes regarding the relationship of humans to the natural world.

The **Kumulipo**, Hawaii's principal creation chant, has been preserved in full. It tells how, after the emergence of the earth "from the source in the slime . . . [in] the depths of the darkness," more complicated life forms developed, from coral to pigs, until finally men, women and "gods" appeared. Not only was there no Creator god, but the gods were much of a kind with humans. It took a hundred generations for Wākea, the god of the sky, and Papa, an earth goddess, to be born; they were the divine ancestors of the Hawaiian people.

Not all Hawaiians necessarily shared the same beliefs; different groups sought differing ways of augmenting their *mana*, or spiritual power. Only the elite *ali'i* may have paid much attention to the bloodthirsty warrior god Kū, while ordinary families, and by extension villages and regions, owed their primary allegiance to their personal *'aumākua* – a sort of clan symbol, possibly a totem animal such as a shark or owl, or a more abstract force, such as that embodied by Pele, the volcano goddess.

Spiritual and temporal power did not lie in the same hands, let alone in the same places. Hawaiian "priests" were known as **kahunas** ("men who know the secrets"), and were the masters of ceremonies at temples called **heiaus**. A *heiau* consisted of a number of separate structures set on a rock platform (*paepae*). These might include the *hale mana* ("house of spiritual power"), the *hale pahu* ("house of the drum"), and the *anuʻu* ("oracle tower"), from the top of which the *kahunas* conversed with the gods. Assorted *kiʻi akua*, wooden images of different gods, stood on all sides, and the whole enclosure was fenced or walled off. In addition to the two main types of *heiau* – **luakinis**, dedicated to the war god Kū, which held *leles* or altars used for human sacrifice; and **māpeles**, peaceful temples to Lono – there were also *heiaus* to such entities as Laka, goddess of the *hula*. Devotees of Pele, on the other hand, did not give their protectress formal worship at a *heiau*. Most *heiaus* were built for some specific occasion, and did not remain in constant use; the best example on the Big Island is the great *luakini* at Puʻukoholā, erected by Kamehameha the Great as proclamation of his plans for conquest (see p.126).

Hawaiian religion in the form encountered by Cook was brought to the islands by the Tahitian warrior-priest Paʻao, who led the last great migration to Hawaii. The war god Kū received his first human sacrifices at *luakini* temples such as those at Moʻokini (see p.148) and Wahaʻula Heiau near Kīlauea, which was recently destroyed by lava flows.

Paʻao is also credited with introducing the complex system of **kapu** – the Hawaiian version of the Polynesian *tabu*, or *taboo* – which circumscribed the daily lives of all Hawaiians. Some of its restrictions served to augment the power of the kings and priests, while others regulated domestic routine or attempted to conserve natural resources. Many had to do with food. Women were forbidden to prepare food or to eat with men; each husband was obliged to cook for himself and his wife in two separate ovens and to pound the *poi* in two distinct calabashes. The couple had to maintain separate houses, as well as a *Hale*

RELIGION

Noa, where a husband and wife slept together. Women could not eat pork, bananas, or coconuts, or several kinds of fish. Certain fish could only be caught in specified seasons, and a *koa* tree could only be cut down once two more were planted in its place.

No one could tread on the shadow of a chief; the highest chiefs were so surrounded by *kapus* that some would only go out at night. The ruling chiefs did not necessarily possess the highest spiritual status. One of Kamehameha's wives was so much his superior that he could only approach her naked, backwards, and on all fours.

The only crime in ancient Hawaii was to break a *kapu*, and the only punishment was death. It was possible for an entire *ahupua'a* to break a *kapu* and incur death, but that penalty was not always exacted. One way guilty parties could avoid execution was by hotfooting it to a *pu'uhonua*, or "place of refuge." The Big Island is thought to have had at least six of these, perhaps one per *ahupua'a*; the one in Hōnaunau remains among the best-preserved ancient sites in all Hawaii (see p.97), while other refuges stood in Waipi'o Valley and Hilo Bay.

The Hawaiian environment

Of all the places in the world, I should like to see a good flora of the Sandwich Islands.

Charles Darwin, 1850

Much of the landscape on the Big Island seems so unspoilt and pollution-free that few visitors realize how fragile the environmental balance really is. Native life forms have had less than two millennia to adapt to the arrival of humans, while the avalanche of species introduced in the last two centuries threatens to overwhelm the delicate ecosystems altogether.

Hawaii is a unique ecological laboratory. Not only are the islands isolated by a "moat" at least 2000 miles wide in every direction, but, having emerged from the sea as lumps of lava, they were never populated by the diversity of species that spread across the rest of the planet.

Those animals that found a foothold evolved into specialized forms unknown elsewhere, some peculiar even to one small part of an island. Because of their uniqueness, these species are particularly vulnerable to external threats; half Hawaii's indigenous plants, and three-quarters of its birds, are already extinct, while 73 percent of all US species classified as threatened or endangered are unique to the islands. More than one hundred species of Hawaiian plants have fewer than twenty remaining individuals in the wild.

The arrival of life

During the first seventy million years after the Hawaiian islands started to arise from the ocean, new plants and animals arrived only by sheer happenstance. A new species only established itself once every 100,000 years. Some drifted, clinging to flotsam washed up on the beaches; others were borne on the wind as seeds or spores; and the occasional migratory bird found its way, perhaps bringing insects or seeds. The larvae of shallow-water fish from Indonesia and the Philippines floated across thousands of miles of ocean to hatch in the Hawaiian coral reefs.

No **birds** other than the strongest fliers made it here, and neither did any land-based amphibians or reptiles, let alone large land mammals. At some point a hoary bat and an intrepid monk seal must have gotten here, as these were the only two mammals to predate the arrival of humans.

As the Hawaiian environment was relatively free of predators, many **plants** prospered without keeping up their natural defenses. Thus there are nettles with no stings, and mint with no scent. Conversely, normally placid creatures turned savage; caterpillars content to munch leaves elsewhere catch and eat flies in Hawaii.

As each new island emerged, it was populated by species from its neighbors as well as stragglers from farther afield. This process can still be seen on the Big Island, where Hawaii's last remaining stand of pristine rainforest attempts to spread onto new land created by Kīlauea. Lava flows destroy existing life, but fresh lava is rich in nutrients, and as water collects in its cavities, seeds or spores gather. The basic building block of the rainforest is the *hāpu'u* tree fern. Patches of these grow and decay, and in the mulch the *'ōhi'a lehua* gains a foothold as a gnarled shrub; in time it grows to become a gigantic tree, forcing its roots through the rock. After several hundred years, the lava crumbles to become soil that will support a full range of rainforest species. In addition, lava flows create isolated "pockets" of growth that develop their own specialized ecosystems – examples include the "bird park" on the Mauna Loa road (see p.246), and the lost world inside the Pu'u Huluhulu cinder cone (see p.240).

The Polynesian world

Many seemingly quintessential Hawaiian species, such as coconut palms, bananas, *taro*, and sugar cane, were in fact brought from Tahiti by the Polynesians, who also introduced the islands' first significant mammals – goats, dogs, and pigs.

The settlers set about changing the island's physical environment to suit their own needs, for example, constructing the terraces and irrigation channels of Waipi'o Valley. While their animals wrought destruction on the native flora, the settlers themselves had a significant impact on the bird population. They snared birds to use their feathers in cloaks, helmets and *leis*; bright red feathers came from the *i'iwi* bird, while yellow became the most prized color of all, as yellow birds such as the *mamo* and *'ō'ō* grew progressively rare. The *nēnē*, a mutated Canadian goose whose feet had lost their webs to make walking on lava easier, was hunted for food, and the *auku'u* heron was driven from its native habitat.

On the whole, however, the Hawaiians lived in relative harmony with nature, with the *kapu* system helping to conserve resources. It was the arrival of foreigners, and the deluge of new species that they introduced, that strained the ecological balance of Hawaii. Among the first victims were the Hawaiians themselves, decimated by foreign diseases.

Foreign invaders

The ships of the European explorers carried food plants and domestic animals around the world, to adapt newly discovered lands to the European image. The Big Island's first cattle, for example, were presented to Kamehameha the Great by Captain Vancouver of the *Discovery* in February 1793. The animals, which initially were allowed to run wild, ate through grasslands and forests, as well as through the Hawaiians' crops. When they were eventually rounded up and domesticated by the Parker Ranch, it formalized the change in land usage they had already effected. Horses had a similar initial impact, and to this day, wild goats remain a problem.

Wild pigs, however, have had an especially devastating effect on the forests of the Big Island. For every twenty humans in Hawaii, there lurks a feral pig. These combine the strong characteristics of the Polynesian pigs brought by early settlers with later European arrivals. Rooting through the earth, eating tree ferns, eliminating native lobelias and greenswords, and spreading the seeds of foreign fruits, the pigs have in most places destroyed the canopy that should protect the forest floor. In addition, they create muddy wallows and stagnant pools where mosquitoes thrive – the resultant avian malaria is the major cause of bird extinctions.

Eradicating the wild pig population is a priority for conservationists. In principle that goal gels with that of the amateur hunters, though so-called "Pig Wars" have arisen because the hunters want to leave enough pigs for their sport to continue, while the scientists want to eliminate the pigs altogether. In the highlands along the Hāmākua coast, men with pickup trucks and packs of dogs fight and kill the tuskers with knives, while riders on horseback, armed with rifles, scour the valleys between Waipi'o and Pololū. Farther south, in Volcanoes National Park, full-time hunters defend the rainforest using modern technology, including placing electronic tags on released "Judas pigs" to lead them to their feral brethren.

Another disaster was the importation to Hawaii of the **mongoose**. It was introduced on the islands by sugar plantation owners in the hopes of keeping down the population of rats, which had arrived by stowing away on visiting ships. Unfortunately, this plan failed to take into consideration the fact that rats are nocturnal and mongooses are not. The rodents continued to thrive, while the mongooses slept, having gorged themselves on birds' eggs during the day. Only Kauai, where the mongoose never became established, now retains significant populations of the many Hawaiian birds who, in the absence of predators, had decided it was safe to build their nests on the ground.

Unwanted alien species continue to arrive. Among those reported within the last five years are the **coqui frog** from Puerto Rico, which has already achieved population densities in excess of ten thousand individuals per acre in over a hundred spots on the Big Island (including Lava Tree State Monument; see p.211) as well as on three other islands, and the Madagascar **giant day gecko**, a foot-long orange-spotted lizard now established on Oahu. Environmentalists fear that Hawaii's next likely arrival will be the **brown tree snake**. Originally found in the Solomon Islands, it has been hitchhiking its way across the Pacific since World War II, sneaking into the holds of ships and planes, then emerging to

FOREIGN INVADERS

colonize new worlds that have never seen a single snake. In Guam it has already established itself in concentrations of up to thirty thousand individuals per square mile, happy to eat virtually anything, and wiping out the local bird populations.

Issues and prospects

The state of Hawaii has a short and unimpressive history of legislating to conserve its environment, and what little has been achieved so far appears to be jeopardized by moves to rein in the powers of the Endangered Species Act. One positive development is that the whole state has been declared a **humpback whale** sanctuary.

On the Big Island, a resurgence in respect for what are seen as native Hawaiian values has dovetailed with the influx of New-Age *haoles* to create an active environmental movement, which has had plenty of issues to occupy its attention. In particular, the depressed state of the island's economy has made it vulnerable to grandiose schemes designed to attract outside funding.

One recurrent theme is the idea that the Big Island's future prosperity might rest in generating **energy** for the rest of the state; at present, Hawaii as a whole imports 92 percent of its fuel. The plan includes such components as harnessing the geothermal power of the Kīlauea region, which has already been achieved by the Puna Geothermal Venture (see p.210), and then exporting electricity via a submarine cable to Oahu. That would involve crossing the deep ʻAlenuihāhā Channel between the Big Island and Maui; the literal translation of ʻAlenuihāhā is "great billows smashing," which suggests why it might not be a good idea.

Another ambitious project was the much-vaunted plan to build a commercial **spaceport** to launch satellites and the Space Shuttle from Pālima Point, just outside Volcanoes National Park in Kaʻū. It was never really necessary for opponents to voice their spiritual and metaphysical objections; the fact that the site is on the flanks of the world's most active volcano, prone to landslides and *tsunamis*, spoke for itself. On the other hand, native Hawaiian campaigners who regard the observatories on top of Mauna Kea as desecrations of a sacred site have had little success in reining in the construction work up there.

The most recent federal scheme to exploit the Big Island's environment is reported to be a plan to address the problem of **global warming** by pumping surplus carbon dioxide into the deep ocean off Honokōhau.

There has also been much debate over what is to become of the island's system of **irrigation channels**. Developed long before European contact and adapted to meet the needs of the plantations, their infrastructure is now rapidly falling into disrepair. As the ancient Hawaiians knew all too well, maintenance is extremely labor-intensive; without swift action, however, the opportunity to revive small-scale agriculture may soon pass.

The power of the **tourism** lobby has for the last few decades been great enough to override environmental objections to the growth of the Kohala resorts. Thus the opening of the *Hapuna Beach Prince* hotel at the island's best beach in 1994, after an islandwide ballot voted narrowly to allow the project, was a blow to campaigners. There are also concerns that the Kohala resorts are damaging their immediate environment; the combination of golf courses and coral reefs may be ideal for vacationers, but that won't last if fertilizer and silt washed down from the greens and fairways end up choking the reef to death. However, it now looks as though the era of resort building is drawing to a close. The huge hotel complex envisaged for Pōhue Bay, below Ocean View at the southern tip of the island, seems unlikely to come to fruition, and perhaps the Big Island is destined for a period of relative equilibrium after its recent hectic changes.

Hula and Hawaiian music

I f your idea of Hawaiian music is Elvis doing the limbo in *Blue Hawaii*, you won't be disappointed by the entertainment on offer in most of the Big Island's hotels. A diet of *Little Grass Shack* and the *Hawaiian Wedding Song*, with the occasional rendition of *Please Release Me* in Hawaiian, is guaranteed. However, the island also boasts its own lively contemporary music scene, and it's still possible to see performances of its most ancient form, *hula*, which embraces elements of theater and dance.

Hula

Although the ancient Hawaiians were devotees of the poetic chants they called **meles**, they had no specific word for "song." *Meles* were composed for various purposes, ranging from lengthy genealogies of the chiefs, put together over days of debate, through temple prayers, to lullabies and love songs. When the chanted words were accompanied by music and dance, as was often the case, the combined performance was known as **hula**.

Musical instruments included gourds, rattles, small hand or knee drums made from coconuts, and the larger *pahu* drums made by stretching shark skin over hollow logs. As a rule the tonal range was minimal and the music monotonous, though occasionally bamboo pipes may also have been played. Complexity was introduced by the fact that the dance, the chant, and the music were all likely to follow distinct rhythmic patterns.

The telling of the story or legend was of primary importance; the music was subordinate to the chant, while the feet and lower body of the dancers served mainly to keep the rhythm, and their hand movements supplemented the meaning of the words. Dancers would be trained in a *hālau hula*, a cross between a school and a temple dedicated to Laka, and performances were hedged around by sacred ritual and *kapus*.

The first Christian missionaries to reach Hawaii saw *hula* as a lascivious manifestation of the islands' lack of morality. No doubt the religious subtleties of the so-called "genital *hula*" dances, for example, which celebrated the genitals of leading members of the *ali'i*, were lost on visiting whalemen.

In consequence, *hula* was largely suppressed for a century. It only returned to public performance at the coronation of the "Merrie Monarch," King David Kalākaua, in February 1883. By then the process of adapting music and dance to suit foreign tastes had started; the grass skirt, for example, was imported to Hawaii from the Gilbert Islands in the 1870s. As a 1923 magazine article complained, "real Hawaiian *hula* has little in common with the coarse imitations served up to sight-seers, magazine readers, and the general public."

Today *hula* persists in two forms. The first, *kahiko*, is closer to the old style, consisting of chanting to the beat of drums; the dancers wear knee-length skirts of flat *ti* leaves, and anklets and bracelets of ferns. *'Auana* is the modern style, featuring musicians playing Western-style instruments.

Both forms have their major showcase on the Big Island

HULA

each April, at Hilo's **Merrie Monarch Festival** (see p.195). Some traditionalists do not participate in the Merrie Monarch, regarding the idea of a competition as contrary to the essential nature of *hula* as a form of religious expression.

Slack-key and steel guitar

The roots of contemporary Hawaiian music lie in a mixture of cultural traditions brought from all over the world by nineteenth-century immigrants. In particular, Spanish and Mexican *paniolos* introduced the guitar, while the *braginha* of the Portuguese plantation workers was adapted to become the Hawaiian *ukulele*. King David Kalākaua had his own ukulele group, and co-wrote Hawaii's national anthem, *Hawaii Pono ʻī*, while his sister Queen Liliʻuokalani composed the haunting *Aloha ʻOe*, since covered by Elvis Presley among others.

The next step towards creating a distinctive Hawaiian sound came roughly a century ago, when the conventional method of tuning a guitar was abandoned in favor of **slack-key** tuning (*kī hōʻalu* in Hawaiian), in which a simple strum of the open strings produces a harmonious chord. Next came the realization that sliding a strip of metal along the strings produced a glissando effect; an Oahu student is credited with inventing the **steel guitar**, as played by early virtuosos such as Sol Hoʻopii.

English words were set to Hawaiian melodies, and the resultant **hapa-haole** music was by World War I the most popular music form in America. The craze for all things Hawaiian took several decades to die down, though it grew progressively more debased. By the time of the nationwide *tiki* craze of the 1950s, when mass tourism was just taking off and Polynesian-themed restaurants were opening all across the United States, pseudo-Hawaiian music such as Martin Denny's cocktail-jazz stylings was still topping the charts.

IZ: MAY 20, 1959 – JUNE 26, 1997

In the summer of 1997, the contemporary Hawaiian music scene lost the man who was in every sense its biggest star. Israel Kamakawiwo'ole, who started out singing in the Makaha Sons of Niihau, and then went solo in 1990, died of respiratory difficulties in a Honolulu hospital. During his twenty-year career, "Iz" came to epitomize the pride and the power of Hawaiian music. His extraordinary voice adapted equally well to rousing political anthems, delicate love songs, pop standards and Jawaiian reggae rhythms, while his personality and love for Hawaii always shone through both in concert and on record. Like his brother Skippy before him – also a founder member of the Makaha Sons – Iz eventually succumbed to the health problems caused by his immense size. At one point, his weight reached a colossal 757 pounds; he needed a fork-lift truck to get on stage, and could only breathe through tubes. His strength in adversity did much to ensure that he was repeatedly voted Hawaii's most popular entertainer, and after his death he was granted a state funeral, with his body lying in state in the Capitol. His enduring legacy will be the music on his four solo albums – *Ka Ano'i* (1990), *Facing Future* (1993), *E Ala Ē* (1995), and *'n Dis Life* (1996) – while his haunting rendition of *Hawai'i 78* (by Big Island songwriter Mickey Ioane, and featured on *Facing Future*) has become the signature song of the Hawaiian sovereignty movement.

The modern generation

The sound created by the newest generation of Hawaiian musicians is a fascinating hybrid, drawing on the tradition of the ancient *meles*, but influenced by mainstream rock, country and even reggae music. It combines political stridency with sweet melodies, and powerful drum beats with gentle *ukulele* tinklings.

THE MODERN GENERATION

The first prominent name in the movement was **Gabby Pahinui**, an exponent of classic slack-key guitar who in the final years before his death in 1980 achieved international fame through his recordings with Ry Cooder. His success encouraged others to stop tailoring their music to suit mainland tastes, and it soon became apparent that there was a market for recordings in the Hawaiian language.

Among the biggest names on the contemporary scene are the duo **Hapa** – Barry Flanagan, originally from New Jersey, and Keli'i Kaneali'i – who combined slack-key guitar instrumentals with soaring harmonies on the huge-selling album *Hapa*, blended ponderous rock with traditional chant on their version of U2's *Pride (In The Name of Love)*, and then riffed their way to heaven with the affectionate spoof *Surf Madness*. The Maui-based *kumu hula* (*hula* teacher), **Keali'i Reichel**, has produced several successful CDs of his exquisite alto singing, of which the first, *Kawaipunahele*, is probably the best, though *E Ō Mai* boasts an enjoyable rendition of the theme from *Babe*. Look out, too, for concert appearances by **Amy Gilliom**; her crystal-clear voice brings out all the beauty of her classic Hawaiian-language material, while she and her partner, guitar virtuoso Wille K, also make a great quick-fire comedy duo.

Finally, visitors may be surprised to encounter the Hawaiian-reggae fusion known as **Jawaiian**, in which the traditional beat of the *pahu* drum is accompanied by a thunderous electrified bass. Reggae is very popular with young Hawaiians, but the home-grown groups don't tend to have the hard edge of the touring Jamaican bands who often perform on the islands. **Ho'ikane**, from the Big Island, is among the best; the group is credited with being the first to introduce an up-to-date dance-hall sound. Other performers include **Titus Kinimaka** – a pro surfer from Kauai's leading *hula* family – and **Butch Helemano**, who has at least nine albums to his name.

Books

An extraordinary number of books have been written about Hawaii and all matters Hawaiian, though you're only likely to come across most of them in bookstores on the islands themselves. All the publishers below are based in the US.

The best places to **buy books** on the Big Island are the two Borders, in Kailua and Hilo, the Middle Earth Bookshoppe in Kailua, and the *Kohala Book Shop* in Kapa'au.

History

Joseph Brennan, *The Parker Ranch of Hawaii* (Harper & Row). This authorized history of the Big Island's famous cattle ranch kicks off well, with lively accounts of the early days, but steadily grows tamer.

Emmett Cahill, *The Life and Times of John Young* (Island Heritage Publishing). Lively biography of one of the most fascinating figures of the imme-diate post-contact era: the Welsh seaman who became Kamehameha's most trusted military adviser.

Gavan Daws, *Shoal of Time* (University of Hawaii Press). Definitive if dry single-volume history of the Hawaiian Islands, tracing their fate from European contact to statehood.

Noel J. Kent, *Hawaii: Islands Under The Influence* (University of Hawaii Press). Rigorous Marxist account of Hawaiian history, concentrating on the islands' perennial "dependency" on distant economic forces.

Liliʻuokalani, *Hawaii's Story by Hawaii's Queen* (Mutual Publishing). Autobiographical account by the last monarch of Hawaii of how her kingdom was taken away. Written in 1897 when she still cherished hopes of a restoration.

Gananath Obeyesekere, *The Apotheosis of Captain Cook* (Princeton University Press/Bishop Museum Press). An iconoclastic Sri Lankan anthropologist reassesses Captain Cook from an anti-imperialist – but, according to most authorities, historically inaccurate – perspective.

A Grenfell Price (ed), *The Explorations of Captain James Cook in the Pacific* (Dover). Selections from Cook's own journals, including entries about his first landfall on Kauai and his ill-fated return to the Big Island.

Marshall Sahlins, *How Natives Think . . . about Captain Cook, for example* (University of Chicago Press). An impassioned and closely argued response to the Obeyesekere book, reviewed above. Sahlins is currently considered to be ahead on points.

Ancient Hawaii

Ross Cordy, *Exalted Sits The Chief: The Ancient History of Hawaiʻi Island* (Mutual Publishing). Cordy has assembled a great deal of valuable raw material about the early history of the Big Island, but the book's poor organization and dry style make it a disappointingly heavy read.

Nathaniel B. Emerson, *Unwritten Literature of Hawaii – The Sacred Songs of the Hula* (Charles E. Tuttle Co). Slightly dated account of ancient Hawaii's most important art form. Published in 1909, its wealth of detail ensures that it remains required reading for all students of the *hula*.

Samuel M. Kamakau, *The People of Old* (Bishop Museum Press, three vols). Anecdotal essays, published in Hawaiian as newspaper articles in the 1860s. Packed with fascinating information, they provide a compendium of Hawaiian oral traditions. Kamakau's longer *Ruling Chiefs of Hawaii* (Bishop Museum Press) details all that is known of the deeds of the kings.

David Malo, *Hawaiian Antiquities* (Bishop Museum Press). Nineteenth-century survey of culture and society, written by a native Hawaiian brought up at the court of Kamehameha the Great.

Valerio Valeri, *Kingship and Sacrifice; Ritual and Society in Ancient Hawaii* (University of Chicago Press). Detailed academic analysis of the role of human sacrifice in establishing the power of the king – an aspect of Hawaiian religion many other commentators gloss over.

Contemporary Hawaii

Michael Kioni Dudley and **Keoni Kealoha Agard**, *A Call for Hawaiian Sovereignty* (Nā Kāne O Ka Malo, two vols). The first of these short books attempts to reconstruct the world view of the ancient

Hawaiians; the second is the clearest imaginable account of their dispossession.

Randall W. Roth (ed), *The Price of Paradise* (Mutual Publishing, two vols). Assorted experts answer questions about life and society in Hawaii in short essays that focus on economic and governmental issues. Of most interest to local residents or prospective migrants, but a useful introduction to ongoing island debates, which sadly has now become somewhat dated.

Haunani Kay Trask, *From A Native Daughter: Colonialism and Sovereignty in Hawaii* (University of Hawaii Press). A stimulating and impressive contribution to the sovereignty debate, from one of Hawaii's best-known activists.

Travelers' tales

Isabella Bird, *Six Months in the Sandwich Islands* (University of Hawaii Press). Enthralling adventures of an Englishwoman in the 1870s, with escapades along the Hāmākua coast and a cold trip up Mauna Loa.

James Macrae, *With Lord Byron at the Sandwich Islands in 1825* (Petroglyph Press). Short pamphlet of extracts from the diary of a Scottish botanist, including the first-known recorded ascent of Mauna Kea, an expedition to Kīlauea and an eyewitness account of the dismantling of the Puʻuhonua O Hōnaunau.

Hunter S. Thompson, *The Curse of Lono* (Bantam Books). Inimitably overwrought account of a winter fishing vacation on the Kona coast, involving such escapades as abandoning a demented Doberman in a suite at the *King Kamehameha* hotel.

Mark Twain, *Letters from Hawaii* (University of Hawaii Press). Colorful and entertaining accounts of nineteenth-century Hawaii, with extensive descriptions of the Big Island. Much of the best material was reworked for inclusion in *Roughing It* (Penguin UK and US).

Natural sciences

Pamela Frierson, *The Burning Island* (Sierra Club Books). The most exciting and original volume written about the Big Island; a history and cultural anthropology of the region around Mauna Loa and Kīlauea, combined with a personal account of living with the volcanoes.

Garrett Hongo, *Volcano* (Vintage Books). The "Volcano" of the title is the Big-Island village where Hongo was born; the book itself is a lyrical evocation of its physical and emotional landscape.

Frank Stewart (ed), *A World Between Waves* (Island Press). Stimulating collection of essays by authors such as Peter Matthiessen and Maxine Hong Kingston, covering all aspects of Hawaiian natural history.

Language

The Hawaiian language is an offshoot of languages spoken elsewhere in Polynesia, with slight variations that arose during the centuries when the islands had no contact with the rest of Polynesia. Among its most unusual features is the fact that there are no verbs "to be" or "to have," and that, although it lacks a word for "weather," it distinguishes between 130 types of rain and 160 types of wind.

Although barely two thousand people speak Hawaiian as their mother tongue, it remains a living language and has experienced a revival in recent years. While visitors to Hawaii are almost certain to hear Hawaiian-language songs, it's rarely spoken in public, and there should be no need to communicate in any language other than English. However, everyday conversations tend to be sprinkled with Hawaiian words, and you'll also spot them in many local place names.

The alphabet

Hawaiian only became a written language when a committee of missionaries gave it an alphabet. The shortest in the world, it consists of just twelve letters – *a*, *e*, *h*, *i*, *k*, *l*, *m*, *n*, *o*, *p*, *u*, and *w* – plus two punctuation marks. When the missionaries were unable to agree on the precise sounds of the language, they simply voted on which letter to include – thus *k* beat *t*, and *l* beat *r*.

Hawaiian may look hard to **pronounce**, but in fact with just 162 possible syllables – as compared to 23,638 in Thai – it's the least complicated language on earth. The letters *h*, *l*, *m* and *n* are pronounced exactly as in English; *k* and *p* are pronounced approximately as in English but with less aspiration; *w* is like the English *v* after an *i* or an *e*, and the English *w* after a *u* or an *o*. At the start of a word, or after an *a*, *w* may be pronounced like a *v* or a *w*.

The **glottal stop** (') creates the audible pause heard in the English "oh-oh." Words without **macrons** (¯), to indicate stress, are pronounced by stressing alternate syllables working back from the penultimate syllable. Thanks to the frequent repetition of syllables, this is usually easier than it may sound. "Kamehameha," for example, breaks down into the repeated pattern *Ka–meha–meha*, pronounced *Ka–mayha–mayha*.

a	**a** as in above
e	**e** as in bet
i	**y** as in pity
o	**o** as in hole
u	**u** as in full
ā	**a** as in car
ē	**ay** as in day
ī	**ee** as in bee
ō	**o** as in hole (but slightly longer)
ū	**oo** as in moon

LANGUAGE

Glossary

'A'ā rough lava

Ahupua'a basic land division, a "slice of cake" from ocean to mountain

'Āina land, earth

Akua god, goddess, spirit, idol

Ali'i chief, chiefess, noble

Aloha love; hello; goodbye.

'Aumākua personal god or spirit; totem animal

'Elepaio bird

Hala tree (pandanus, screw pine)

Halāu long house used for *hula* instruction; also a *hula* group

Hale house, building

Hana work

Haole (white) non-native Hawaiian, whether foreign or American resident

Hapa half, as in *hapa haole*, or half-foreign

Hāpu'u tree fern

Heiau ancient place of worship

Honua land, earth

Hui group, club

Hula dance/music form (*hula 'auana* is a modern form, *hula kahiko* is traditional)

Imu pit oven

Kahuna priest(ess) or someone particularly skilled in any field; *kahuna nui* chief priest

Kai sea

Kālua to bake in an *imu* (underground oven)

Kama'āina Hawaiian from another island; state resident

Kāne man

Kapa the "cloth" made from pounded bark, known elsewhere as *tapa*

Kapu forbidden, taboo, sacred

Kapu moe prostration

Kaukau food

Keiki child

Kiawe thorny tree, mesquite

Ki'i temple image or petroglyph

Kīpuka natural "island" of vegetation surrounded by lava flows

Koa dark hardwood tree

Kōkua help

Kona leeward (especially wind)

Lānai balcony, terrace, patio

Lau leaf

Lehua *or* **'Ōhi'a lehua** native red-blossomed shrub/tree

Lei garland of flowers, feathers, shells or other material

Liliko'i passion fruit

Limu seaweed

Lomi Lomi massage or raw salmon dish

Luakini temple of human sacrifice

Lū'au traditional Hawaiian feast

Mahalo thank you

Mahimahi white fish or dolphin fish (not the mammal)

Makai direction: away from the mountain, towards the sea

Malihini newcomer, visitor

Mana spiritual power

Mauka direction: away from the sea, towards the mountain

Mele ancient chant

Menehune in legend, the most ancient Hawaiian people, supposedly dwarfs

Mu'umu'u long loose dress

Nēnē Hawaiian goose – the state bird

Nui big, important

'Ohana family

'Ōhelo sacred red berry

'Ōhi'a lehua see *lehua*

'Ono delicious

'Ō'ō yellow-feathered bird

'Ōpae shrimp

Pāhoehoe smooth lava

Pali sheer-sided cliff

Paniolo Hawaiian cowboy

Pau finished

Pili grass, used for thatch

Poi staple food made of *taro* root

Poke raw fish dish

Pua flower, garden

Pūpū snack

Pu'u hill, lump

Taro Hawaiian food plant

Tsunami tidal wave

Tūtū grandparent, general term of respect

Wahine woman

Wai water

Wikiwiki hurry, fast

INDEX

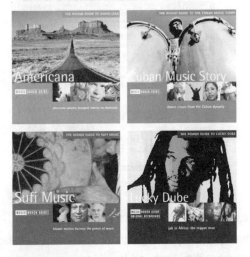

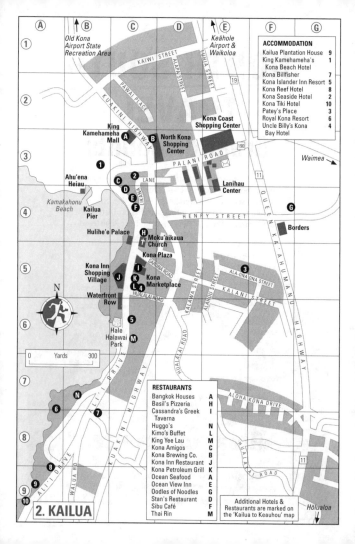

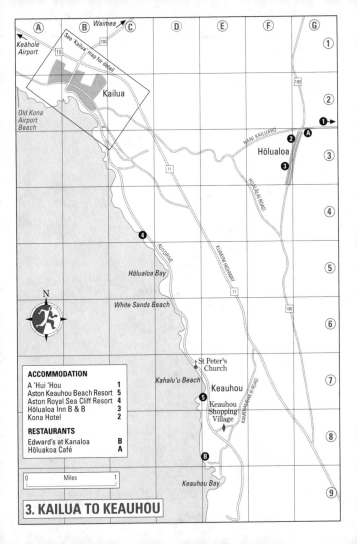

Keāhole Airport

Waimea

See Kailua map for detail

Kailua

Old Kona Airport Beach

Hōlualoa

MANI KAILUAHO

HUALALAI ROAD

ALII DRIVE

Hōlualoa Bay

KUAKINI HIGHWAY

White Sands Beach

N

St Peter's Church

Kahalu'u Beach

Keauhou

KAMEHAMEHA III ROAD

Keauhou Shopping Village

ACCOMMODATION

A 'Hui 'Hou	1
Aston Keauhou Beach Resort	5
Aston Royal Sea Cliff Resort	4
Hōlualoa Inn B & B	3
Kona Hotel	2

RESTAURANTS

Edward's at Kanaloa	B
Hōluakoa Café	A

0   Miles   1

Keauhou Bay

3. KAILUA TO KEAUHOU

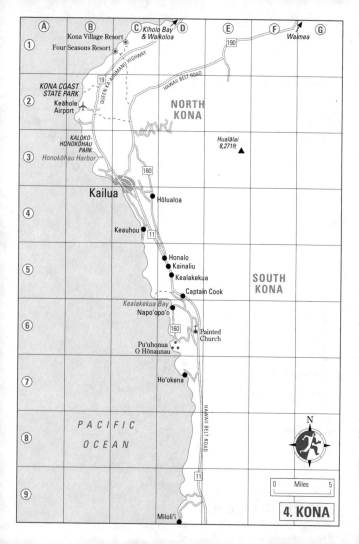

4. KONA

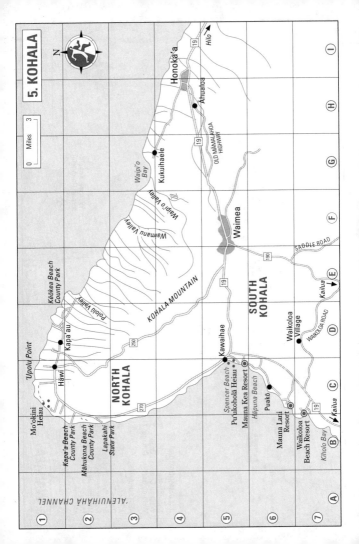

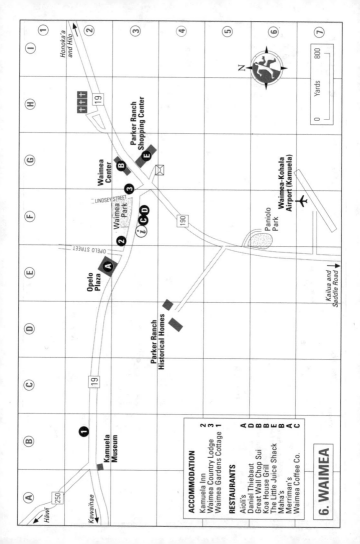

Honoka'a
and Hilo

Parker Ranch
Shopping Center

Waimea
Center

B
E

LINDSEY STREET

Waimea
Park

3

i C D

2

Opelo Plaza

A

OPELO STREET

19

Parker Ranch
Historical Homes

Kamuela
Museum

1

250

Hāwī

Kawaihae

190

190

Paniolo
Park

Waimea-Kohala
Airport (Kamuela)

Kailua and
Saddle Road

N

0   Yards   800

ACCOMMODATION

Kamuela Inn   2
Waimea Country Lodge   3
Waimea Gardens Cottage   1

RESTAURANTS

Aioli's   A
Daniel Thiebaut   D
Great Wall Chop Sui   B
Koa House Grill   E
The Little Juice Shack   E
Maha's   B
Merriman's   A
Waimea Coffee Co.   C

6. WAIMEA

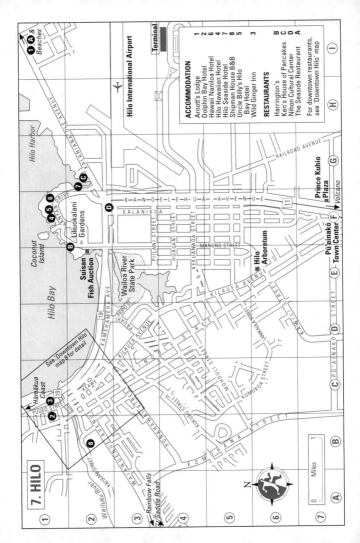

7. HILO

Hilo International Airport

Terminal

ACCOMMODATION

Arnott's Lodge	1
Dolphin Bay Hotel	2
Hawaii Naniloa Hotel	6
Hilo Hawaiian Hotel	4
Hilo Seaside Hotel	7
Shipman House B&B	8
Uncle Billy's Hilo	5
Bay Hotel	
Wild Ginger Inn	3

RESTAURANTS

Harrington's	B
Ken's House of Pancakes	C
Nihon Cultural Center	D
The Seaside Restaurant	A

For downtown restaurants, see 'Downtown Hilo' map

Hilo Harbor

Hilo Bay

Coconut Island

Hanākua Coast

KALANIANAOLE AVENUE

KAMEHAMEHA AVE

Liliuokalani Gardens

Suisan Fish Auction

Wailoa River State Park

See Downtown Hilo map for detail

Rainbow Falls

Saddle Road

Wailuku River

PUEO STREET

KEAWE

PIOPIO

PIILANI STREET

HUALANI STREET

KEKUANAOA STREET

K·A·N·O·E·L·E·H·U·A — A·V·E·N·U·E

KALANIKOA

MANONO STREET

KILAUEA AVENUE

KUMUKOA STREET

KUKUAU STREET

MOHOULI STREET

KOMOHANA STREET

PONAHAWAI AVENUE

WAIĀNUENUE AVE

KINOOLE STREET

KAMANA STREET

RAILROAD AVENUE

Prince Kuhio Plaza

Volcano

Pū'ainakō Town Center

Miles

N

0   1

11

19

① ② ③ ④ ⑤ ⑥ ⑦

Ⓐ Ⓑ Ⓒ Ⓓ Ⓔ Ⓕ Ⓖ Ⓗ Ⓘ

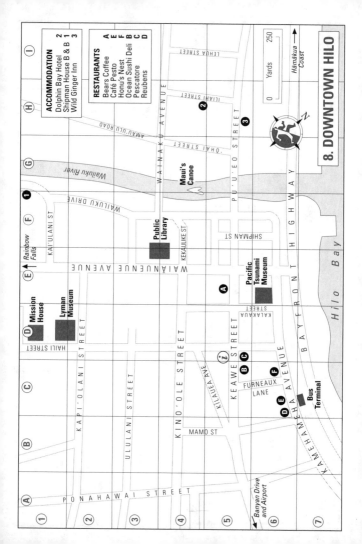

ACCOMMODATION
Dolphin Bay Hotel   2
Shipman House B & B   1
Wild Ginger Inn   3

RESTAURANTS
Bears Coffee   A
Café Pesto   E
Honu's Nest   F
Ocean Sushi Deli   B
Pescatore   C
Reubens   D

Hāmākua Coast

0   Yards   250

8. DOWNTOWN HILO

Hilo Bay

Banyan Drive and Airport

Bus Terminal

PONAHAWAI STREET

MAMO ST

FURNEAUX LANE

KAMEHAMEHA AVENUE

BAYFRONT

KALAKAUA STREET

KEAWE STREET

KILAUEA AVE

KINO'OLE STREET

ULULANI STREET

KAPI'OLANI STREET

HAILI STREET

Mission House

Lyman Museum

WAIANUENUE AVENUE

Pacific Tsunami Museum

SHIPMAN ST

KEKAULIKE ST

KAI'ULANI ST

Public Library

WAILUKU DRIVE

Wailuku River

Rainbow Falls

AMAU'ULU ROAD

Maui's Canoe

WAINAKU AVENUE

PU'U'EO STREET

OHAI STREET

ILIAHI STREET

LEHUA STREET

HIGHWAY

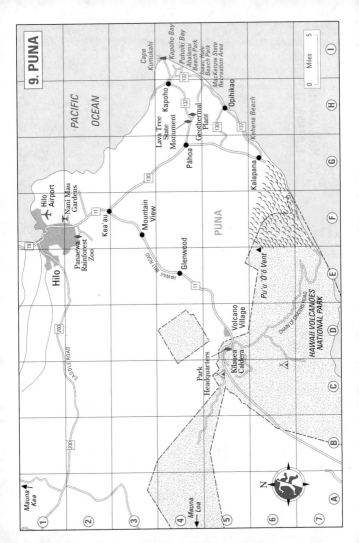

PACIFIC OCEAN

Cape Kumukahi

Kapoho Bay

Pohoiki Bay
Ahalanui Beach Park
Isaac Hale Beach Park
MacKenzie State Recreation Area

Kapoho

Lava Tree State Monument

Geothermal Plant

Pāhoa

Opihikao

Hilo Airport

Nani Mau Gardens

Panaewa Rainforest Zoo

Hilo

SADDLE ROAD

Mauna Kea

Keaʻau

Mountain View

Glenwood

HAWAII BELT ROAD

PUNA

Kalapana

Kehena Beach

Park Headquarters

Volcano Village

Kīlauea Caldera

Puʻu ʻŌʻō Vent

CHAIN OF CRATERS ROAD

HAWAII VOLCANOES NATIONAL PARK

Mauna Loa

N

0   Miles   5

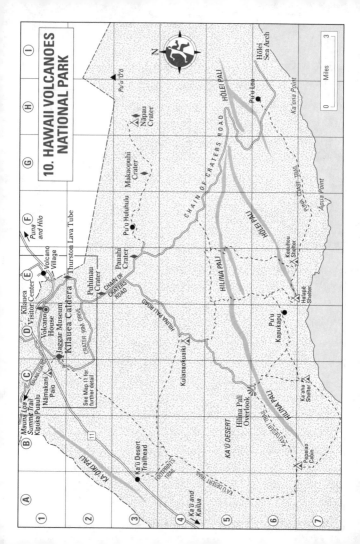

10. HAWAII VOLCANOES NATIONAL PARK

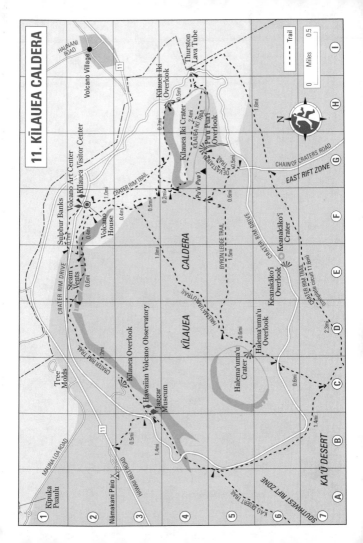

11. KĪLAUEA CALDERA

HAUNANI ROAD

Volcano Village

Volcano Art Center

Kīlauea Visitor Center

Sulphur Banks

Volcano House

Steam Vents

CRATER RIM DRIVE

CRATER RIM TRAIL

Kīlauea Iki Overlook 0.5mi

Kīlauea Iki Crater

Thurston Lava Tube

Pu'u Pua'i Overlook

KĪLAUEA IKI TRAIL 2.4mi

0.7mi

1.8mi

DEVASTATION TRAIL 0.5mi

CHAIN OF CRATERS ROAD

EAST RIFT ZONE

'Pu'u Pua'i

0.2mi

0.6mi

CALDERA

KĪLAUEA

BYRON LEDGE TRAIL 1.5mi

HALEMA'UMA'U TRAIL

1.8mi

EAST CRATER RIM DRIVE

Keanakāko'i Crater

Keanakāko'i Overlook

CRATER RIM TRAIL

0.6mi

0.6mi

2.3mi

(complete circuit 11.6mi)

Halema'uma'u Overlook

Halema'uma'u Crater

0.6mi

1.4mi

KA'Ū DESERT

SOUTHWEST RIFT ZONE

KA'Ū DESERT TRAIL

1.4mi

Hawaiian Volcano Observatory

Jaggar Museum

Kīlauea Overlook

0.5mi

1.4mi

Tree Molds

CRATER RIM TRAIL 2mi

Nāmakani Paio X

MAUNA LOA ROAD

HAWAI'I BELT ROAD

Kīpuka Puaulu

N

- - - - - Trail

0   0.5
Miles

1   2   3   4   5   6   7

A   B   C   D   E   F   G   H   I